THE PC UPGRADE HANDBOOK

Clive V. Smith

SIGMA PRESS
Wilmslow, United Kingdom

First published in 1988 by
Sigma Press 1 South Oak Lane, Wilmslow, SK9 6AR, England.

British Library Cataloguing in Publication Data

Smith, Clive
      The PC upgrade handbook.
      1. Microcomputer systems. peripheral
      equipment
      I. Title
      004.7'16

ISBN: 1-85058-118-5

Distributed by
John Wiley & Sons Ltd., Baffins Lane, Chichester, West Sussex, England.

Printed by Manchester Free Press

Cover design by Professional Graphics, Warrington, UK

Acknowledgments:

The author is most grateful to all people, organisations and societies that have given him assistance during the proparation of this book. Many firms have been of great assistance in providing data and details of various products.

In particular we would like to mention: APL; Callbox; Citadel products; Dataflex Design; Dowty Systems; Fairhurst Instruments; Miracle Technology; Oxford hard Cards; Peripherals Connections Ltd; Tandon.

Numerous trademarks and registered trademarks are referred to throughout the text and we are pleased to fully acknowledge all of these.

PREFACE

This book first examines many of the upgrades/enhancements available for the ubiquitous PC. The PC is taken as being a genuine or clone of the IBM PC XT. This includes both the Amstrad 1512 and 1640 models plus the myriad of named and un-named varieties. Mention is made of some of the incompatibilities, if known, and where upgrades can and cannot be made.

The theme of the book then transfers to the communication aspect, whether it be another PC, a modem or radio link. Both serial and parallel communications are examined and various commercial solutions considered and this leads to the concepts of data transfer and the use of shared resources. The book then goes on to examine data acquisition and industrial control followed by a look at small area networks which are suitable for confined locations. The final chapter covers at specialist communications, especially packet radio as used by radio amateurs (hams).

In carrying out upgrades beware they do not invalidate any warranty - some manufacturers/suppliers are very sharp on this ! There is variation in statutory law between countries with regard to consumers' rights. The author and publisher cannot be held responsible for any damage caused - always read your hand book first.

Wherever possible, information has been checked from at least two sources, a full I/O and memory map is given so that it can be seen where the add-ons are accommodated. This memory and I/O map are as accurate as possible but unfortunately all suppliers/manufacturers do not keep to it strictly and there will inevitably be some variations. New products are appearing on the market all of the time and these may well have to use unallocated slots as they do not fall into any previous category.

I have no connection with any firm that supplies additional units for the PC and if there is any bias it is because those firms have been most helpful in providing information and these are duly acknowledged in the Appendix. Some firms I wrote to did not even have the courtesy to reply to my letters and I would have liked to have included these in a "don't buy from" list. The list also does not include all suppliers, it would be a Herculean task to find them all out. I would, however, be willing to include them in any future editions if they will tell me of their presence and give a good list of the products they deal with.

Clive Smith

CONTENTS

GENERAL INTRODUCTION

Introduction

Developments in semiconductor design and manufacture have gone in leaps and bounds from the inception of the transistor in 1947 to the present production of very complex integrated circuits. The first commercially available ICs appeared in the mid 1960s with much more complex units available by the early 1970s. With this, the microprocessor as we know it was born and the small computer gradually came onto the market.

The first of the microcomputers appeared in the mid/late 1970s and ever since, better and better units have appeared at generally lower and lower prices. Up to this time the computer had been enshrouded by mystique and lesser mortals had been made to feel beholden to the "computer people" for being able to run even small programs and applications. The microcomputer has now broken this hold and computing power is available to anyone that has the need.

With the obvious success of the microcomputer, IBM, one of the strongholds of mainframe mystique and unintelligible manuals, was suddenly shaken into the reality of Power to all the People. The first offerings were the PC and PC Junior with small amounts of memory. Following these came the PC with extended memory and the PC XT was born. This product was initially very expensive and it was not until the advent of the "clones" that prices started to tumble. IBM was reluctantly dragged along, and the chance was there for many more people to own desktop computers with reasonable processing ability. This, of course, opened the door for many software firms to expand into somewhat larger markets.

However, whatever one thinks of IBM, they had created a standard which had hitherto been missing, and the opportunity was available for many innovative firms to take advantage. This included the production of the printed circuit boards for the various options, external units, power supplies, housings and complete computers. The subject of this book is the add-on boards and external expansion units and how they can be used, especially with regard to communications.

Many firms are now moving on to producing and supplying newer, better and faster models of computer. Whatever happens, the faithful XT and equivalents will be around for quite a while and in many applications jogging along at 4.77 or 8 Mhz may well be all that is required. Do not be pushed into buying a "souped" up, Turbo, GT model with go faster stripe just because the media is getting all "hyped" up about it. Many expansion possibilities exist for the PC XT and clones and these should be examined first.

Whenever the latest computer and electronic journals are opened new add-on equipment is described and it has been a difficult task to keep pace. The contents of this book must be regarded as typical of the options available.

Book Layout

It has been quite difficult to find an optimum way in which to explain each of the various upgrades and their requisite knowledge. Chapters on communications do require the reader to be familiar with parallel and serial communications. If this is not so, Chapter 9 has been included in order to remedy the situation. A bibliography is provided at the end of the book (Appendix 6) where readers will find texts on similar topics or where fuller study of a certain sphere of interest can be followed up.

More information has been given in the chapters than is needed to install a given option - do not let it put you off - some people will find this of use as it aids an understanding of the computer as a whole. It has certainly been very helpful to the author in gaining a better comprehension of the topic under discussion.

To make explanations easier the book examines add-on facilities as though only one item is added per unit. This certainly has been useful for writing the book but in reality several features may be included in one add-on unit and so the reader can gain knowledge by looking at the appropriate sections and pooling the information.

The PC (or Personal Computer)

There are now many varieties of this machine on the market - from the genuine IBM to the many un-named versions; IBM has now in fact ceased to manufacture the PC XT. Most of the machines follow the same physical pattern but the two Amstrad models (1512 and 1640) are arranged differently (see Chapter 2).

It is now possible to buy all of the component parts, including casings, and to assemble one's own machine from scratch. On a quick pricing of parts, however, it is not possible to match an assembled unit for price and of course there is no guarantee on the whole product - only on the individual sub-assemblies. For industrial control applications, though, this may be a good route as no keyboard or housing may be required in the final product. What is probably a good way, and this book will provide assistance here, is to buy a basic unit with a single floppy drive and a minimum of 256 kBytes of memory and add the extras as required.

Add-On Equipment

These fall mainly into two categories:-

internal units, and
external units.

However, life is never that simple, and some add-on units will require both the external unit plus an additional internal unit. The appropriate information must then be gleaned by reading both of the following sections.

A summary of typical suppliers is added at the end of each chapter and an address list of suppliers has been included in Appendix 7. This is by no means exhaustive and really only represents advertisements seen by the authorand those firms responsive to requests for information. Products tend to be cheaper in the USA and the typical £1 = $1 syndrome exists in most of the market.

To find out more information look through the suppliers at the end of each chapter or any computer magazine which includes the PC, typical examples are:-

Personal Computer World
PC Plus
Personal Computing with the Amstrad
Which Micro ?
Micro Decision
Personal Computer Magazine

Choose one or two suppliers and then request information on the particular product. Better still, visit them; but for many people this is not an economic proposition. Ask to see a sample of the documentation and fitting instructions; if they cannot provide any then go somewhere else. Because of the popularity of the Amstrad machines some firms now advertise complete kits of parts and it is hoped that the documentation provided matches their advertising. Documentation costs money to produce and it may add a few pounds to the cost of a board but is generally worthwhile in the long run.

This book in no way claims to be a substitute for any manual for an add-on unit but it gives an insight to what is on the market and the possible operations that a buyer/user has to make in installing their newly bought "goodie". The author has added several features to his machine and there have not been any specific problems. One problem was forgetting to take an insulating disk off the bottom of a nickel cadmium battery on a real time clock board and wondering why it would not store the time when it was switched off !!

Internal Expansion Cards

Many of the add-on cards available have more than one option fitted but to understand how everything fits together it was thought worthwhile to examine options topic by topic. Where a card having more than one option alters any parameters (eg memory or I/O map assignments) this has been mentioned if the information is available. The cards are mainly of far east (e.g. Taiwanese) or US origin but are generally of a high standard. Sad to say, but the UK electronics industry has really not responded to this growing market very positively, but there are notable exceptions, mainly in the industrial control and data acquisition sphere.

The expansion card fits into one of the 62-way expansion sockets on the computer motherboard. The expansion card must communicate with the computer and this is done via input/output addresses, interrupts and direct memory access (see Figure 1.1) discussed further in the next chapter. There may be various settings of these parameters and if so they can usually be pre-set by means of links or dual-in line switches (DIP switches) located on the add-on card (see Figure 1.2).

An expansion card is normally quoted as being full length, three quarters length or half length. This refers to the longitudinal dimension and they are, respectively, approximately 325mm, 250mm and 150mm long. The height of the board is nominally 100mm.

External Expansion Units

These units will normally require an internal board to be fitted but the boards that come initially fitted to the computer may have the necessary facilities. Typical of these is a spare parallel or serial port (RS232).

Many of the units under this category may be of UK origin. This is certainly so with the modem market as this has been aided by the fact that the American modem standards are not permitted on the public telephone circuits in the UK.

What is Required in Installation

First of all it is useful to have the manual on the computer in question and, of course, the manual that comes with the associated add-on. Read all of the relevant sections in these thoroughly and if necessary have a "dry-run" at fitting the unit. The tools required for internal units are usually a screwdriver - cross-point and/or flat blade and maybe a small pair of pliers.

Make sure the computer is switched OFF and disconnected from the mains supply. The first task is then the removal of part or all of the computer case. On some machines this merely involves unclipping and raising a hinged lid, on others the removal of part of the case (e.g. Amstrad) or having to undo screws and slide the case off: it all depends on make - (see Figure 1.3). The add-on cards are a single screw fixing and a typical unit is shown on Figure 1.2. Be careful with the screw as it is a ***** to get out if it is dropped into the computer!

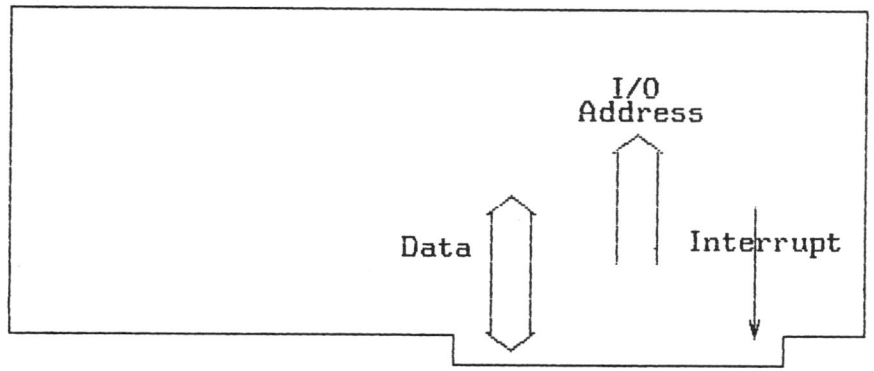

Figure 1.1 Relationship of Expansion Board and Computer Bus

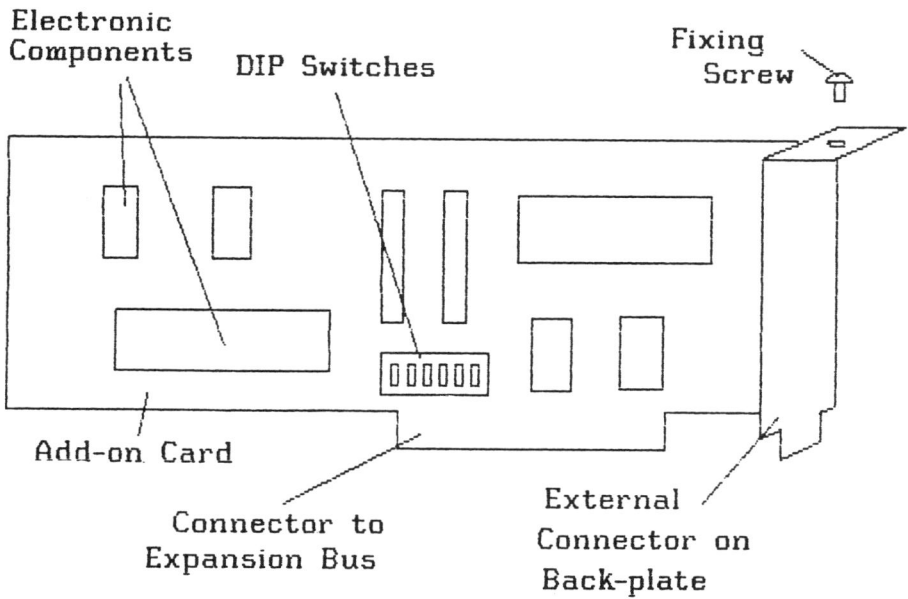

Figure 1.2 Typical Arrangement of Add-on Card with Fittings

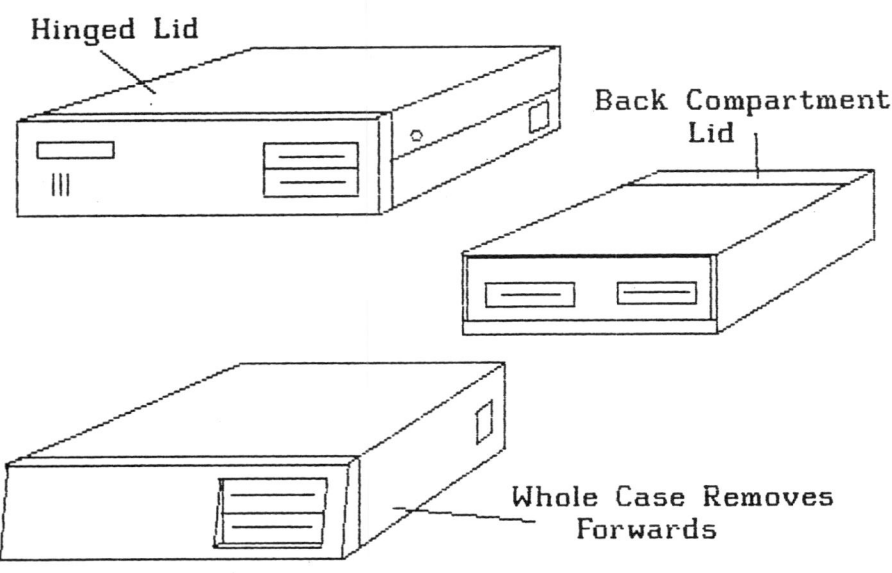

Figure 1.3 Three Ways of Getting into the System Board

A blanking plate must be removed from the computer before the board can be fitted, make sure the board is pressed firmly and squarely into the expansion socket. It does not matter which socket it is fitted to as all sockets are identical. If the unit is heavy on current consumption it might be wise to fit it as near as possible to the power supply connection on the motherboard. There may then be some wiring to connect to other internal units (e.g. disk drives), make sure these leads are fitted correctly.

On external units it is often merely a matter of connecting the equipment to the mains and a cable to the computer. For modems, of course, connection to the telephone circuit by means of a BT600 series connector is also necessary. Figure 1.4 shows the typical connection of an external unit.

6

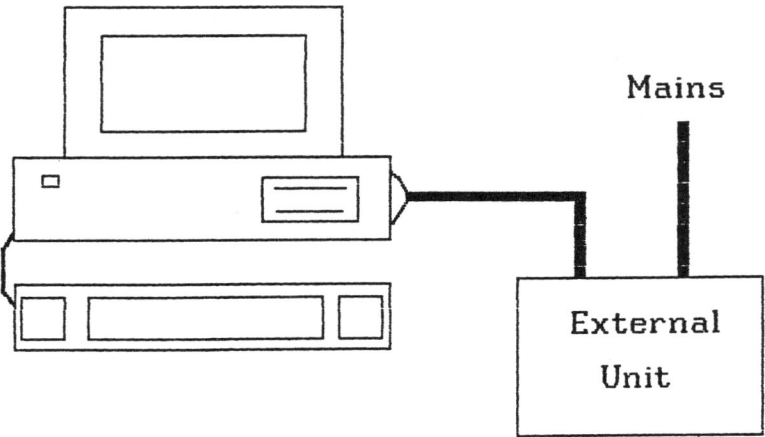

Figure 1.4 Connection of External Unit to PC

Software Routines

Often the add-on will come with software capable of driving it, other cards already have the driving routines in the operating system, e.g. serial RS232. There may come the time when expertise is at hand for additional driving routines to be provided by the buyer. Look at the manual with the expansion unit carefully as some manuals are no more than fitting instructions and written in pretty poor English at that !

All that can be added is Good Luck.

2

GENERAL ARCHITECTURE
OF THE PC

Introduction

This chapter examines the hardware and software of the basic PC or clone. Although there may be constructional differences, the make up of the various clones must be very similar and the memory and I/O maps must conform to a standard. In order to help the reader understand why some add-on cards need switches or links set this chapter tries to explain why certain functions occur and how they are used by the rest of the system. Because of the variations that can occur with expansion cards it is strongly recommended that users make a list of their own memory map, I/O map, interrupt usage and DMA channels used.

The Physical Arrangements

The PC consists of several parts, viz:-

> the mother or system board
> the plug-in boards
> the power supply
> the permanent storage
> the keyboard
> the visual display unit.

These have been assembled in various ways to give varying characteristics and it may be this fact that limits expansion capabilities. The units fall into two main camps: those following an IBM pattern and those after Amstrad. There are differences between the Amstrad 1512 and 1640 as there may well be between models in another manufacturer's range.

The general arrangement of the types is given in Figures 2.1 and 2-2, with Figures 2.3 and 2-4 showing typical subdivisions on the motherboard. From Figures 2.1 and 2-2 it can be seen that the main difference in construction is the location of the power supply. In the Amstrad models it is located within the monitor, hence a monitor change requires the purchase of a monitor/power supply - something that may not be acceptable to industry.

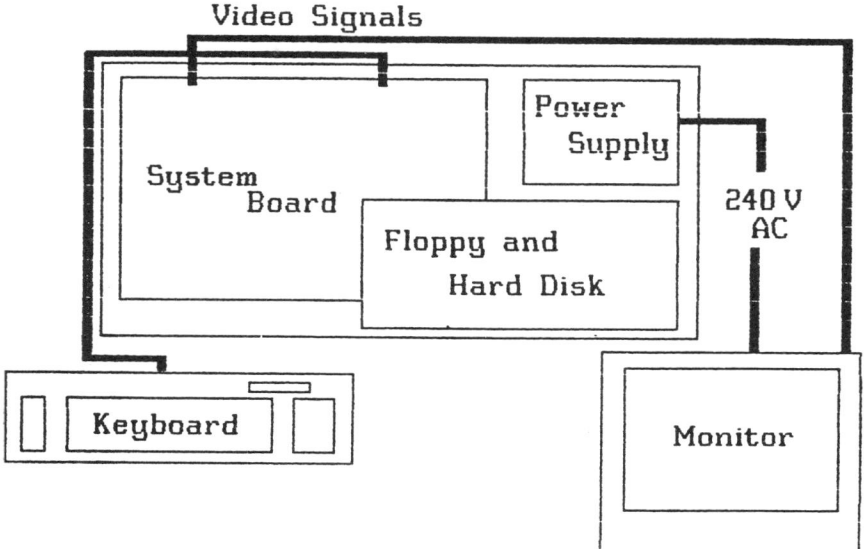

Figure 2.1 Typical Arrangement of IBM Clone

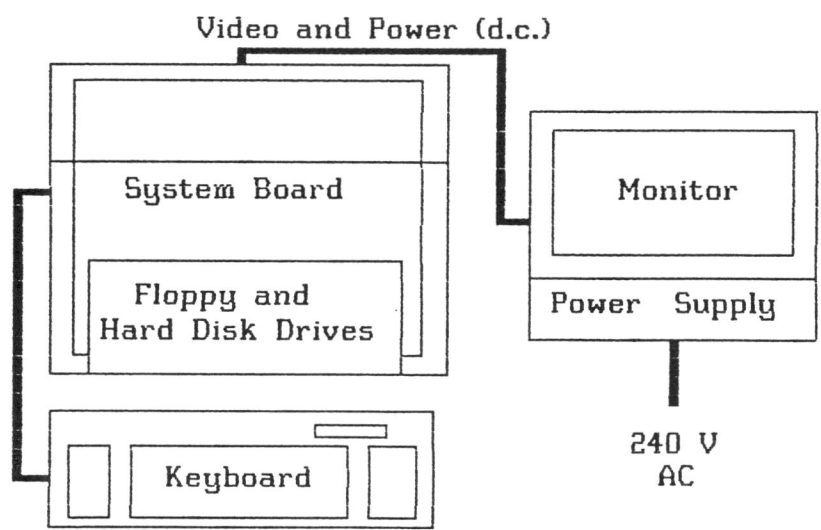

Figure 2.2 Typical Arrangement of Amstrad Machines

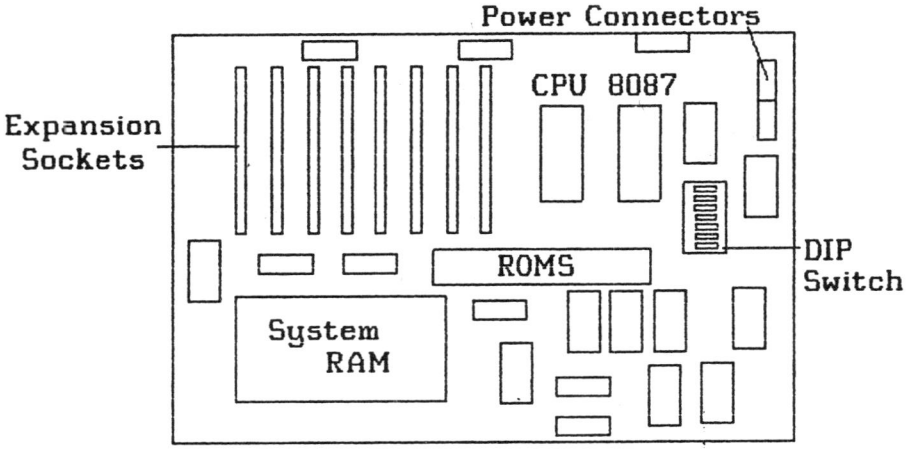

Figure 2.3 Typical Layout of PC Clone

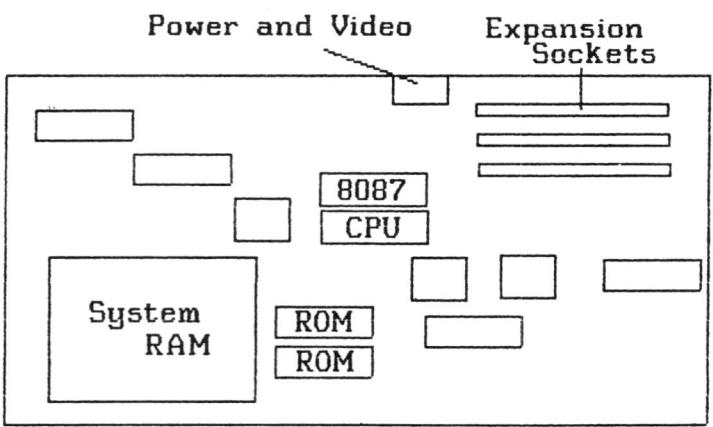

Figure 2.4 Typical Layout of Amstrad 1512

In the 1512 the power supply is not fan cooled, something that is evident in all other compatibles as well as IBM and the later Amstrad 1640. This fact did cause some controversy and various comments in the computer press. With all non-Amstrad units the 240v power supply for the monitor can be taken direct from a 13 amp socket or from the mains outlet on the back of the system box which uses a CEE22/IEC style plug and socket.

On examining the motherboards depicted in Figures 2.3 and 2-4, one of the main differences is the number of expansion sockets provided. The IBM and true compatibles all offer 8 expansion sockets, but Amstrad in both the 1512 and in the 1640 offers only three readily available sockets, with an additional one inside the 1640 for a hard disk controller card. However, Amstrad have included certain features on the motherboard which would be in an expansion slot in the other machines. Table 2.1 below gives some comparisons.

Feature	IBM/Compatibles	Amstrad
Serial output (COM1)	Plug-in card	On motherboard
Parallel output (LPT1)	Plug-in card	On motherboard
Video Controller	Plug-in card	On motherboard
Serial Mouse	Use a serial port	N/a
Bus Mouse	Plug-in card	On motherboard
Clock	Plug-in card	On motherboard
Floppy disk controller	Plug-in card	On motherboard
Hard disk controller	Plug-in card	Plug-in card

Table 2.1 Comparison of Features

From the table it may appear that the compatibles use up most of the expansion slots. This is not true however as several features may appear on one board, e.g. serial and parallel output plus clock or video board plus parallel printer.

Another factor that must be considered generally is that of radio interference. Because of the pulse nature of the internal waveforms, computers can cause interference to sensitive radio equipment. This should be considered when purchasing equipment: metal cases generally provide some inherent screening, whereas plastic cases provide nothing unless treated with a metallised spray. The same can be said for the keyboard, monitor and any other attached devices. The UK authorities have dragged their heels over this matter but in the USA the FCC have set standards. On some units of equipment it may be seen stated, "meets FCC Class B standard" or similar.

Software

Without any software included the computer is a collection of electronic components, printed circuit boards and other miscellaneous hardware that will do very little. On switching on a machine nothing can happen unless certain software routines exist. The purpose of these routines is to perform some form of self test, see what configuration exists, access a hard or floppy disk in order to load the operating system and perform basic input/output. The difference here between various clones is the BIOS (Basic Input Output System) ROM - termed ROS for the Amstrad - and the software in this is copyright. This means that the manufacturers of all compatibles will have to have a BIOS ROM that simulates the genuine IBM product yet does not infringe copyright. The machine coding therefore has to be different and this is where some of the incompatibilities may arise. A good test is software packages that have extensive use of graphics such as AutoCad and Flight Simulator.

Hardware

The original IBM XT ran at 4.77 MHz but most compatibles are either hardware or software switched to give the option of 4.77 or 8 MHz; Amstrad offers only 8 MHz. Some compatible machines are now advertised at 10 MHz. There will be differences in printed circuit board (pcb) layout so that copyrights are not infringed but many of the motherboards are very similar in the positioning of the ICs.

Many of the compatibles have power supplies with greater power capacity, i.e. 155 watts instead of 135 watts, to cope with the additional expansion boards. The Amstrad 1512 and the 1640 have power supplies to supply the motherboard and the limited expansion sockets. The power supplies are all of the switched mode design in order to minimise heat generation and keep the size small and its position in the monitor is peculiar to the Amstrad models. All other models tend to follow a similar pattern, the power to the motherboard being via a 6 way connector and to other units such as disk drives via a 4 way connector. The pin designations are given in Table 2.2 and the connectors will only mate one way round.

	6 pin connectors		4 pin connector
	PL1	PL2	
pin			
1.	+5V dc	0V	+12V dc
2.	n/c	0V	0V
3.	+12V dc	-5V dc	+5V dc
4.	-12V dc	+5V dc	0V
5.	0V	+5V dc	
6.	0V	+5V dc	

Table 2.2 Pin Designations

The Central Processing Unit (CPU)

The choice of processor is either the 8088 or 8086 (or the V20/V30 series - see Chapter 4). The 8088 is not a fully fledged 16 bit microprocessor as it uses an 8 bit data and I/O bus, the 8086 is a true 16 bit processor. Both, however, are software compatible. Figure 2.5 shows the outlines and pin designations for the 8088 and 8086 and table 2.3 gives a brief description of the pin functions, a fuller description needs a deeper understanding of the CPU.

Vcc ..	+5 V dc, GND .. 0 V ..... power supply pins
Axx ..	this denotes an Address pin only
ADxx ..	this denotes an Address pin on one part of the bus cycle and Data on another part of the bus cycle.
Axx/Sx ..	denotes Address pin at the beginning of a bus cycle and the processors internal status otherwise
RD ..	Read, active low
READY ..	Acknowledgement from addressed memory or I/O device that it will complete the data transfer
INTR ..	non-maskable interrupt request
TEST ..	wait for test control
NMI ..	non-maskable interrupt
RESET ..	causes processor to terminate and initialise to a known set state
CLK ..	basic timing clock for CPU operations
MN/MX ..	minimum or maximum mode, PC works in Max. mode
Sx ..	machine cycle status
RQ/GTx ..	local bus priority control, GT1 not used in PC design
QSx ..	instruction queue status
LOCK ..	bus hold control, not used in PC design
M/IO ..	memory or I/O access
WR ..	write control
ALE ..	address latch enable
DT/R ..	data transmit or receive
DEN ..	data enable
INTA ..	interrupt acknowledge
HOLD ..	hold request
HLDA ..	hold acknowledge

Table 2.3 Pin Functions

The 8086 and 8088 can be split internally into two units (see Figure 2.6), these are referred to as the:-

> bus interface unit (BIU)
> execution unit (EU)

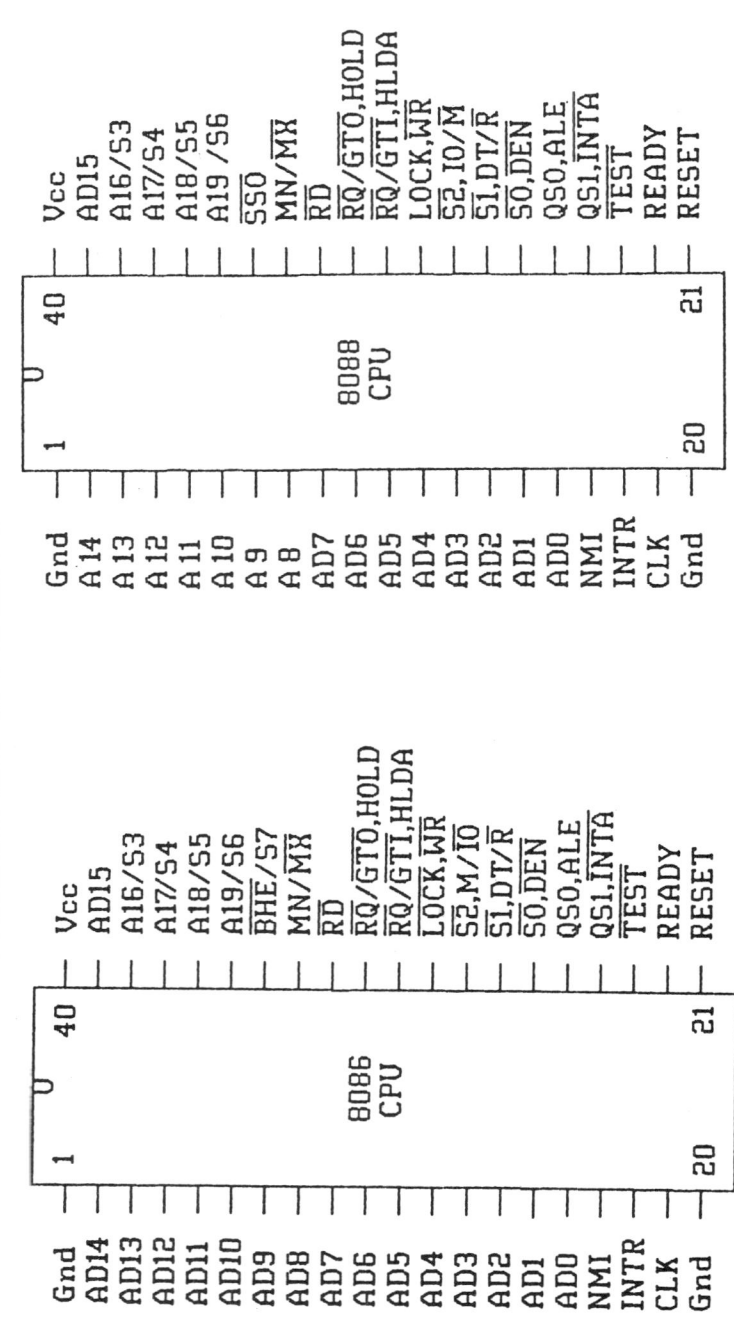

Figure 2.5 Pin Connections for 8086 and 8088 CPUs

14

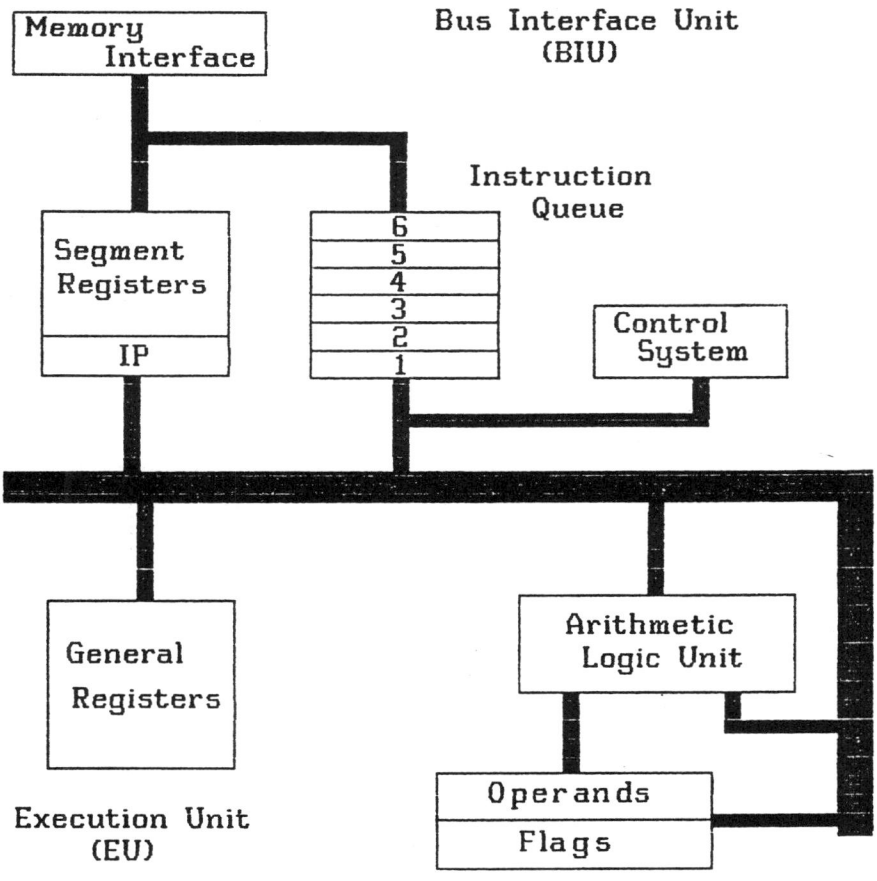

Figure 2.6 Block Diagram of CPU

The bus interface unit deals with communication with external integrated circuits and handles instruction fetching and queuing, operand access, address relocation and control of the bus. The instruction queue can hold up to 6 bytes from the instruction stream whilst they are awaiting decoding and execution. This effectively speeds up the instruction cycle and allows the BIU to use the memory very effectively.

The execution unit accepts the pre-fetched instruction from the BIU queue with any memory operands, executes the instruction and passes the result back to the BIU for memory storage.

The 8088/8086 contains various registers that are used in the performance of its operations and these are depicted in Figure 2.7 and described in the following paragraphs. The CPU has 8 general purpose registers, each containing a 16 bit word (i.e. 2 bytes). The AX and DX registers are known as the accumulators and used for operations such as addition and multiplication. Registers BX, SI and DI are base and index registers for memory addressing, BP and SP are used as stack pointers whilst CX is used as a count register. AX, BX, CX and DX can each be split into two 8 bit registers, e.g. AH (high order byte) and AL (low order byte). These 8 bit registers can be used independently of each other for 8 bit manipulation.

The segment registers require a little explanation but the concept will appear in utility programs such as DEBUG. The processors have 20 address lines which means that they can access 1 MByte of memory (00000H to FFFFFH). However, the maximum number of bits a register can hold is 16, i.e. 4 bits short. To overcome this the memory is split into blocks of up to 64 kByte referred to as segments, each boundary falling on a 16 byte boundary, i.e. hex addresses always ending with a zero, e.g. 01200H, AF4F0H or bits A0 to A3 all zeros. There are four different types of segment and these are labelled CS, DS, SS and ES which refer to code, data, stack and extra segments respectively. Within a segment there can then be an offset of up to 16 bits or 0000H to FFFFH. This offset information is contained within the BX, DI or SI registers. To obtain the true address the BIU shifts the segment data four places to the left and adds four zeros. The BIU then adds the offset address and hence can put the true 20 bit address on the bus.

Figure 2.8 shows how the segment and offset address are implemented. The segment address is derived from the four rightmost hex digits (16 bits) of the complete address on a 16 byte boundary. The offset can then address up to 64 kBytes from that address, the complete address being determined by the combination of segment and offset address. It is possible for segments to overlap as indicated on Figure 2.8.

At this level the machine is controlled by its own instruction set and is beyond the scope of this book. Interested readers are referred to some texts in the bibliography.

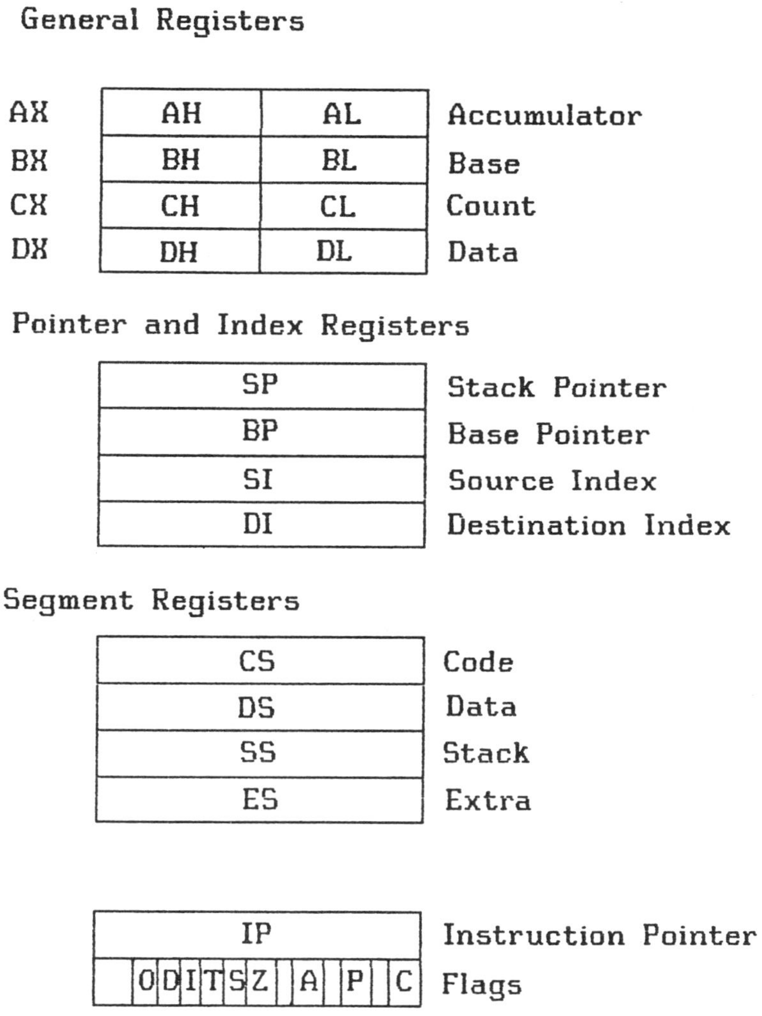

General Registers

	AH	AL	Accumulator
AX			Accumulator
BX	BH	BL	Base
CX	CH	CL	Count
DX	DH	DL	Data

Pointer and Index Registers

SP	Stack Pointer
BP	Base Pointer
SI	Source Index
DI	Destination Index

Segment Registers

CS	Code
DS	Data
SS	Stack
ES	Extra

IP	Instruction Pointer
O D I T S Z A P C	Flags

Figure 2.7 8086/8088 Registers

Complete Address

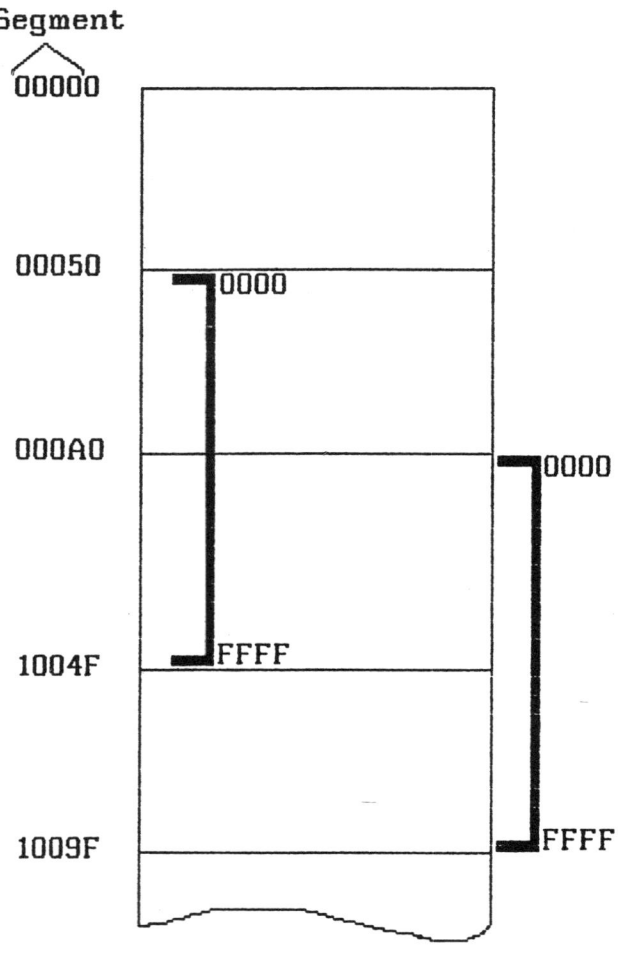

Figure 2.8 Construction of Segment Addresses

Memory

The CPU can address 1 MByte (i.e. 10 bits) and the way this is split is further discussed in the following section. The purpose of this section is to examine the ICs themselves and how the CPU accesses them. The memory may be split into blocks:-

- that used by MSDOS and application programs (640 kBytes maximum) which is usually on the motherboard (RAM)

- RAM/ROM used for video displays, hard disks and so forth (usually on the appropriate board)

- read only memory containing BIOS and so forth on the motherboard (ROM)

The RAM is usually of the dynamic type, i.e. its contents must be refreshed on a regular basis, whilst the read only memory may be ROM, EPROM or equivalent and is permanent.

The user RAM is usually together in a block (see Figure 2.3) on the system board and may consist of 36 sockets (some older models only had 32). It is generally grouped as in Figure 2.9, the data being arranged as one bit columns, 8 columns making one byte (D0-D7). It will be noted that the system memory is nine bits wide - one bit being used for parity checking. Parity is generated on every memory write cycle and stored in the parity bit. On a read cycle parity is regenerated and compared to the stored bit. If the bits are the same it is assumed that the data is good, if not a parity error is generated and reported to the processor via a non-maskable interrupt. The system will then generate an error message for the video display and the operation is aborted. Some very early products did not use parity !

The RAM integrated circuits used are depicted in Figure 2.10 which gives the pinout for the two types. Type 4164 is 64 K x 1 bit and 41256 is 256 K x 1 bit (65,536 and 262,144 memory locations respectively). To decode these the first type needs 16 address lines and the latter 18 address lines. To minimise the number of pins per package the address is given in a two part process, the first part specifies Row, when RAS is low, and the second part specifies Column, when CAS is low. RAS and CAS are derived from the higher order memory bytes and split into RAS0-RAS3 and CAS0-CAS3 - i.e. the four banks of memory. This is shown diagrammatically in Figure 2.11.

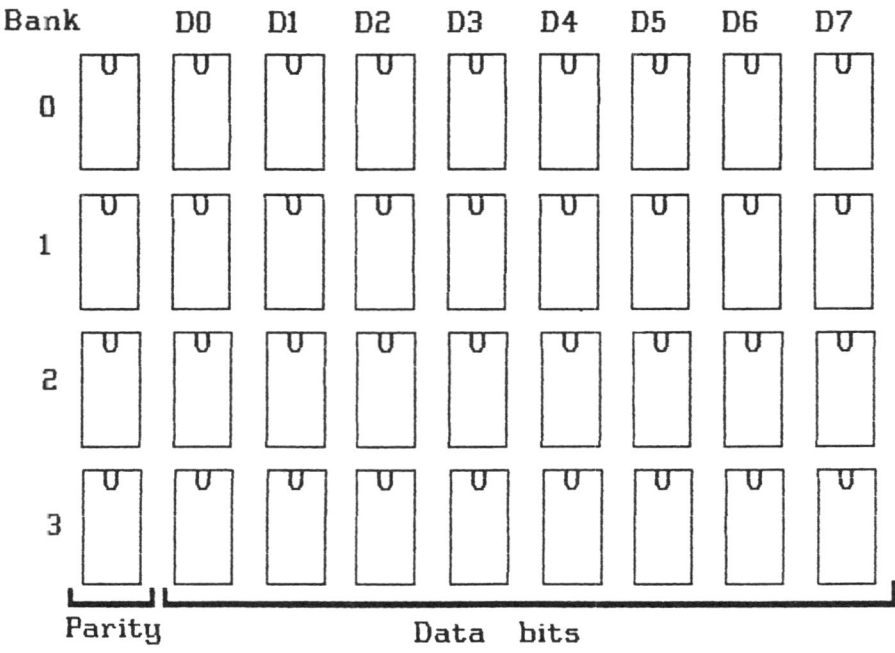

Bank   D0   D1   D2   D3   D4   D5   D6   D7

Parity   Data   bits

Figure 2.9 RAM Grouping

4164	41256	Pin		Pin	4164	41256
NC	A8	1		9	A7	A7
Din	Din	2		10	A5	A5
$\overline{\text{WRITE}}$	$\overline{\text{WRITE}}$	3		11	A4	A4
$\overline{\text{RAS}}$	$\overline{\text{RAS}}$	4		12	A3	A3
A0	A0	5		13	A6	A6
A2	A2	6		14	Dout	Dout
A1	A1	7		15	$\overline{\text{CAS}}$	$\overline{\text{CAS}}$
+5v	+5v	8		16	Gnd	Gnd

Din/Dout   data in/out $\overline{\text{CAS}}$ column add. strobe
$\overline{\text{WRITE}}$ read write control $\overline{\text{RAS}}$ row address strobe
An   address lines

Figure 2.10 RAM Integrated Circuits

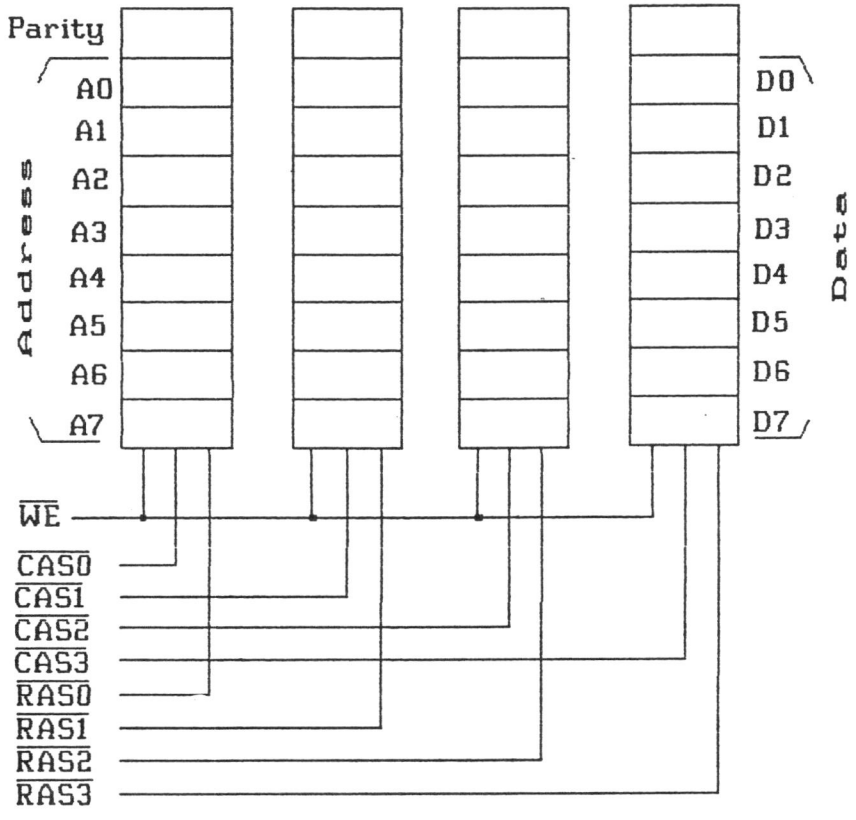

Figure 2.11 Typical RAM Addressing

Comparing the two types of memory chip it can be seen that the only difference is pin 1 - not connected in the 4164 and an extra address line in the 41256. Both types will therefore fit the same IC socket and the memory therefore can consist of a mixture of device types. Hence, assuming the system board can cope with a maximum of 640 kBytes typical arrangements are:-

128 kB	2 rows of 4164 (64k x 1 twice)	- 18 sockets
256 kB	1 row of 41256 (256K x 1)	- 9 sockets
	or 4 rows of 4164 (64k x 1 four times)	- 36 sockets
512 kB	2 rows of 41256 (256k x 1 twice)	- 18 sockets
640 kB	2 rows of 41256	
	and 2 rows of 4164	- 36 sockets

The ROM is accessed slightly differently as it has 8 bit data lines. The higher order bytes are decoded to give a CS (chip select) signal and then all the data bits are output. This is shown diagrammatically in Figure 2.12.

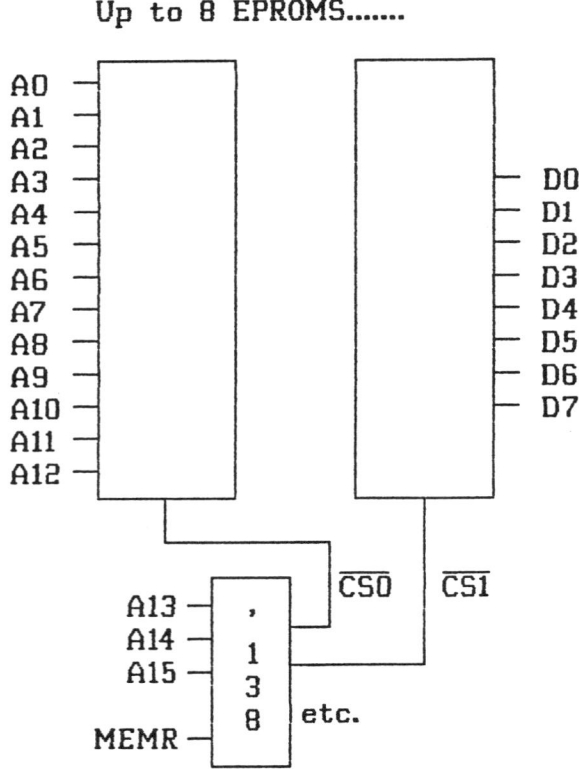

Figure 2.12 Typical Arrangement for ROM Addressing

Address (Hex)	Comments
00000	0000 - 03FF Interrupt Vectors
10000	0400 - 04FF BIOS Variables
20000	
30000	
40000	
50000	User RAM - 640 kBytes
60000	to 9FFFF
70000	
80000	
90000	
A0000	Video RAM Area
B0000	EGA A0000 - BFFFF CGA B8000 - BBFFF Herc. B0000 - BFFFF
C0000	Possible Memory Expansion Area
D0000	C8000 - C9FFF Hard Disk BIOS
E0000	
F0000	F4000 - FFFFF ROM Sockets
FFFFF	FE000 - FFFFF System BIOS

Figure 2.13 Memory Map for PC

Memory Map

As already mentioned, both the 8088 and 8086 processors are capable of addressing 1 MByte of memory. However MSDOS and PCDOS can only handle 640 kByte of user RAM for program purposes, the remaining 384 kBytes being used for video displays, hard disks and system ROM. Figure 2.13 shows the memory map of the machines and depicts the use of the various areas of memory. There may be some spare RAM in the memory map, depending on the options fitted, but it would require special software to make use of it.

The user RAM lies from 00000H to 9FFFFH (640 kBytes), but 0000H to 03FFH is normally used for system vectors and 0400H to 04FFH for BIOS data. The next main block of memory (A0000H to BFFFFH) is for the various video displays. The amount of memory used here depends on the type of video card employed and the maximum memory required lies from A0000H to BFFFFH (i.e. 128 kBytes) - this is discussed further in Chapter 5.

The area C0000H to EFFFFH is the possible memory expansion area of 192 kBytes but requiring special software for its use. However, it is required for the hard disk BIOS ROM (C8000H-C9FFFH) and possibly local area networks. The area F0000H to F3FFFH is generally quoted as Reserved. The area from F4000H to FFFFFH can cope with 6 ROM sockets, the BIOS being generally located from FE000H to FFFFFH (ROS in Amstrad 1640 is FC000H to FFFFFH). F4000H to F5FFFH is generally vacant, any BASIC interpreter or part thereof residing from F6000H to FDFFFH. Not all machines have all sockets provided and most machines will have the BASIC interpreter completely on disk, e.g. GWBASIC.

Input/Output Map

The 8086 and 8088 processors can cope with a maximum of 65,536 I/O ports and use the IN and OUT instructions for this purpose. In the PC XT design only the lower 10 bits of the address are used as shown below:

bits 0 - 8	defines 512 port addresses
bit 9	defines if port address is on system board or expansion socket
bits 10-15	not used in PC XT design
bits 16-19	not used in 8086/8088 architecture

As bits 0-9 are used in addressing this gives a maximum of 1024 I/O ports but they are restricted as follows. When bit 9 is low, data cannot be received from the expansion I/O sockets, only from the motherboard and when high it allows data from the I/O expansion channels. Thus for inputs the I/O is divided into two groups, 512 each from system board and expansion channels. There is no restriction on the 1024 output ports.

I/O Port Address (Hex)	Comment
000 - 00F	DMA Controller
010 - 01F	-
020 - 021	Interrupt Controller
022 - 03F	-
040 - 043	Timer Counter
044 - 05F	-
060 - 063	PPI 8255A IC
064 - 07F	-
080 - 083	DMA Page Registers
084 - 09F	-
0A0	NMI Mask Bit
0A1 - 1FF	-
200 - 20F	Game Control Adapter
210 - 277	-
278 - 27F	Parallel Printer Port LPT2
280 - 2F7	-
2F8 - 2FF	Serial Port COM2
300 - 31F	Protoype Card
320 - 32F	Hard Disk Controller
330 - 377	-
378 - 37F	Parallel Printer Port LPT1
380 - 3AF	-
3B0 - 3BF	Monochrome and Printer Adapter
3C0 - 3CF	EGA Adapter
3D0 - 3DF	CGA Adapter
3E0 - 3EF	-
3F0 - 3F7	Floppy Disk Adapter
3F8 - 3FF	Serial Port COM1

Notes: after 3FF I/O address may "wrap around"
         - denotes not specified but may NOT be vacant

Figure 2.14 Typical PC XT Input/Output Address Map

The input/output address space is divided as follows:

	Input	Output
0000H-01FFH	for motherboard	no restriction
0200H-03FFH	expansion I/O slots	no restriction
0400H-FFFFH	not used in basic computer design	

The general arrangement of the I/O map of the PC is given in Figure 2.14 and a more detailed description is given, when required, in succeeding chapters under the various types of expansion considered. **Care must be exercised** with some of the I/O map as there may be minor differences between options as more expansion cards become available. A good idea is to draw a memory map similar to Figure 2.14 for your computer and the options fitted.

Interrupts

The computer system serves little use if it cannot communicate with the outside world. This is normally accomplished by means of the keyboard, monitor, printer, disk drives and other options attached such as RS232 links and industrial controllers. To be able to perform these functions the computer must have an efficient I/O system and recognise when it has to carry out an operation. In order to see if these units require attention there are three methods commonly used:-

    polling
    interrupts
    direct memory access

The first method uses software routines and checks all devices on a periodic basis to see if they require servicing. When it finds a unit requiring attention it will attend to it, then carry on with the polling and then return to whatever else it was doing. This is a very simple solution but can result in the computer spending a lot of time just polling devices. Also, a device will not be serviced until the next poll - an unsatisfactory situation if the unit requires immediate attention.

A better approach is to allow the device requiring attention to signal to the computer that attention is required. This is known as "interrupts" and provides an efficient method of communication. It is explained in detail below. The third method still relies on interrupts but these signify that an operation is required that does not require information to be passed via the CPU but directly with memory. This is discussed in the next section.

When an interrupt is detected the CPU will finish the immediate operation, store the information held about the present operation (i.e. status registers, flags, program counters on the system stack) service the interrupt and then recall the parameters from the stack and resume whatever it was doing. Interrupts are classified into three groups:-

interrupts (INTR)
non-maskable interrupts (NMI)
reset (RESET)

These all have a separate pin on the CPU and the responses are described in the next few paragraphs. Figure 2.15 represents how the various interrupts are interfaced into the system.

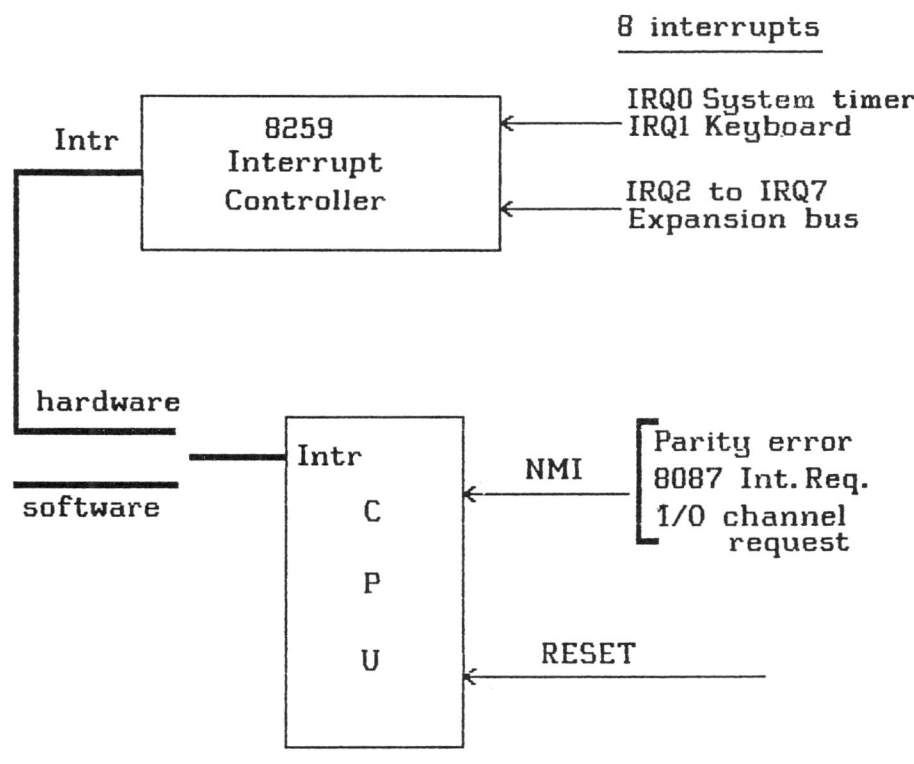

Figure 2.15 Hardware Arrangement for IRQ0 to IRQ7

INTR

This type of interrupt has the lower order of priority. It can be software masked (i.e. ignored) until a more appropriate time for the CPU. The CPU can handle 256 types of interrupt and these may be generated by either software or hardware and the hardware interrupt is recognised by INTR going high (i.e. logic 1). Figure 2.16 gives a typical list of the various interrupts (although it may not be accurate for all clones). The interrupts that appear on the expansion bus are IRQ2 - IRQ7 and these are obviously used by the expansion cards, IRQ2 has a higher priority than IRQ3 and so on. Some of these interrupts are already reserved so that if it is necessary to select an interrupt be very careful in its choice. To enhance the interrupt system an 8259 programmable interface controller (PIC) is fitted. In machines such as the Amstrad PCs some expansion is on the system or motherboard.

When an interrupt has been acknowledged, then the computer must go to a routine to deal with that interrupt, the addresses (or vectors) for these routines being obtained from memory locations 0000H to 03FFH (1024 bytes).

The sequence of events on receiving an interrupt are:-

1. Interrupt acknowledge sent, INTA (active low).

2. Interrupt type code (N) read from data bus, D0-D7.

3. Flag register pushed on to system stack.

4. Interrupt and single step mode disabled.

5. CS and IP registers saved on to system stack.

6. IP register loaded with data from memory locations 4*N an 4*N + 1 (N interrupt type).

7. CS register loaded with data from memory locations 4*N + 2 and 4*N + 3.

8. CPU obtains next instruction from 20 bit address generated by the new IP and CS values.

9. Interrupt then serviced.

10. Old values of IP, CS and flag register recalled from stack.

11. Original operation resumed.

Interrupt Type Dec.	Hex.	Designation	Function
0	00		Divide by zero
1	01		Single Stepping
2	02		Parity Error (NMI)
3	03		Break
4	04		Overflow
5	05		Print Screen
6	06		–
7	07		–
8	08	IRQ0	Time of Day
9	09	IRQ1	Keyboard
10	0A	IRQ2	RTC Interrupt
11	0B	IRQ3	COM2
12	0C	IRQ4	COM1
13	0D	IRQ5	Hard Disk
14	0E	IRQ6	Floppy Disk Drive
15	0F	IRQ7	Parallel Port
16	10		Video I/O
17	11		System Configuration
18	12		Memory Size
19	13		Disk I/O
20	14		Serial I/O
21	15		–
22	16		Keyboard I/O
23	17		Printer I/O
24	18		System Restart/resident BASIC
25	19		Bootstrap
26	1A		Time of Day Clock
27	1B		Keyboard BREAK
28	1C		Ticker
29	1D		Video Initialisation
30	1E		Diskette Parameters
31	1F		Video Graphics Characters
32–39	20–27		Disk Operating System
40–95	28–5F		Reserved
96–103	60–67		Reserved – user software
104–127	68–7F		Not Used
128–133	80–85		Reserved by BASIC
134–240	86–F0		BASIC Interpreter when running
241–255	F1–FF		Not Used

Figure 2.16 Typical Use of Interrupts and Types

NMI

This is the non-maskable interrupt and cannot be "ignored until a suitable opportunity has arisen" as with the previous type and is on pin 17 of the CPU. It serves three basic functions:-

reporting a parity error

8087 co-processor interrupt
I/O channel request.

It is assumed to be of type 2 (see Figure 2.16) and the sequence of events is:-

1. Flag register pushed on to system stack

2. INTR interrupts disabled

3. TF cleared, no single step may occur

4. CS and IP registers pushed on to system stack

5. IP register loaded with 16 bit data from 00008H and 00009H memory locations

6. CS register loaded with 16 bit data from 0000AH and 0000BH memory locations

7. CPU fetches the next instruction (interrupt service routine) from the 20 bit address generated by the IP and CS registers.

8. Interrupt then serviced

9. Recalls flag register from system stack

10. Recalls CS and IP from system stack

11. Original operation resumed

Reset

This interrupt is generated by the system timer and goes to pin 21 of the CPU. It occurs when the computer is switched on and has the following effect:-

FLAG	cleared
IP	0000H
CS register	FFFFH
DS register	0000H
SS register	0000H
ES register	0000H

The first instruction after a reset is taken from FFFF0H and Intel recommends that memory locations from FFFF0H to FFFFFH are not used except for their intended purpose or the computer may become confused on initialisation.

DMA Channels

Direct memory access (DMA) allows direct transfer of information from the computer's memory to a peripheral device without going via the CPU. The reason for this is that some devices can pass data at a rate faster than the CPU can keep up with, e.g. floppy disk units and hard disk units. A DMA controller (DMAC) - 8237 - is provided in the PC design to handle this data transfer, this IC is programmable by certain registers it contains via I/O ports. It allows 4 channels of DMA data transfer and can transfer in blocks of 64 kBytes.

Before a DMA transfer can occur the IC must be initialised and the following information provided:-

> Read or write to memory
> Type of transfer - single or block transfer
> Byte count
> Channel priority
> Starting memory address
> Enable channel's request signal

The initialisation is carried out by writing control words to the DMAC via the I/O ports at 0000H to 000FH. These are divided into two groups, 0000H to 0007H and 0008H to 000FH. The first group contain read/write registers holding memory information whilst the second group contain status and control registers. They are defined as follows:-

0000H	
0001H	Start memory address for each channel
0002H	
0003H	Current memory address for next DMA cycle
0004H	
0005H	Byte count to be transferred for each channel
0006H	
0007H	Current byte count for each channel

on I/O port Read

0008H	Read status register
0009H-000CH	Not used
000DH	Read temporary register
000EH-000FH	Not used

on I/O port Write

0008H	Write command register
0009H	Write request register
000AH	Write single mask bit register
000BH	Write mode register
000CH	Clear byte pointer flip-flop
000DH	Master clear
000EH	Clear mask register
000FH	Write all mask registers

The DMAC can handle four channels and these are designated below:-

Channel 0	supports memory refresh	highest priority
Channel 1	not allocated	
Channel 2	floppy disk drive adapter	
Channel 3	hard disk drive (if fitted)	lowest priority

If a DMA channel is required for an additional expansion option then a DMA channel must be chosen carefully. Channel 3 can be used if no hard disk drive is fitted, otherwise the only choice is channel 1. The expansion unit should give the option of using the DMA channel and will be set by switches or links on the appropriate add-on board.

Input and Output Expansion

As mentioned above many of the compatibles have a total of 8 expansion sockets but Amstrad has nominally only three. These I/O channels are essentially an extension of the microcomputer system bus. They are de-multiplexed, re-buffered and use the additional facilities provided by interrupts and DMA functions. In all designs the expansion socket on the mother or system board must conform to a given standard and this is shown on Figure 2.17 with all pin designations (the 16 bit PC Bus). It is a 62 pin connector with 0.1 inch pin spacing and the connections are as described below. The signal lines are TTL compatible and provide 2 LSTTL loads per slot.

32

Signal	Pin	Pin	Signal
Gnd	B1	A1	I/O CH CK
Reset Drv.	B2	A2	D0
+5V dc	B3	A3	D1
IRQ2	B4	A4	D2
-5V dc	B5	A5	D3
DRQ2	B6	A6	D4
-12V dc	B7	A7	D5
Not used	B8	A8	D6
+12V dc	B9	A9	D7
Gnd	B10	A10	I/O CH RDY
MEMW	B11	A11	AEN
MEMR	B12	A12	A19
IOW	B13	A13	A18
IOR	B14	A14	A17
DACK 3	B15	A15	A16
DRQ3	B16	A16	A15
DACK 1	B17	A17	A14
DRQ1	B18	A18	A13
DACK 0	B19	A19	A12
CLK	B20	A20	A11
IRQ7	B21	A21	A10
IRQ6	B22	A22	A9
IRQ5	B23	A23	A8
IRQ4	B24	A24	A7
IRQ3	B25	A25	A6
DACK 2	B26	A26	A5
T/C	B27	A27	A4
ALE	B28	A28	A3
+5V dc	B29	A29	A2
OSC	B30	A30	A1
Gnd	B31	A31	A0

Figure 2.17 Expansion Socket and Designations

Data Lines (D0-D7) - 8 lines

These are bi-directional and active high. D0 is LSB and D7 MSB.

Address Lines (A0-A19) - 20 lines

These lines can be used for addressing memory and I/O ports. A0 is LSB and A19 MSB and active high.

Interrupt Request Signals (IRQ2-IRQ7) - 6 lines

These are six input only lines generating interrupt requests to the processor. IRQ2 has highest priority and IRQ7 the lowest. The interrupt signal is a low to high transition and is held until the processor acknowledges.

Direct Memory Access Request (DRQ1-DRQ3) - 3 lines

These lines go directly to a DMA controller (e.g. 8237 DMA) and are asynchronous channels used by the interface to request DMA cycles. This allows the device to transfer information between itself and memory without the intervention of the CPU. DRQ1 has highest priority and DRQ3 the lowest.

Direct Memory Access Acknowledge (DACK0-DACK3) - 4 lines

These signals are sent by the DMA controller to acknowledge receipt of a DRQ signal and are active low. DACK0 is used to refresh the system dynamic memory.

I/O Channel Check (I/O CH CK)

This is an input only signal and active low. It is used to report an error condition on an interface card.

I/O Channel Ready (I/O CH RDY)

This is to enable a slow device to communicate with the I/O channel without difficulty. This signal is input only and is used by the memory or I/O device to extend the length of a bus cycle. It goes low to cause this condition.

Memory Write (MEMW)

This is an output signal and tells the memory to store the data at present on the data bus. It originates from the bus controller (e.g. 8288) on CPU initiated bus cycles.

Memory Read (MEMR)

This is an output only signal and is active low. It instructs the memory to output data on to the data bus. The signal comes from either the bus controller or the DMA controller.

Address Latch Enable (ALE)

This is active high and an output only from the bus controller. It is used to indicate that the address bus is valid for the beginning of a bus cycle.

Address Enable (AEN)

This signal is used by the DMA controller to indicate that a DMA bus cycle is in progress. When high the DMA controller takes control of the address bus, data bus and read/write command lines.

Oscillator (OSC)

An output only signal with a clock frequency of 14.31818 MHz. This is derived from the main crystal oscillator on the system board.

Clock (CLK)

This is the system clock and depends on the setting on the system board viz. 4.77 or 8 MHz. It is an output only signal.

Reset Driver (RESET DRV)

An output signal that provides a power-on reset signal to bus-attached interface logic or I/O devices.

Terminal Count (TC)

This is used by the DMA controller to indicate that one of the DMA channels has reached its terminal count. The signal is active high.

I/O Read (IOR)

This is an output signal from the bus controller and informs the I/O device to read the data from the data bus. It is active low and can also be provided direct from the CPU or DMA controller.

I/O Write (IOW)

This is the same as above except that it informs the I/O device to write to the data bus.

Voltage Supplies

These provide voltages to drive the I/O boards and are allocated as below with typically expected tolerances.

+5V DC	+/- 5%	pins B3 and B29
-5V DC	+/-10%	pin B5
+12V DC	+/- 5%	pin B9
-12V DC	+/-10%	pin B7
Ground (GND)		pins B1, B10 and B31.

System Board Switch Settings

There is usually an 8 way DIP switch on the motherboard. This provides the computer with information when it is switched on or reset, i.e. the operating system is configured. They are allocated as follows:-

Position	Function
1	Normal operation OFF
2	8087 co-processor option
3 & 4	RAM available
5 & 6	Type of display adapter
7 & 8	Number of floppy disk drives

The DIP switch has one side labelled ON and the other OFF. The position of the small switches is defined below.

Position 1   leave in OFF always

Position 2   ON no 8087 processor   OFF 8087 processor installed

Position 3	Position 4	Memory Installed
OFF	ON	128 kBytes
ON	OFF	192 kBytes
OFF	OFF	256 kBytes or greater

Position 5	Position 6	Display Configuration
ON	ON	No display adapter
OFF	ON	Colour/Graphics (default 40x20)
ON	OFF	Colour Graphics (default 80x25)
OFF	OFF	Monochrome display adapter

Position 7	Position 8	No. Floppy Disk Drives
ON	ON	1
OFF	ON	2
ON	OFF	3
OFF	OFF	4

Because the arrangement is somewhat different in the Amstrad machines it is best to consult their manuals.

3

MEMORY UPGRADES

Introduction

This chapter examines two possible forms of semiconductor memory upgrade; disk and tape storage are dealt with in Chapter 6. The first to be examined is the expansion of the normal user RAM to 640 kBytes. The second memory expansion is the use of add-on boards that permit memory expansion to about 8 MBytes but it can only be used with special software because of the limits imposed by MSDOS/PCDOS and the processors used. It will however enable speed improvements in the use of databases and spreadsheets that support this facility.

The expansion of any computer using MSDOS/PCDOS to 640 kBytes is the first step that anyone should consider in memory expansion. The very earliest of the IBM PCs only had a very mean 64 kByte on the motherboard! This form of memory expansion also represents the cheapest option. Some programs require upwards of 512 kBytes to run, and this is especially true in the big desktop publishing packages. It is difficult to see why any manufacturer/supplier only places 512 kBytes on the motherboard when it is almost as cheap, and more useful, to fit the full 640 kBytes.

Basic Memory Expansion

As already mentioned, without special software, the maximum amount of user RAM that MSDOS or PCDOS can handle is 640 kBytes. Not all of the PCs supplied contain this amount of memory and it is easy to upgrade to the maximum although some of the original ICs installed may become redundant. BEWARE - some of the early machines only had sufficient room for 256 kBytes on the motherboard or could only cope with a certain type of RAM, others use RAM ICs to give this amount yet fill all the sockets. The starting point is reading your manual and looking inside the computer. If the motherboard can only hold a certain amount of memory then it will be necessary to install an expansion board.

Expansion of On-board RAM

This section really only deals with adding ICs to the system board but if the system board will only hold 256 kBytes then read the next section on memory expansion boards - there is a solution to the problem.

Chapter 2 gives an explanation of the types of IC used, how they are arranged and how they are accessed. From this information it should be possible to work out the type of memory ICs required - i.e. 4164 or 41256 dynamic RAMS (or DRAMS). Before obtaining these items another important factor to determine is the speed of access of the chip. In the older 4.77 MHz only units the chip was specified as 200 ns (-20). In the dual 4.77/8 MHz units a 150 ns (-15) device must be used, and if a 10 MHz board is used then the device must be 120 ns or 100 ns access time (-12 or -10). The types are designated, for example, 4164-15 or 41256-15 for a 150 ns device.

When ordering these ICs specify the correct speed type with the correct suffix. Shop around for the ICs, a 41256-15 is typically £2.50 and the 4164-15 about £1.00 although having stated this there is a dearth of the 41256 type around at the moment and prices are being pushed up.

Inserting the Ram Integrated Circuits

Make sure from your computer reference manual whether there is any restriction in which rows the different type of RAM can reside in. Make sure the computer is switched off and be careful in the handling of the RAM. Ease any ICs out of their sockets that must be extracted and carefully push the new ones in - taking great care with the correct alignment (the notch or spot on the IC case). Whilst the computer case is open make sure all the other RAM is firmly in its sockets by pressing them in. The only item left is whether any system board switch settings need be altered. This is discussed towards the end of the previous chapter and informs the operating system how much memory is available.

Some firms advertise upgrade memory kits for such machines as the Amstrad PC1512 together with complete instructions - see suppliers at the back of this book.

Memory Expansion Boards

This is a means of expanding the base memory from typically 256 kBytes to 640 kBytes with an add-on board where it is not possible to implement this with ICs, as discussed in the previous section. These will give typically an extra 384 kBytes of memory and, providing the system board contains 256 kBytes, allows expansion to the full 640 kBytes for MSDOS/PCDOS. Some boards will provide more memory BUT the base memory can only be extended to 640 kBytes, the remainder must be used as extended memory (see next section). One normally has the option of buying the boards with or without the memory ICs - do your own sums as prices fluctuate. By buying the board with the memory the supplier is responsible for the overall guarantee.

If the board is bought unpopulated (i.e. no RAM ICs fitted), insert the memory ICs but note the comments above regarding the ICs themselves and about inserting the RAM integrated circuits. In addition read the manual for the expansion board very carefully as this will give any link/switch settings required both on the expansion board and the motherboard. These settings typically denote where the board has to sit in the computer's memory map as well as denoting the amount of memory available for the system. This is required by the operating system when it is booted up as MSDOS/PCDOS must have contiguous RAM and know how much there is. Insert the board into an expansion socket, fix it in properly with the screw provided and then turn the computer on . All should now function and the system will recognise the extra memory available - normally shown in some form in the boot-up routine on the screen.

Extended Memory Expansion

As stated in the previous section the MSDOS/PCDOS operating system can only cope with 640 kBytes of memory although the 8088/8086 microprocessors themselves can cope with 1 MByte. The option offered by adding an extended memory card is expanding the base memory above the user 640 kByte RAM limit by adding additional banks of memory which can only be used with application packages containing the requisite software for bank switching.

The memory is intended as an expansion to the basic 1 MBytes that the microprocessors can address and requires special software to access it. This is typically contained in some programs such as Lotus 1-2-3, DBASE3, AUTOCAD and some programs used in image capture. In addition, with software typically provided with the expansion card, it can act as a Ramdisk and Print Spooler. These types of board may also be referred to as Intel above board expansion units, as it was Intel who first produced such equipment. The actual specification is referred to as the Lotus/Intel/Microsoft (LIM) Expanded Memory Specification (EMS) and usually allows up to an extra 8 MBytes to be fitted in the typical XT type clone if there is sufficient physical space in the expansion sockets. The latest version of the EMS/LIM specification is 4.0.

A typical board can contain up to 2 MBytes of additional RAM (some allowing part of the memory to fill the base memory as mentioned earlier). It is also possible to have several boards residing (up to 8 MBytes) provided that the software in use can handle it. The memory of course has to be addressed but it is split into banks of memory as explained below. It sits in parallel with the main memory and is accessed as necessary.

Each board need not be fully populated but a DIP switch will normally have to be set to indicate amount of memory present. Each 2 MByte board is split into 128 x 16 kByte pages of memory and 64 kBytes of this can be switched into a "window" in the main 1 MByte memory map (see Figure 3.1). An expansion memory board is controlled by I/O addresses or page registers. These denote which board is to be accessed and which 16 kByte page(s) are to be used. As mentioned earlier a total of four boards can be used which means that there must be four independent groups of I/O addresses in total. The DIP switches on a board allow these to be set independently but must not conflict with each other OR any other expansion facility. This may in fact restrict the number of boards that can be added. A total of 4 x 16 kBytes (64 kBytes) can be switched into an area of the 1 MByte main memory, e.g. A0000H to AFFFFH .

The bottom 7 bits of the register select which of the 128 pages (00H to 7FH) is to be switched into the region whilst the most significant bit denotes if the region is enabled into address space (if 0 then not enabled, if a 1 it is enabled). Figure 3.1 shows diagrammatically how the boards are arranged whilst Figure 3.2 shows how four pages are placed into the four regions of the 64 kBytes of contiguous memory. Although A0000H to AFFFFH are shown here it may have to be changed as this memory space clashes with that required for EGA and VGA video cards (see Chapters 2 and 5).

Fitting the Expansion Board

This is a fairly painless affair. First of all read the manual and ascertain the settings of any links or DIP switches on the board. If memory ICs have to be fitted then take careful note of the exact types required and make sure that they are fitted with the correct orientation. The board is the normal screw fitting and easy to install after removing the case from the computer.

Software

There may be some form of extended memory manager program that comes with the board that allows the memory to be partitioned for disk caching, RAM disk and printer spooling as well as providing test routines. The application software to be used with this option may need to be re-configured so that it is aware that EMS is available.

Suppliers

AST - memory and extended memory boards
Atomstyle - memory cards
Citadel Products Ltd - memory and extended memory boards
Dataflex Design - extended memory boards, RAM ICs
Digitask - memory boards, RAM ICs
DRAM Electronics - RAM ICs
First Software - extended memory boards
Link International - extended memory boards
Orchid (Europe) Ltd - extended memory boards
RS Components - RAM ICs
Technomatic - memory expansion cards, RAM ICs
Verospeed - RAM ICs

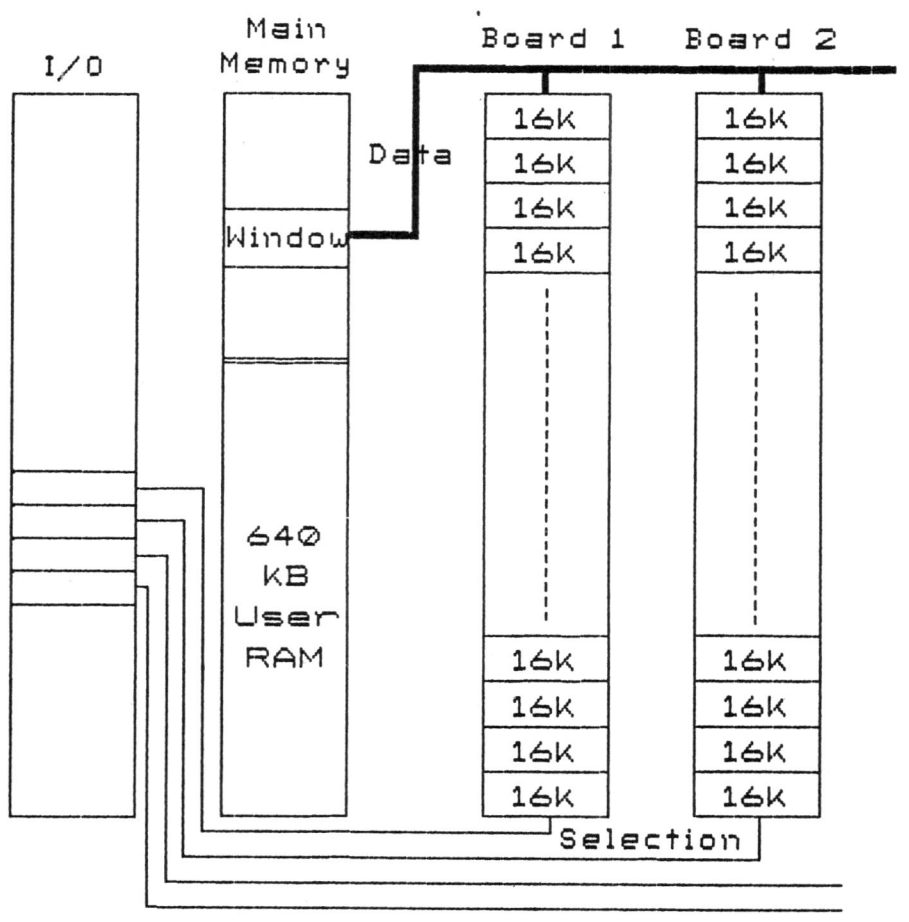

Figure 3.1 Selection and Use of EMS RAM

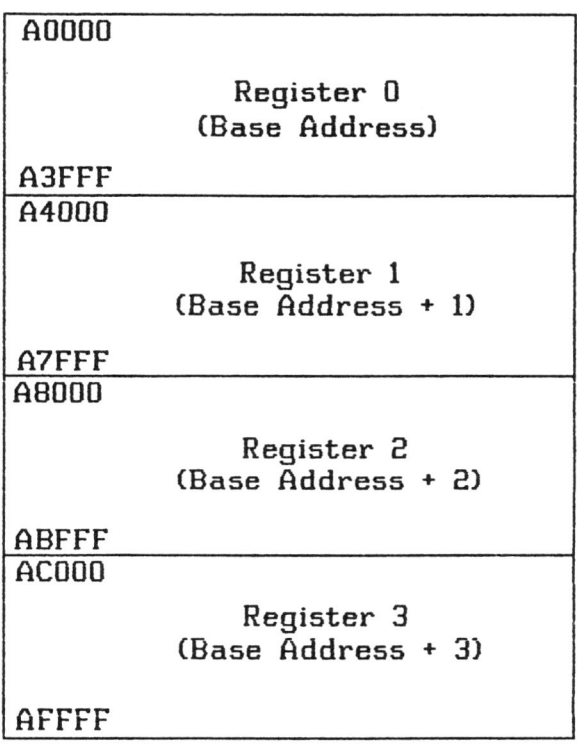

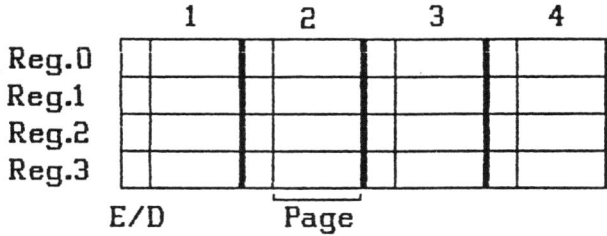

Figure 3.2 Arrangement of Page Memory and Registers

4

SPEED ENHANCEMENTS

Introduction

This chapter examines a variety of methods of increasing the speed of the basic PC XT and compatibles. There is no need to consider this option "just for the sake of it", one must examine the whole gamut of operations to see why an increase in throughput is required and if this is actually the computer itself or a slow peripheral device.

This can be accomplished in a variety of methods but only one is relatively cheap and as might be expected it does not offer the biggest benefit. The newer PC XT compatibles all operate at 8 MHz with some giving the option of the slower 4.77 MHz. Also, some of the latest types on the market give a 10 MHz operating speed. However, it is assumed that one already has a computer of a given breed and wishes somehow to speed its operations.

Obviously the slow 4.77 MHz machines will benefit the most but a good economic case has to be established for an upgrade of this variety. It is only software that uses extensive computing manipulation that will show any real benefits, a straightforward program in BASIC (although it will run faster) will not necessarily show any great increase in throughput.

The upgrades available in this chapter go from a simple replacement of the basic microprocessor IC to replacement boards for the microprocessor itself or even a new mother/system board.

Microprocessor Replacement

This section deals solely with the replacement of the microprocessor IC (an 8086 or 8088) by another device and represents the cheapest possible upgrade. The 8088 and its true 16 bit brother the 8086 are used in various machines and have a designator after the type number, e.g. 8088-2. The designator denotes maximum clock rate permissible and one accepted form is:-

designator	clock speed
-4	4 MHz
none	5 MHz (e.g. 4.77 MHz)
-2	8 MHz
-1	10 MHz

The computer must always contain the microprocessor IC that will cope with the maximum clock rate to be used, e.g. a 4.77/8 MHz turbo system board must have a 8086-2 or 8088-2 CPU installed to provide the faster speed.

The Nippon Electronics Corporation (NEC) of Japan brought out their own pin compatible versions of the 8086 and 8088. These units run faster and in a typical test, using the SYSINFO program of the Norton Utilities suite, at a clock speed of 4.77 MHz a computer gave a speed increase of 1.7 (8088 substitution) and at 8 MHz an increase of three times the bog standard 4.77 MHz/8088 combination. This dramatic increase is, however, not realised in practice as the coding has not necessarily been optimised for use with these NEC devices.

The device codes and equivalents of the NEC devices are:

NEC replacement	INTEL code
V20 (D70108)	8088
V30 (D70116)	8086

These units use the designator -5 for 5 MHz and -8 for 8 MHz, viz V20-8 or D70108-8, V30-8 or D70116-8 for 8 MHz devices. As these devices are pin for pin compatible with the INTEL devices, the pin coding can be taken as for the 8088/8086 given in Chapter 2.

Carrying Out the Upgrade

The upgrade is cheap - about £12 if one shops around - but do not anticipate fantastic improvements, expect about a 15% to 30% increase in speed, dependent very much on application. Make sure the computer is switched off, open the case and carefully remove the old CPU from its socket - for positioning see diagrams in Chapter 2 (Figures 2.3 and 2-4). Be careful with this device as it is sensitive to static, as is the new replacement, and store it away in an anti-static foam or equivalent. Ease the new CPU into the same socket - the rows of pins may need to be bent slightly in order to fit the DIL socket and PLEASE - note the correct alignment of the integrated circuit.

There is no other operation to perform, replace the unit's cover and turn the computer on and make sure it functions. If you have a copy of Norton Utilities, run SYSINFO and see if the same results occur as mentioned above.

Maths Co-Processor

This single IC can give the greatest increase in computing speed, especially for work that entails many mathematical operations. Such packages include mathematical modelling, statistical analysis and CAD/CAM work. Speed increase of up to 100% can be expected for programs that are very heavily dependent on mathematical routines with long periods between screen displays and which are carefully coded. More typical increases are in the 30% - 40% range. This IC can only be utilised with application packages which are written to support it.

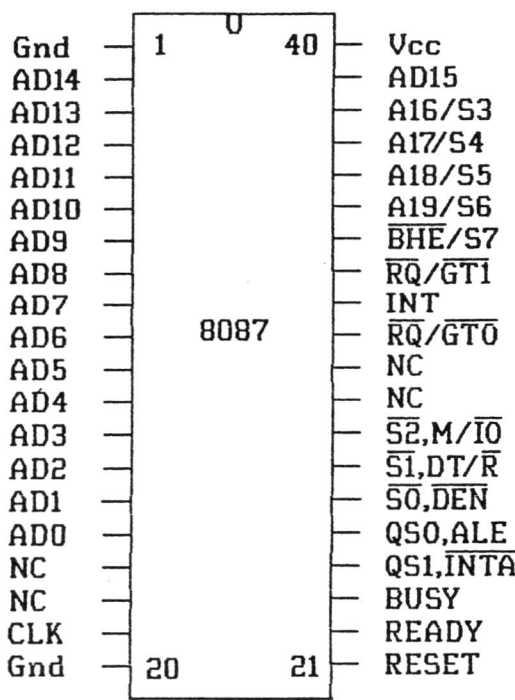

Figure 4.1 Pin Connections for 8087 Co-Processor

The general purpose microprocessor (8088 etc.) performs mathematical functions relatively slowly, especially with non- integers. Non-integers have to be dealt with by means of special software routines and then, for any type of number, the mathematical function is performed by sets of software sub-routines.

The maths co-processor (or floating point co-processor as it is sometimes called) copes with many mathematical functions internally rather than relying on externally called software routines. A typical device will have internal routines for addition, subtraction, multiplication and division plus square roots, absolute values and the common trigonometric functions. It provides floating point calculations up to 80 bits wide and integers up to 18 digits in length. The device for assisting the 8086 or 8088 microprocessor is the 8087 co-processor and has the same designators as the 8086/8088 devices for clock rating (i.e. -5, -8 etc.). The pin diagram is shown on Figure 4.1 whilst the position for it on the motherboard can be ascertained from Figures 2.3 and 2.4 in Chapter 2.

Carrying Out the Upgrade

Now comes the crunch. It is such a shame that this IC is so expensive, if it were cheaper more units would definitely be sold. The price of the 5 MHz version is about £100 and for the 8 MHz version about £135 with prices dropping slightly. Shop around for the device as there is quite a range of prices but buy it from a reputable dealer. If you buy one treat it like gold dust - you can buy an awful lot of bottles of whisky for that price!

On the mother or system board there will be an empty 40 pin socket adjacent to the main processor socket and this may be named Aux. Processor Socket. Make sure that the computer is switched off and handle the IC carefully - it can also be damaged by static. The co-processor device needs to plugged into this socket, taking great care of the alignment. Having placed it into its socket and making sure it is firmly seated and the correct way round, set the DIP switch on the motherboard (see Chapter 2) - this informs the operating system on booting up that a 8087 co-processor exists. If this switch is not changed the 8087 will not be recognised.

All that can be said is that it is hoped the outlay in cash will produce the desired increase in computing speed.

Go-faster Boards

Some application packages are now demanding an awful lot from the humble 8088 and 8086 microprocessors. Typical of these packages are Excel from Microsoft and some of the large CAD/CAM packages. One solution would be to start afresh with a new computer using devices such as the 80286 (16 bit) or even better an 80386 (32 bit) microprocessor. For many, though, this cannot be justified economically and one would prefer to try and inject some more life into the trusty PC. There is no need to change machines like a fashion conscious youngster, as some manufacturers and columnists keep trying to persuade us. A word of warning however - this form of up-grade may prove somewhat complex and troublesome as much of the testing work has been done with only the IBM XT and very close compatibles.

Many of the speed comparisons have been done with the slow 4.77 MHz XT and so the faster units running at 8 MHz, and especially with the V20 series microprocessor, will not show anywhere near the same advantages. It's a pity that this is all the advertisements go for. Likewise, if the 8087 co-processor has been fitted. Because a faster microprocessor needs faster memory it may be that all of the existing 640 kBytes of memory may become redundant - possibly another source of expense - or wait states added to allow the memory to respond. These boards also address memory so there may be conflicts between different expansion boards and there could be a conflict in addressing - **BEWARE**. The best solution is to use a reputable dealer and if possible one supplying all of the additional expansion features. These upgrades are not cheap and one does not wish to throw money away.

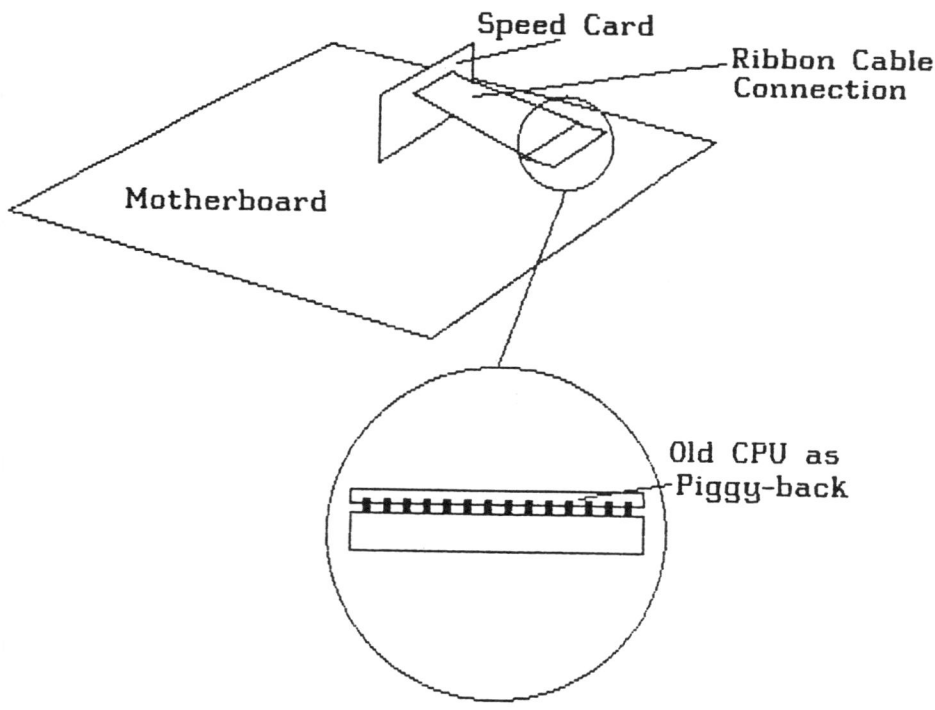

Figure 4.2 One Method of Connection for Speed and Accelerator Card

The aim of these add-on units is to speed up the relatively slow compatible computer or clone. Certainly with the 8088 it has a bottle neck when it comes to its data and address structure, with the 8086 really only being slightly better. The additional speed is obtained by using a faster microprocessor such as an 80286, to perform the manipulation of data. This can be approached in basically three ways, but with possible variations on a theme:-

a) replacement of the 8086/8088 microprocessor by a board with possibly the 8088/8086 still *in situ* (Figure 4.2)

b) an expansion board with a fast processor and the 8088/8086 used mainly for I/O

c) complete replacement of the system or motherboard

Speed/Accelerator Cards

In a) an additional board is added to the computer with a microprocessor that runs faster than the 8088/8086. This also has a flying lead that plugs into the original 8088/8086 socket with a possible piggy-back arrangement for the original microprocessor (see Figure 4.2). Depending on manufacturer this allows the original microprocessor to be switched in for running as necessary. There are several variations in how this option is implemented and this section is only representative. If an 8087 co- processor has been previously fitted, it is sad to say that this may no longer be of any further use.

The arrangement for a) still uses the data from the 8088/8086 socket and to help speed up operations it may have something like 8 or 16 kBytes of fast "cache" RAM on board or even its own 640 kBytes - it depends on manufacturer. It will use a faster microprocessor like an 80286 or even possibly a fast 8086.

In b) the 8088/8086 is still left in place but a new board is added. This board comes with all the memory needed for the new microprocessor and the old 8088/8086 acts merely as I/O which unfortunately will slow things down somewhat. The faster board comes with associated software that will ensure that the data is routed to the correct places. This board may also be able to accept additional memory for EMS as mentioned in Chapter 3. Typically this new board must have dual ported RAM with the host microprocessor to act as a window, it must use NMI and IRQ lines and have allocated a set of contiguous I/O ports which are switch/jumper selectable.

These boards are fitted the same as any other expansion card. Make sure the computer is OFF, READ THE MANUAL, remove the lid, remove the blanking plate, make the appropriate settings on the card and plug in the board and fix using the single hole screw fitting. If ICs or other connectors are to be used make sure that pins do not get bent and that they are the correct way round.

Replacement of Motherboard

This is option (c) and seems at first like really major surgery but with the cost of motherboards falling sharply it may be similar in cost to some of the above options. All that happens here is that a new board is fitted inside the same case with new faster memory and microprocessor fitted (e.g. 80286). Many of the new motherboards will give expansion provision for both 8 and 16 bit expansion cards. However, to be cost effective, it is used with the existing add-on cards such as the disk drive controllers, video cards and serial/parallel ports. The hard disk on the older PCs is relatively slow and may slow down the operation of the system somewhat. This can in part be remedied by the use of RAM disk although this subtracts usually from the user RAM.

Suppliers

AST - speed/accelerator board, replacement motherboards
Atomstyle - speed/accelerator board
Golden Gate - speed/accelerator boards
HK Systems - speed/accelerator boards
Ideal Hardware - speed/accelerator boards
Intel - speed/accelerator boards
Mektronic Ltd - NEC microprocessors, co-processors
Orchid - speed/accelerator boards
Specialix Systems -speed/accelerator boards
Technomatic - speed/accelerator board, replacement motherboards, ICs

5

DISPLAY DEVICES AND DRIVERS

Introduction

Without the display device (e.g. monitor or projector) and driver, the computer cannot normally communicate with us. There are some applications in industrial control however where this condition is satisfactory and it makes the controlling computer cheaper. When considering displays, one must look at what the unit is to be used for and, hopefully consider the future as well. Because of the way in which the Amstrad PCs are arranged some of the options described here may already be implemented or the Amstrad only upgrade route must be followed. In other cases it may be hard to implement an option.

The format of the display splits into two types - text and graphics. Sometimes these are desired separately and sometimes in combination. Both of these can be subdivided: typically text is displayed as 80 characters horizontally by 25 lines or 40 characters by 25 lines, the choice is dictated by the viewer and the end product. For typical word processing an 80 character screen is most useful but if the screen is to be viewed from slightly further away, for example as a general information screen, then the 40 character display is more appropriate. It is possible to get displays of up to 132 characters wide as well as displays with much larger characters for such uses as railway and airline public information systems. The latter is generally handled as a graphics problem. Other monitors are also produced that look as if they "are on their side" but this is to accommodate a full A4 page - very useful for full page display and editing in desktop publishing applications. Monitors are now available with screen sizes from about 12 inches up to a massive 37 inches, this latter being useful in CAD/CAM applications. For use in the lecture room, projection type display devices are now available and allow the display of a computer screen on to a much larger screen.

With graphic displays it is the number of colours required, the accuracy in placing a line and the definition afforded by the pixel size which is important. The range goes from typical monochrome business bar and pie charts to sophisticated multi-coloured CAD/CAM displays. There is a link between the number of colours required and the pixel size and this is manifested in the amount of memory required for video storage, the type of adapter to use and the standards the monitor employs. Unfortunately the different types of display adapter and monitor input standards are not necessarily compatible. Changing one will probably mean that the other must be changed - a double cost is normally always involved. Sometimes two display adapters cannot co-exist in the same computer due to memory conflicts.

Monitors

These are the normal devices on which the majority of people will expect the computer to output information to them. There are obvious differences which one recognises such as screen size and whether colour or monochrome - all visual aspects and it probably is easy to make the decision. There are, however, more detailed differences internally which means that the appropriate monitor must be chosen for the fitted video adapter card which is discussed later in this chapter. The following descriptions will give a brief insight into how the monitor functions and the various standards that may be mentioned with respect to the video cards.

The familiar cathode ray tube (CRT) has not been replaced yet for these devices and so is a good starting point. The picture is made up from a number of lines on the screen and Figure 5.1 shows the two typical forms. The line is made up from a beam of electrons hitting the screen which is coated with a chemical (normally a phopshor) and this emits energy in the form of light that we can see. This electron beam is controlled by electronic circuits which cause the beam to deflect both horizontally and vertically as well as to brighten up. All of this information must be derived from the input signal, which in this application comes from the computer.

As can be seen from Figure 5.1 the display (frame) can be either of the interlaced or non-interlaced type - this may be switched by software when appropriate. Figure 5.2 gives a typical block diagram of a monitor and leads to a discussion of various matters. The electron beam needs to "know" when to start its horizontal or line scan and also when to begin the downward movement - frame scan. These are signals that are generated by the computer and may be termed vertical or frame synchronisation (sync for short) and horizontal or line synchronisation. Added to this information must be a signal that determines where the beam must brighten up in its horizontal movement (left to right). The beam is automatically "blanked" as it travels at fast speed from right to left ready for the next line. This introduces two concepts, that of line scan rate and that of frame scan rate - both of which are important when considering the various types of display adapter.

To complicate matters further a colour display is composed from three primary colours - red, green and blue (usually referred to as RGB). It has three electron beams which fall on various types of phopshor and cause the appearance of the colour display. It is the mixture of R,G and B and the intensity or brightness of each which gives the many hues possible. By restricting the number of signals required there is a limitation on the number of colours obtainable. This is also limited by the memory capacity of the computer, as explained later.

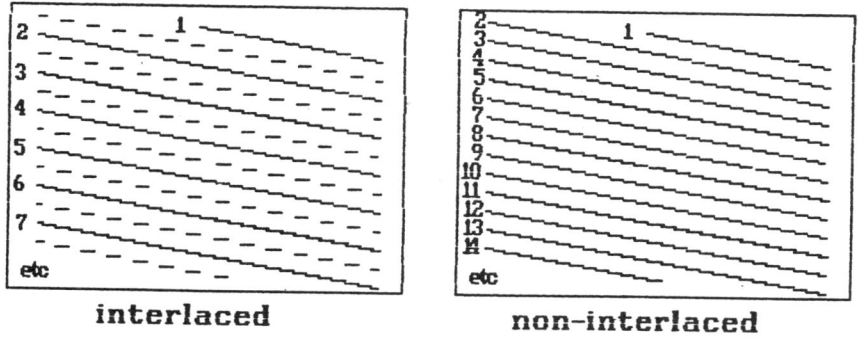

interlaced   non-interlaced

Figure 5.1 Formation of Dislay Screen (Frame)

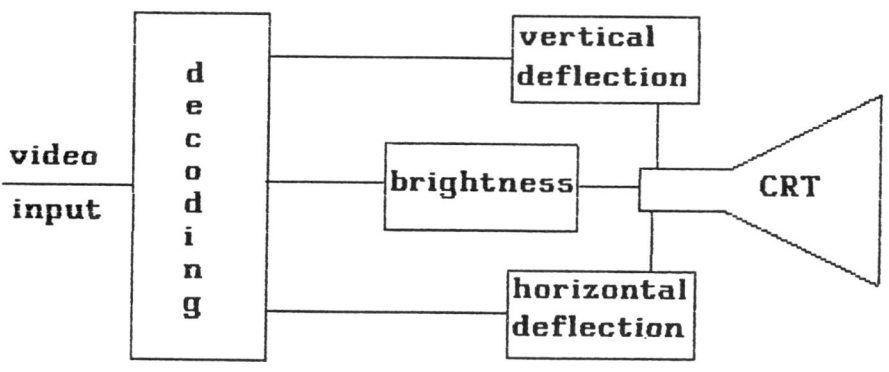

Figure 5.2 Basic Block Diagram of Monitor

Monochrome Signals

Figure 5.3 shows the various ways in which the frame, line and intensity signal can be combined for a monochrome system. In Figure 5.3 (a) the three signals are all separate and sent on different wires, whilst in (b) the synchronisation signals have been combined to produced what is known as mixed sync. In both (a) and (b) the signals are normally TTL digital signals (0 and +5 volts). When combined as a composite signal (c) the waveform is much more complex and cannot be transmitted as a digital signal. It is then an analogue signal and a typical standard is 1 v (pk-pk) into a 75 ohm load. On receiving a composite signal the monitor must split it up into its constituent parts again, likewise for a digital mixed sync. signal. As might be expected the transmission of the three individual signals is the arrangement that provides best definition as something is always lost in the combination and splitting process. An intensity line may also be added to enable bold text and similar.

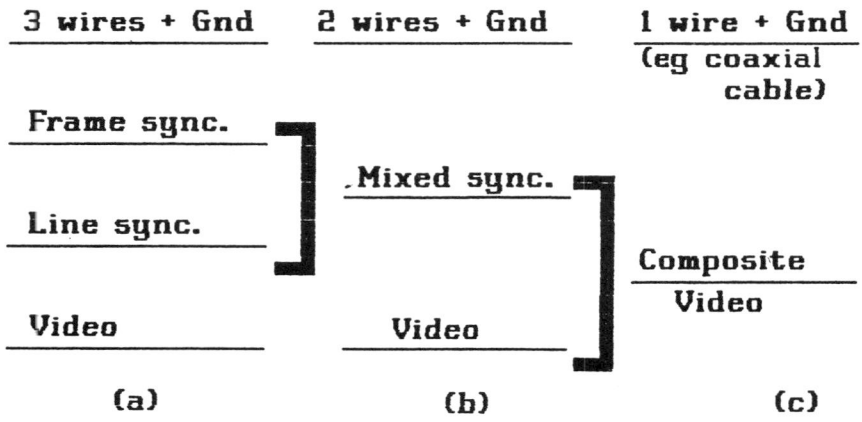

Figure 5.3 Monochrome Signals

Colour Signals

With a colour signal there are again complications as it depends on the number of wires and colours required. Figure 5.4(a) shows the simplest possibility for colour using individual lines and the number of wires required, all TTL levels. This will give a total of 8 colours, including black and white. By adding another line (intensity) it is possible to double the number of colours. Figure 5.4 (b) shows the arrangement when the synchronisation signals are combined whilst Figure 5.4 (c) provides the typical composite colour signal using a single co-axial cable. This analogue composite signal is now a complex signal. The best definition is to be expected from a system using individual wires for each signal function. To obtain even more combinations of colour the next step is an intensity line for each colour and this leads to the designation RrGgBb or RR'GG'BB'. Each of these is again a TTL signal with the associated line and frame sync pulses. This combination gives up to 64 colours.

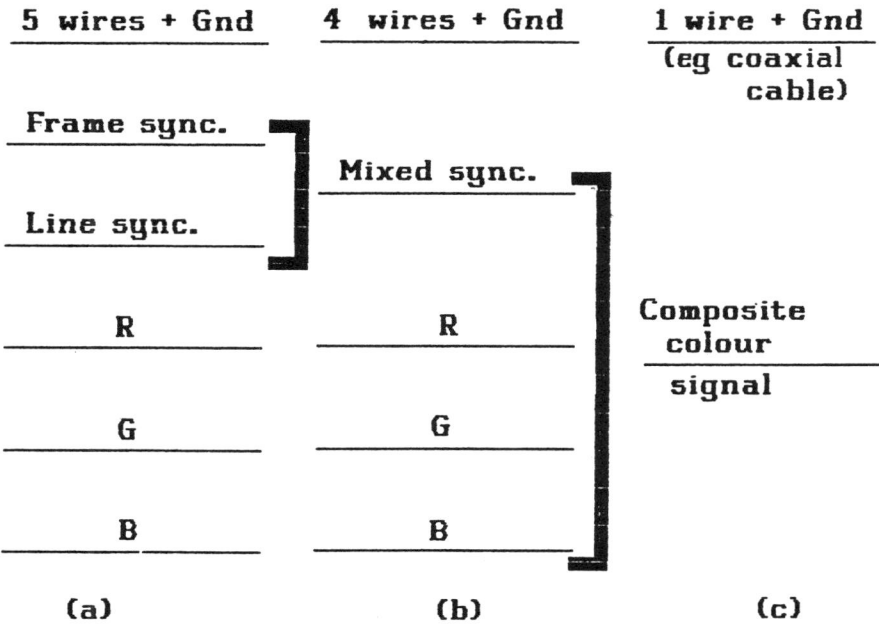

Figure 5.4 The Simplest Colour Arrangement

Monitor Parameters

As the resolution desired increases it is necessary to use monitors with increased line or scan frequency and at the top end of the scale increased frame rates. Also, to get sharp edges to images the amplifier circuits used within the monitors must have a greater bandwidth. All this of course tends to increase the cost of the monitor.

It is possible to go and buy a monitor with a given specification but because of the various standards now required by some of the display adapters many manufacturers have produced models that can cope with different line and scan rates and these are referred to as multi-sync. monitors. One must examine the advertising literature in order to pick out suitable models and then to choose the supplier. One may in fact get a video lead to couple the computer with the monitor, otherwise it must be purchased separately or made from its individual parts by someone good with a soldering iron. Many of the compatible computers have an IEC mains connector on their back plate so that a monitor can plug into that and be controlled by the computer ON/OFF switch instead of an additional mains socket being required - but check on the power rating of the computer switch and fusing.

Amstrad units come in a form whereby the monitor must be plugged into the computer.

There are a host of monitors available on the market and the suppliers list at the end of this chapter can only hope to give a few of the names. Monitors range from monochrome to colour, single scan frequency to multi-synchronisation types. Remember, choose one to match your video adapter and possibly bear in mind future expansions. There are some monitors that have a very white screen and these are most suitable for use with desktop publishing and similar applications. Generally normal monochrome monitors are relatively cheap and many appear also on the surplus market, still in good condition.

The advertising literature with monitors gives a fair indication of the video adapters the monitors will work with. It is thus worthwhile collecting a fair amount of advertising material before the monitor choice is made. Many new systems come with a video option and it may be hard to better the price by buying separately.

Light Pens

This is a small hand held device very similar to a large pen that can be used in conjunction with the monitor screen and Figure 5.5 shows a sketch of such a device. The light pen contains a light sensor that will respond to the light emitted by the electron beam falling on the screen phosphor.

When the electron beam, during one of its scans, passes the light pen, a pulse is produced by the light pen and is sent to the computer (the CRT controller IC). The time difference between the start of the frame scan and the light pen pulse will determine its position on the screen. This can then be used by appropriate software for drawings, menu selection and similar.

The connection for the light pen is often a 6 way pin connector and provides:-

1. light pen input
2. not used
3. light pen switch
4. chassis ground
5. +5volts
6. +12 volts

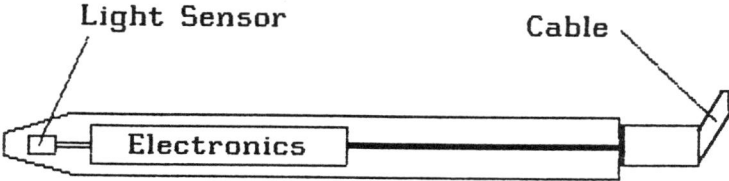

Figure 5.5 Typical Light Pen

Video Adapters

Figure 5.6 shows essentially how the video card relates to the main system board and external units (for most PC systems) whilst Figure 5.7 shows the block diagram of a typical video adapter board. The video information derived from the computer program running is passed to the video card through several I/O ports and the expansion socket. This data includes information relating to the screen display such as characters per line, pixel arrangement used, colour information and of course the data/characters to be displayed on the screen. A good reference for the display arrangements is the PC1640 technical manual (see bibliography).

This information is split between the video RAM and the various control registers in the CRT and adapter controller (if fitted). Random access memory is required to hold the screen information continuously as the CRT itself will only display information for fractions of a second unless it is refreshed. The CRT controller is responsible for sending the information to the monitor and generating frame and line synchronisation pulses, causing the correct readout from the video RAM and the display characteristics. The type of output generated depends on the card used and a summary of typical display modes for various video cards is shown in Table 5.1, there being some variation between suppliers as to what is included. The definitions do not necessarily correspond exactly to the original IBM cards!

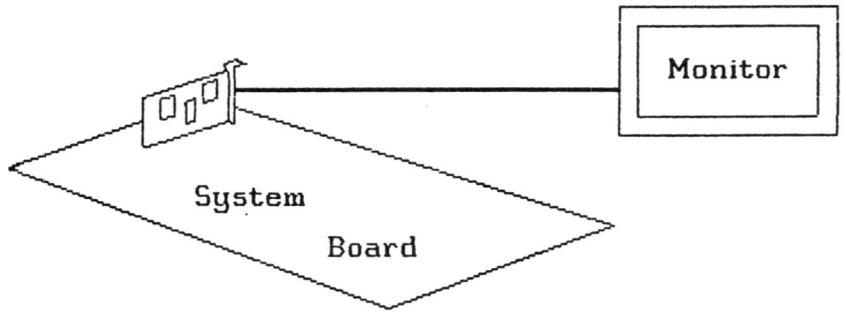

Figure 5.6 Typical Arrangement for Video Board and Monitor (non Amstrad)

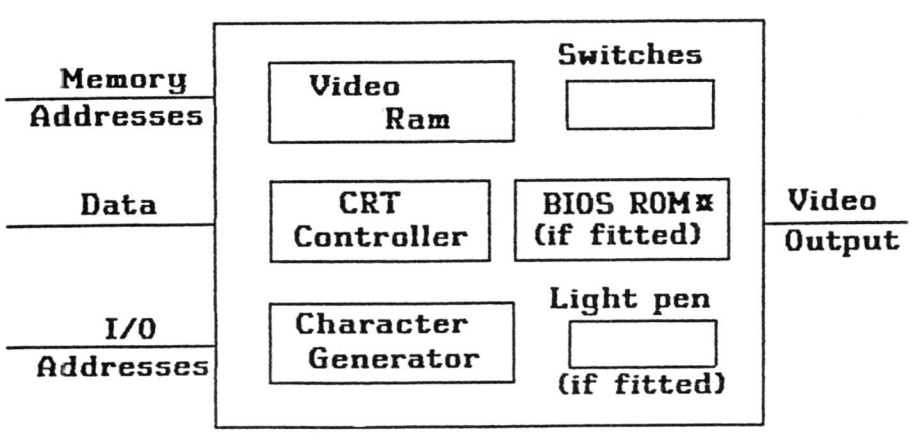

Figure 5.7 Typical Block Diagram of Video Card

	TEXT			GRAPHICS			LINE SCAN kHz	FRAME SCAN Hz	VIDEO OUTPUT
	Char.	Col.	P	Pixels	Col.	P			
Mono.	40x25	2	1	None			18.43	50	Mono (TTL)
	80x25	2	1						
Herc.	80x25	2	1	720x348	2	2	18.8	50.9	Mono (TTL)
CGA	40x25	2	8	320x200	4/16	1			RGBI (TTL)
	40x25	16	8	320x200	2	1	15.75	50	Composite
	80x25	2	8	640x200	2	1			
	80x25	16	8						
EGA	40x25	2	8	320x200	4	1			RrGgBb (TTL)
	40x25	16	8	320x200	2	1	15.75		
	80x25	2	8	320x200	16	8			
	80x25	16	8	640x200	2	1		50/60	RGBI (TTL)
	80x25	2	8	640x200	16	4	to		
	80x25	16/64	8	640x350	2	1			Mono (TTL)
	80x43	16/64	4	640x350	2	2	21.85		
	80x43	2	4	640x350	4/64	1			Composite
				640x350	16/64	2			
				720x348	2	2			
VGA	40x25	2	8	320x200	256✗	1			RrGgBb (TTL)
	40x25	16	8	320x200	16✗	8			
	80x25	16	8	320x200	4	1			RGBI (TTL)
	80x25	16	8	320x200	2	1	15.75		
	80x25	2	8	640x200	2✗	1		50	Mono (TTL)
	80x25	16	8	640x200	16✗	4		60	
	80x25	2	8	640x350	2	1	to	70	IBM PS/2
	80x60	16	2	640x350	2	2			Analogue
	132x43	16	4	640x350	4	1			
	132x43	2	4	640x350	16✗	2	31.5		Composite
				640x480	2✗	1			
				640x480	16✗	1			
				720x348	2	2			

Char. = no of characters   Col. = number of colours

P = number of pages   16/64 denotes 16 colours out 64

✗ out of palette of 262144 colours

Table 5.1 Summary of Typical Display Adapters

Depending on the I/O addresses and memory buffers used, some adapter boards may co-exist with others but certain boards will provide all the options available anyway. In many compatible machines these boards all plug into one of the eight expansion slots. Both Amstrad models have the video circuitry all on the system board and this makes it awkward to upgrade; this is especially true with the PC1512 model, but the PC1640 already has the equivalent of an enhanced graphic display and this will cope with all the other lesser display modes. Also, the Amstrad machine has the power supply in the monitor and if a non-Amstrad monitor is used the old one must still be connected in order to provide power to the system board . This unfortunately does not provide a very neat arrangement.

When IBM first brought out the PC XT the choices for display adapter were poor - more or less take it or leave it, but since then several variations on a theme have been produced and Table 5.1 gives a summary of various types that are available. The market is changing very fast at the moment and it is almost impossible to keep track of the latest offerings and the best course is to peruse the latest magazines before making the final decision. Variations on a theme do exist and so all cards are not necessarily identical in performance and the following discussions must therefore be taken as representative of the standard.

When software packages are bought they usually have to be installed for a particular configuration and this will include the type of video adapter in use. Many of the software packages include an INSTALL routine and this allows the user to specify the video card to be used by a YES/NO or choice routine.

Monochrome Adapter (Text Only)

This was the initial monochrome option provided by IBM and now seems somewhat mean compared with present offerings from all of the compatible and expansion card producers. This card is monochrome only and provides text at 80x25 or 40x25 and the only reason for including it is to provide a complete picture of the options available and the monitor standards used. Fairly crude graphics can be obtained using block text characters but these now seem rather pathetic with more recent offerings. It requires only 2kBytes of video RAM and these reside from B0000H to B0800H. This board uses the 6845 CRT controller, as do many other boards.

Whilst only being monochrome it did allow highlighting, blinking, underlining and reverse video. This board was usually combined with a parallel printer port having the fixed designation LPT1. The I/O addresses for this board are:-

3B0H	Not used
3B1H	Not used
3B2H	Not used
3B3H	Not used
3B4H	6845 Index register
3B5H	6845 Data Register

3B6H	Not used
3B7H	Not used
3B8H	Mode Select register
3B9H	Reserved (light pen)
3BAH	CRT status register
3BBH	Reserved (light pen)
3BCH	Parallel printer data port
3BDH	Printer status port
3BEH	Printer control port
3BFH	Display control register (if used)

The output was TTL levels and Figure 5.8 covers the display video connections.

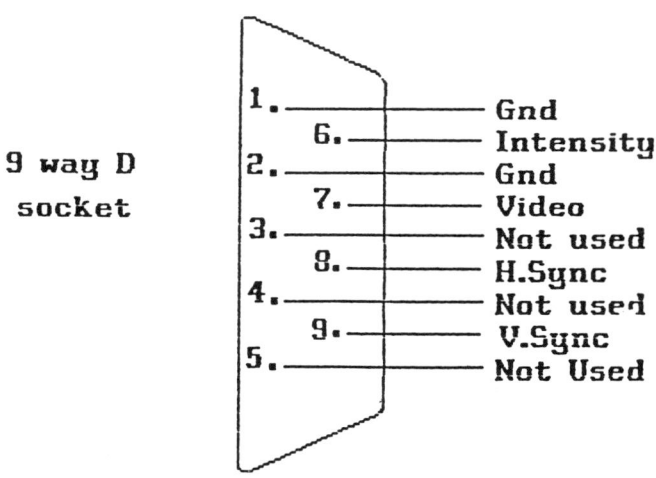

Figure 5.8 Monochrome Adapter Connections

Hercules/Monochrome Adapter - Text and Graphics

This board was an extension of the previous video adapter and developed by the Hercules Computer Corporation to give high resolution monochrome graphics. It provides monochrome 80 x 25 text and 720 x 348 graphic displays (see Table 5.1). The Hercules option requires a horizontal scan rate of 18.8 kHz and the cost of a typical card is between £50 and £90.

The Hercules/Monochrome board requires a total memory of 64 kBytes and the full memory buffer is capable of supporting two full-size graphic screen displays. It is still based on the 6845 controller chip and may also have a parallel printer port on the same card and the above I/O port designations are still valid for this card.

In text mode characters are stored one per byte, with another byte for the attributes described below. The memory requirement is therefore 80x2x25 = 4000 bytes per screen (B0000H-B0FFFH). The text character is made from a 9 x 14 dot pattern and an eight bit code in the associated byte controls the attributes as described below.

Attribute	Bit -	7	6	5	4	3	2	1	0
Normal video		B	0	0	0	I	1	1	1
Reverse video		B	1	1	1	I	0	0	0
Underline		B	0	0	0	I	0	0	1
Blank		B	0	0	0	I	0	0	0

Where:-   I = 0 normal intensity body
                                 I = 1 for high (bold) intensity body

Bit 5 = 0 (blinking disabled)   Bit 5 = 1 (blinking enabled)

B=0, normal background   B=0, no blinking
B=1, bold background   B=1, blinking

In graphics mode a line of 720 pixels is stored in 90 consecutive bytes in the screen buffer. If a bit=0 then the pixel is off and if a 1 then it is on.

The total screen RAM required for a full board is 64 kBytes, extending from B0000H to BFFFFH in the main memory map. This is described as a full screen buffer but it is possible to select only a half screen buffer, either by a hardware setting (e.g. jumper) or software - see the manual on the card involved. By splitting into two it is possible to hold two graphics screens, the selection being accomplished by bit 7 of the display mode control port 3BF, 0 is page 0 (B0000H-B7FFFH) and 1 is page 1 (B8000H-BFFFFH).

The output from this board is at TTL levels and is a 9 way D connector and the pin connections are shown in Figure 5.8. The output is not suitable for colour monitors and damage may ensue if one is connected.

Colour Graphics Adapter (CGA)

This board is a very popular choice and may be regarded as a middle of the road solution in that it provides monochrome text and graphics as well as colour but at a reduced number of pixels per screen (see Table 5.1 for typical specifications). This adapter is the colour/graphic option that IBM initially provided for the PC and it usually costs between £40 and £80 and comes as a long or short board, depending on the supplier. It has two forms of video output - composite video (may or may not be colour) and RGB with intensity (this allows 16 colours in total). The horizontal scan rate is 15.7 kHz, and vertical is 60 Hz. In text mode it supports 80x25 or 40x25 text and each character is formed within an 8x8 matrix. The characters can be monochrome or in colour with up to 8 background colours and 16 foreground colours.

In monochrome the characters can be made to blink, be highlighted or produced in reverse video. In memory each character display position requires one byte for the character code (eg ASCII) and the other for its attributes. Hence a memory requirement of 80x25x2, or 4000 bytes, of RAM for one screen display (B0000H-B0FFFH). As before, the display code is in an even numbered location and its attribute is in the following odd numbered location. For a 40x25 display the memory requirement is only 2000 bytes and sits at B0000H to B07FFH.

On the board, the ROM character generator provides drive for 256 different characters. This comprises 96 standard ASCII characters plus special characters for supporting games, text processing, international characters and symbols, line graphics, scientific notation and Greek characters. This requires a 7x7 dot pattern in an 8x8 box. There may also be a light pen interface and printer port, depending on whose board you buy. The ubiquitous 6845 CRT controller is used and multiple pages of text are stored in the CGA RAM.

When used for graphics there are two modes possible, a 320x200 four colour mode and a 640x200 monochrome mode. In the 320x200 mode there are two sets of four colours and require four horizontal pixels per byte, i.e. two bits per pixel. The two sets of colours are:

	Set 1 background	Set 2 foreground
1	Cyan	Green
2	Magenta	Red
3	White	Brown

A typical byte is arranged thus:-

Bit number -	7	6	5	4	3	2	1	0
	C1	C0	C1	C0	C1	C0	C1	C0

The total memory requirement for this mode is $\dfrac{320 \times 200}{4 \times 4} = 16000$ bytes.

The screen is divided into two buffers - each of 8000 bytes. B8000H-B9F3FH contains the information for the even lines of the scan and BA000H-BB3F3H for the odd lines. Bit 7 and 6 of the first byte is the top left hand corner of the screen.

In the 640x200 monochrome display mode, there are 8 pixels per byte i.e. one bit per pixel - black is zero and white equals a logic one. Thus the memory requirement is 640x200/8 = 16000 bytes. This is the same as before. Memory allocation for the lines is the same as the 320x200 mode. The pixels go horizontally and hence B7 of the first byte is the top left hand corner.

Graphics and text can be mixed but the text must be generated from a separate area in the ROM from the text only option. A table of the first 128 characters similar to the text mode is stored, each character being defined by 8 consecutive bytes.

When this data is transferred to video RAM it has to be split into even and odd rows and sent to the appropriate buffer. These patterns will be accessed as codes 128-255 by the ROM INT 10H graphics character routines if the user points to the table with interrupt vector 1FH.

The 6845 CRT controller is initialised by accessing its internal registers. The register number is first output to the address register (port 3D4H) followed by the data byte to port 3D5H. The I/O address range allocated for this board is:-

3D0H |	
3D1H |	not used
3D2H |	
3D3H |	
3D4H	6845 register number
3D5H	data for register in 3D4H
3D6H |	
3D7H |	not used
3D8H	mode select register (o/p)
3D9H	colour select register (o/p)
3DAH	input status register
3DBH	clear light pen latch (o/p)
3DCH	set light pen latch (o/p)

The wiring connections from the CGA card are depicted in figure 5-9 and as shown it will cope with monitors with various inputs, all modes of operation being able to drive all monitors.

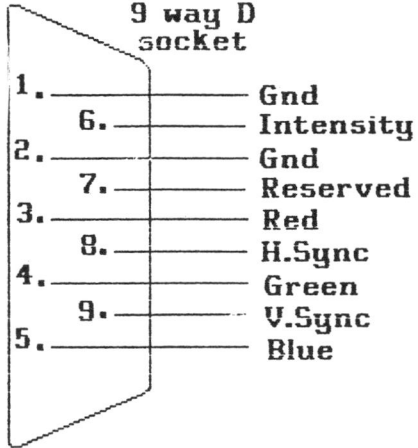

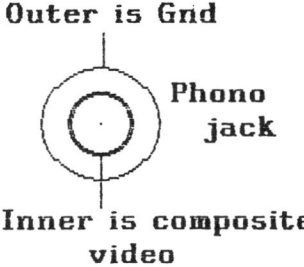

9 way D socket

1. ─────── Gnd
6. ─────── Intensity
2. ─────── Gnd
7. ─────── Reserved
3. ─────── Red
8. ─────── H.Sync
4. ─────── Green
9. ─────── V.Sync
5. ─────── Blue

Outer is Grid

Phono jack

Inner is composite video

[n.b. two phono jacks may be fitted, one for monochrome, other colour composite]

Figure 5.9 CGA Card Video Connections

Enhanced Graphics Adapter (EGA)

This type of board used to be the top of the range in display adapters and was brought out by IBM to compete, if not surpass in some areas, the Hercules offering mentioned above. It has been displaced by the VGA type (next section) and in consequence prices have fallen and this type of board can be bought for between £100 and £200. These boards will emulate all of the lower forms of display adapter (e.g. Monochrome Text, Hercules and CGA) and are therefore very versatile. However, to achieve the highest resolutions offered by this card a monitor must be used capable of synchronising at up to 21.85 kHz line scan rate (see earlier section on monitors re multi-sync monitors). All modes can normally be displayed on the high scan rate monitor but if a monitor is used with a lower scan rate only the lower graphic modes can be displayed.

These boards are supplied with 256 kBytes of DRAM (usually split as 4x64 kBytes) and support varying numbers of video pages (up to 8). The allocation in the main memory map is A0000H to BFFFFH (128 kBytes), and so the full 256 kBytes cannot be used all at one time unless "tricks" are played. A typical 640x350x16 colour display requires 128 kBytes. The cards are normally of half length although some of the earlier ones are full length. Some of these boards will co-exist with CGA or monochrome display adapters in other expansion slots but it is wise to seek further advice from the supplier. However, these other boards do not need to exist as the EGA board will perform all the functions. A character is formed in the high resolution mode in a 9 x 14 dot matrix and a self-contained RAM character generator allows the creation of up to four sets of 256 different characters.

The range of outputs are as for the previous card (CGA) plus an RrGgBb or RR'GG'BB' TTL positive output option(see Figure 5.10). This option is on the 9 way D connector and set by a DIP switch on the back panel. A CGA monitor should NOT be connected if the option is set for EGA characteristics as the monitor or display card may be damaged electrically. On the metal plate at the back of the board are normally the following:-

> 1 or 2 Phono Jacks with composite video
> 9 pin D connector - connections as per CGA board Figure 5.9,
> externally accessible DIP switch to set default mode of display.

On the board itself there is a 32 pin EGA compatible "feature connector" plus light pen socket. The feature connector seems to have been included for future use and little information is around as to its detailed use.

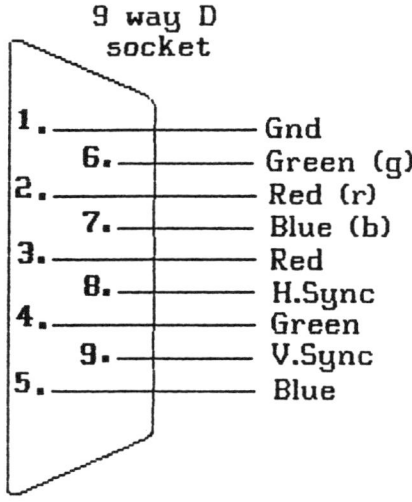

Figure 5.10 Connections for RrGgBb

When the EGA card is accessed it is via various I/O addresses which are specified below. Also, when accessed, control is passed from the BIOS on the system board to a BIOS on the EGA card. This is because the system BIOS may not support any higher resolution graphic/text output than the CGA standard. There may be a problem with equipment with very early BIOS ICs, e.g. IBM models with a BIOS date prior to October 27, 1982. This BIOS will not allow control to pass to the EGA BIOS and will need to be replaced - see your dealer for further information.

The following list of I/O addresses used is from a typical EGA manual (there may however be the option to set a different range).

3C0H	attribute/palette address source
3C1H	-
3C2H	miscellaneous output (write only)
3C3H	-
3C4H	sequencer address select register (write only)
3C5H	data read/write address
3C6H	-
3C7H	-
3C8H	-
3C9H	-
3CAH	graphics controller, graphic 1 position
3CBH	-
3CCH	graphics controller, graphic 2 position
3CDH	address select register
3CEH	graphics controller address register
3CFH	graphics controller data read/write

(- denotes not specified)

The 6845 CRT controller is accessed as for the previous cards via 3B4H/3B5H or 3D4H/3D5H - selectable on a DIP switch. If a light pen is fitted this is controlled typically by 3DBH and 3DCH as defined for earlier adapters.

As already indicated there is a DIP switch or link settings on the board and these will be more fully discussed in the accompanying EGA manual. These typically control:-

if another video board can co-reside and which
    is the primary video adapter
the initial mode of operation to select
the EGA BIOS location
the printer port setting (e.g. LPTx)
the type of colour monitor attached
which video output connection
possibly an address port selector (e.g. 3xx or 2xx).

Video Graphics Array (VGA)

This board is included mainly for the sake of completeness. It is the next development in the search for quality graphics on the PC and probably represents the end of the line for the typical XT clone. This is the standard for the new PS/2 type machines from IBM and various add-on suppliers have been very quick to bring out boards to fit the older machines. This board is typically under £300 and offers additional facilities such as graphic 640x480 (2 and 16 colour) and 320x200 (256 colour) modes. It also requires the use of monitors with even faster line and scan rates for the highest resolutions, the top VGA standard on many cards requires a horizontal scan rate of 31.5 kHz.

Some of the early VGA boards that came onto the market were merely EGA boards "souped up" with software to emulate the VGA BIOS and they did not necessarily produce every display mode that the genuine VGA adapter could. Gradually all of this type of board is being replaced so that they are all register compatible with the true IBM VGA hardware. This is something to look out for if considering going for this option.

Various boards are produced and they seem to be available with 256 kBytes or 512 kBytes of RAM. This memory still sits at A0000H to BFFFFH (a 128 kByte slot) as for the EGA board and so for the higher resolutions some form of memory switching must be used. The outputs from these boards are TTL compatible except for the analogue output which gives the highest number of colours (256 out of a palette of 262,144) but only in CGA format, i.e. 300 x 200 pixels. The best output from the VGA system is represented by a 640 x 480 pixel by 16 colour display.

The output connections of these boards are typically:-

> 9 way D type - TTL output compatible with EGA and CGA, etc.
> 32 pin EGA "feature connector"
> 15 pin PS/2 compatible analogue video (1 pin missing)
> 6 pin light pen connector (possibly)

Fitting the Video Adapters

The fitting of these adapters into the computer is straightforward and simply involves plugging the card into an expansion socket and fixing the screw. Before this is carried out make sure the computer is switched OFF and set any DIP switches or links on the expansion board. These should be detailed in the accompanying manual and are briefly mentioned under appropriate video adapter headings. There may also be a system board setting - see Chapter 2.

The Amstrad PC1640 has a switch determining display settings and this is located on the back of the machine.

Video Projectors

These displays are fairly expensive and would only be justified if much use is to be made of computer generated displays in a lecture room environment or similar. They certainly allow images to be displayed greater in size than the conventional CRT display. The units all obtain their video information from the video board in the computer but the method of projection from thereon differs. Figure 5.11 and 5.12 show the basic types available, the difference being from where the light is obtained for projection. Depending on type and model it is possible to illuminate screens from about 1 m x 0.75 m to 6 m x 4.5 m.

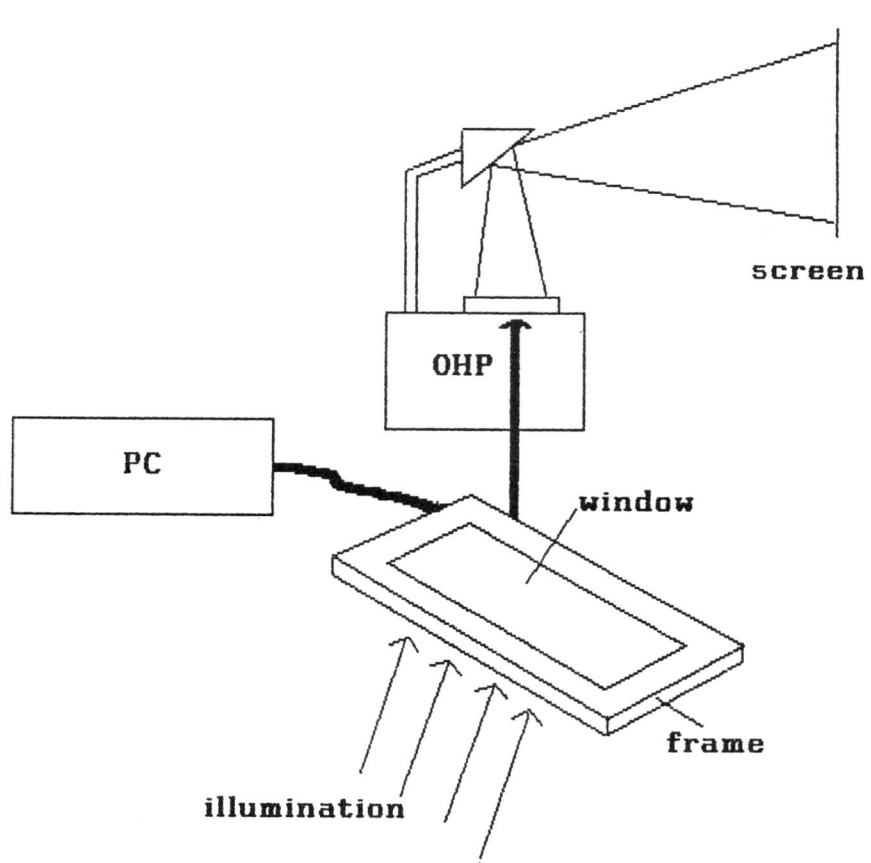

Figure 5.11 Projection with External Illumination

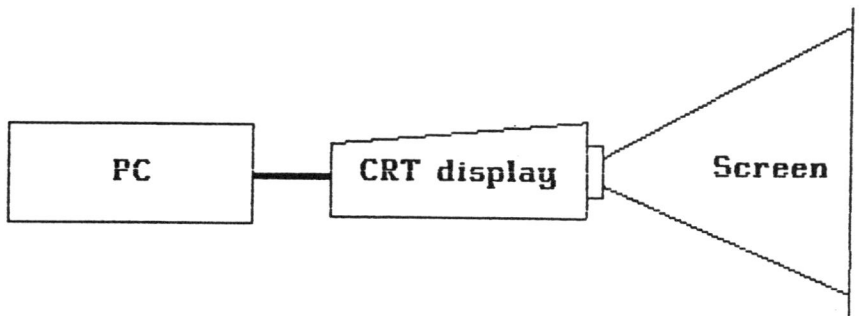

Figure 5.12 Projection with CRT Projector with Internal Illumination

External Illumination

These are the cheaper form for projection but do not produce the quality or colour generated by the next form. They are normally used with an overhead projector, are portable and derive the video information from the RGBI output from a CGA card or EGA card in CGA mode.

The clear window, as shown in Figure 5.12, contains a super twisted high contrast monochrome liquid crystal display (LCD). This LCD display can be activated to either allow light through or not, thus giving a monochrome projected image. Software provided gives various enhancements such as storage of the projection sequence, various lettering styles and frame grabbing facilities. The unit itself also gives the facility for manual control of background and contrast. A typical unit is the Sharp model QA25.

Internal Illumination

These models are the more expensive and are both more complex and less portable - they are more suitable for fixed locations. However, the quality of the projected image is better and they do provide colour projection.

Figure 5.13 depicts the typical construction of one of these units. The input video signal, which could possibly be any of the forms shown, is decoded and used to drive high brightness projection CRTs. These are red, green and blue (RGB) and the combined image is produced at the screen. These units are of the multi-sync variety (as with monitors) and will synchronise with various line and frame speeds. Various units are therefore compatible with CGA, EGA and VGA standards.

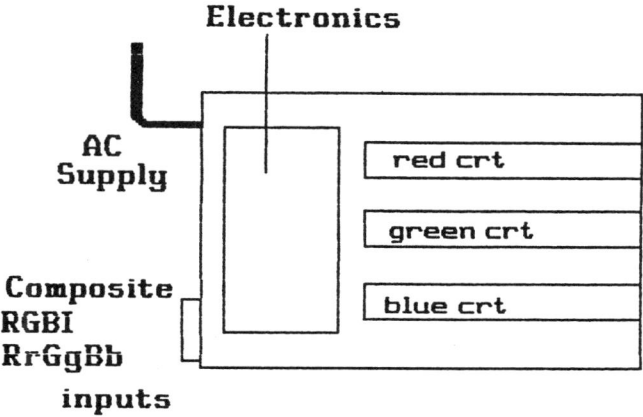

Figure 5.13 Typical Construction of Internally Illuminated Projector

Suppliers

AST Europe Ltd - various video cards
Atomstyle Ltd - various video cards
Aydin Controls - monitors, video cards
Continental Ltd - various video cards
Cristie - externally illuminated LCD type projectors
CRT Displays Ltd - internally illuminated projectors
Digivision - monitors
First Software - various video cards
Hitachi - monitors
Manitron Displays - monitors
Microvitec - monitors
Mitsubishi - monitors
NEC - monitors
Orchid (Europe) Ltd - various video cards
P & P Micro Distributors Ltd - various video cards, monitors
Philips - monitors
Samuelson Communications Ltd - internally illuminated projectors
Semaphore - various video cards
Sharp - LCD type projection equipment
Sony (UK) Ltd - internally illuminated projectors
Taxan (UK) - monitors
Vanilla Computers Ltd - monitors, display adapters
Visualex - LCD type projection equipment
Zenith - monitors

6

ADDING PERMANENT STORAGE

Introduction

Permanent storage can be defined as the storage of information without the need for a continuously present power supply source. For many this is the typical floppy or hard disk where the results of toils and tribulations are stored at various times. It is also convenient to be able to move some storage media away from the vicinity of the computer for both security and safety reasons - it could be disastrous for a business to lose all of its financial data because the computer caught fire!

It is possible to have in semiconductor form or optical disks the storage of absolutely permanent data, but for most applications this data may need to be altered or updated on a regular basis. One form of permanent storage in our computer is the BIOS chip which is a read only memory (ROM). The true IBM XT has part of its BASIC interpreter also held on ROM and in most of the compatibles sockets are provided for additional permanent programs on ROM. Optical storage media (CD-ROM and WORM) have now appeared on the market, these are optical disks read by a laser and can hold 500+ MBytes of information and these are examined towards the end of the chapter.

To cope with the need for changing data on a regular basis, and that is what this chapter is really about in the main, one comes back to the familiar magnetic surface type of storage. This comes in three forms - the floppy disk, the hard disk and the magnetic tape. This chapter will examine all the forms and some of the technical details of how they are connected to the computer. They will be dealt with in the order floppy disk, hard disk and tape so please go to the section of interest. The first two represent storage media that are accessed during normal program operation whilst the final one is really for back-up and archive storage.

The Floppy Disk

The minimum configuration the computer will come with is a single 5.25" floppy disk unit, now normally of half height (about 45 mm). Early models had units of twice this height and this obviously restricts space for further additions. The operating system can cope with a maximum of four floppy disk drives, although probably two of these will have to be external to the computer itself. On the system or motherboard there is a DIP switch to specify the number of floppy disk drives attached - the settings are given in Chapter 2.

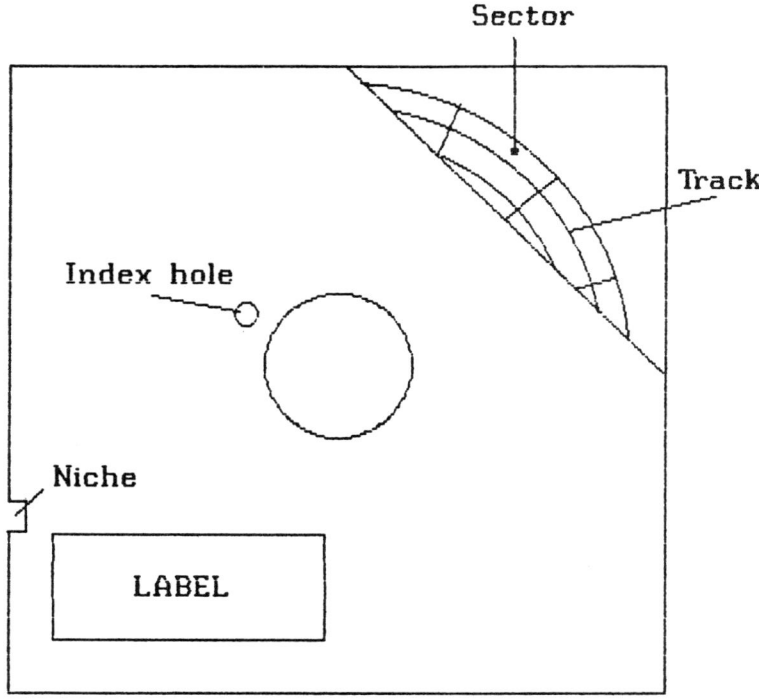

Figure 6.1 Typical Layout of Floppy Disk

The floppy disk itself is normally bought unformatted and then formatted by the user with a format program (e.g. FORMAT under MS-DOS). The disk is split into tracks and sectors as show in Figure 6.1 and as it is classified as double density will hold 512 bytes of information per sector (there are additional bytes on top of this for addressing, synchronisation and so forth). The standard is now 9 sectors per track, 40 tracks per side and as both sides of the disk are used, this will hold 512x9x40x2 (or 360 kBytes) in total. Earlier systems may only have 8 sectors per track, so the total capacity is then 320 kBytes. When the operating system goes to read a disk it will automatically determine if it is 8 or 9 sectors per track . The small hole on the disk allows the floppy disk unit to recognise the start of the disk, sector 0. The floppy disk also has a niche on one side (see Figure 6.1). If this is left uncovered then the disk is read and write, if covered by a tab then the disk is read only ‑ a condition detected in the disk drive unit and a signal sent back to the floppy disk controller.

Figure 6.2 shows the block diagram of a floppy disk controller card.

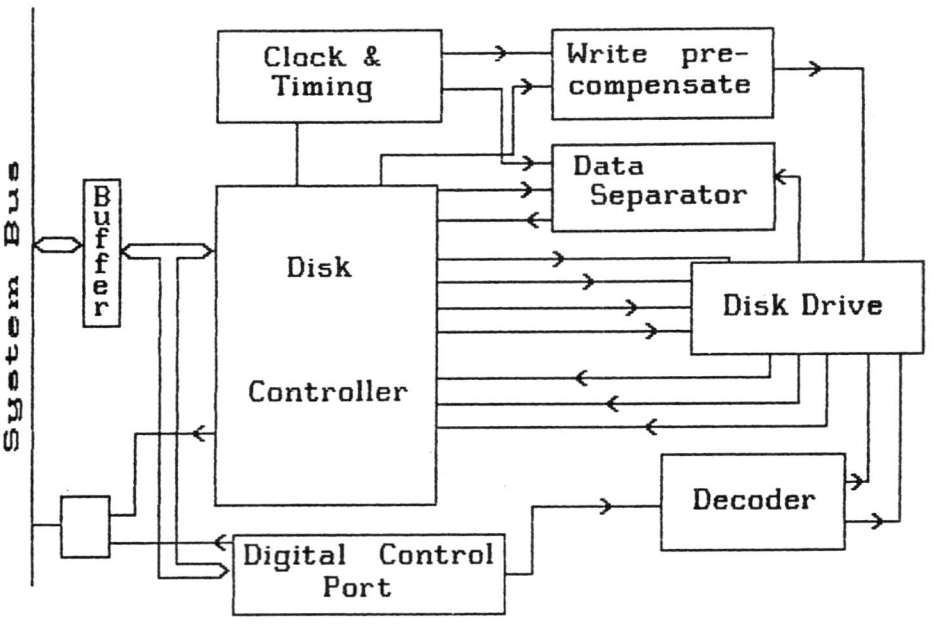

Figure 6.2 Block Diagram of Typical Floppy Disk Controller Card

The floppy disk drive can be split into three main components - the spindle drive system, head positioning system and the read/write/erase system. All of these need to be controlled from the computer via the interface card. The spindle drive system is driven by a servo-controlled motor running at 300 rpm and the read/write head system driven by a four phase stepper motor. When a disk is inserted it locates over the drive hub, and when the door latch is closed it is clamped to the hub. Only on request for a disk access is the disk rotated and the head positioned from information obtained (normally) from the directory on the disk which is on track 0. The power for the disk drive(s) is obtained from the system power supply.

The interface card for the floppy disk drive(s) is plugged into one of the expansion sockets on the motherboard (in the Amstrad PC it is part of the motherboard). The floppy disk interface is thus coupled to the system bus (data and address) and the interrupt circuits.

The functions of the floppy disk contoller card (FDC) can be summarised as follows:-

1. Select the correct drive
2. Check to see if R/W head is over track 0 (for directory)
3. Look for READY signal to see if a disk is properly inserted
4. Look for INDEX signal to see if R/W head is on this system
5. Look for WRITE PROTECT signal (tab on disk)

The data to be read or written to the disk is normally passed via the DMA controller and so does not go via the CPU. However, the floppy disk controller has to be set up by the operating system and this is done via I/O ports (03F0H to 03F7H, see I/O map Figure 2:14) and the CPU. The data is then passed serially from the FDC card to the disk drive as the information is stored sequentially. Only three I/O ports are used and these are defined as :-

03F2H	Drive select	output only
03F4H	FDC status register	input only
03F5H	FDC data register	input/output

These are further subdivided as:-

The digital output register controls the drive selection, drive motors and various resets and enables.

03F2H**	Bit 0	Bit 1	Drive select
	0	0	drive 0
	0	1	drive 1
	1	0	drive 2
	1	1	drive 3

Bit 2	FDC	Bit 3
0	reset FDC	0 disabled
1	enable FDC	1 enable INT
		and DMA request

Drive stepper motor

Bit 4 = 1	drive 0 selected
Bit 5 = 1	drive 1 selected
Bit 6 = 1	drive 2 selected
Bit 7 = 1	drive 3 selected

** **Please note:** not all floppy disk controllers will cope with four drives, some only two, see appropriate manual for further details.

The FDC status register contains, as its name implies, status information about the FDC. It provides information about whether the FDC is busy, if a command can be sent to the FDC and whether the status should be read after a command has been executed.

03F4H	Bit 0 = 1	drive 0 in seek mode
	Bit 1 = 1	drive 1 in seek mode
	Bit 2 = 1	drive 2 in seek mode
	Bit 3 = 1	drive 3 in seek mode
	Bit 4 = 1	read/write command in process
	Bit 5 = 0	FDC in DMA mode
	= 1	FDC not in DMA mode
	Bit 6 = 0	data transfer CPU to FDC
	= 1	data transfer FDC to CPU
	Bit 7 = 1	data register ready for FDC<>CPU

The FDC Data Register (035H) consists of a stack of registers and these contain data, commands and floppy disk drive status information. Data is written into these registers in order to program a particular command and the address is read afterwards to obtain the result.

The FDC can carry out 15 different commands. This is accomplished by a multi-byte data transfer from the CPU and after execution of the command it can provide a multi-byte transfer back to the CPU. A command is divided into 3 phases:-

Command Phase - FDC receives information required for carrying out an operation from the CPU.

Execution Phase - FDC performs operation as instructed.

Result Phase - at end of execution status and other information made available to CPU.

The Physical Connections

The above describes both how the FDC and floppy disk drive are accessed from the operating system via the expansion bus, and the purpose of the FDC. The main question is, "How do I connect the Floppy Disk Drive (FDD) ?" All of these operations must be done with the power OFF and Figure 6.3 shows the components now necessary and the cabling required (the FDC card shown is fictitious). The floppy disk drive has two connectors - one for power and the other to the FDC.

The power connection is a four way plug from the power supply, the pin connections are:-

1	+12 V
2	0 V
3	0 V
4	+ 5 V

There may be several connectors from the power supply but they are all identical. This should be attached to the appropriate connector on the FDD.

The main control/data cable (supplied with the FDC) for the internal drives is a flat grey ribbon cable with three 34-way connectors on it. This is known as a Daisy Chain arrangement. The connectors on the FDC and FDD will only fit one way round as there is a keyway to prevent reverse connection. The two connectors close together are for the FDD and the other at the far end is for the FDC card. The one red core of the ribbon cable denotes pin 1 of the connectors, and the connector specification for controller to floppy disk drive is given in Figure 6.4.

To fit an additional disk drive all of the above apply but in addition the operating system must be able to address the individual diskdrives. This is normally accomplished in one of two ways:-

1) a setting must be made on the FDD itself or
2) a cable is used with some of the wires swapped round (or twisted) on the second plug.

It is hoped that the method used is explained in the documentation you receive with the disk drive.

In the first case a straight through control/data cable is used and the drive address must be set on the FDD, i.e. drive 0,1,2 or 3. This is the only way the FDC knows which drive to access. The setting is normally a link with a small plug or shunt. Unfortunately the designations on the FDD itself do not follow a strict pattern. Logical Drive 0 (A) is usually address DS0 on the FDD but occasionally it is called DS1 - read your manual very carefully!

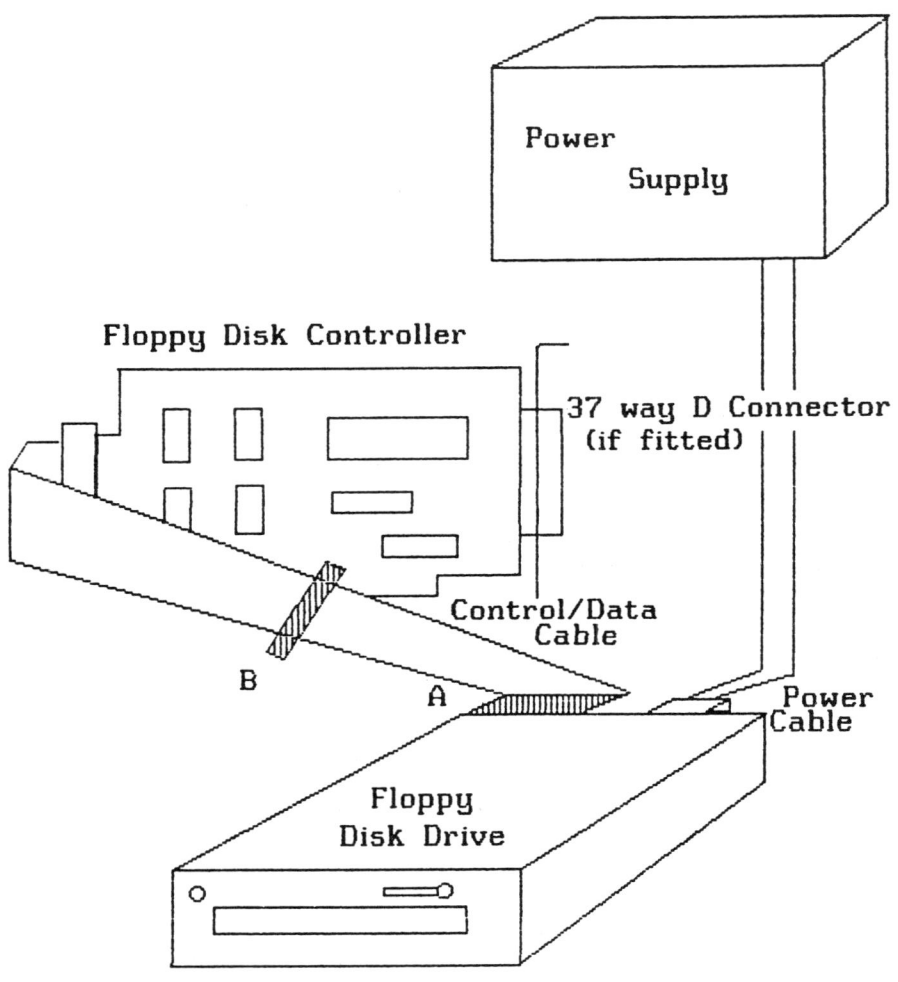

Figure 6.3 Connections for Internal Disk Drive(s)

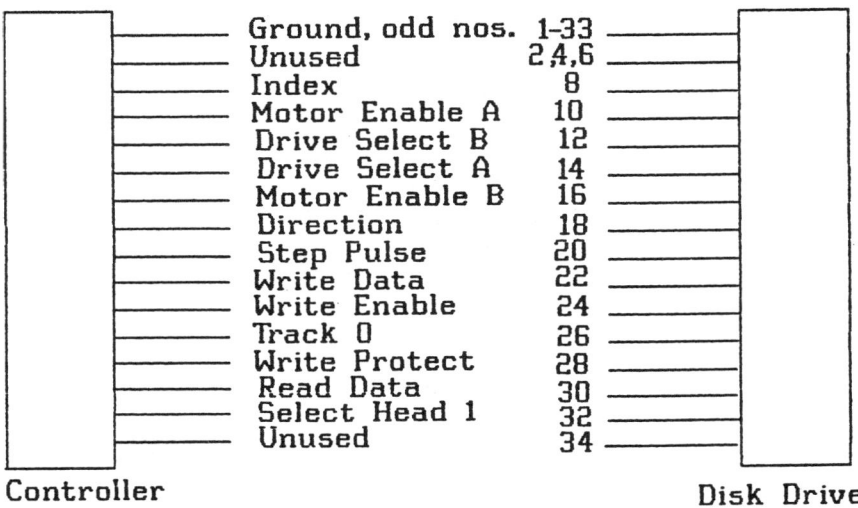

Ground, odd nos. 1-33
Unused   2,4,6
Index   8
Motor Enable A   10
Drive Select B   12
Drive Select A   14
Motor Enable B   16
Direction   18
Step Pulse   20
Write Data   22
Write Enable   24
Track 0   26
Write Protect   28
Read Data   30
Select Head 1   32
Unused   34

Controller   Disk Drive

Figure 6.4 Internal Cable Specification for Floppy Drives

If a twist cable is used five wires (two address and three ground wires) are transposed so that addressing is effectively carried out on the cable. In this arrangement logical address line 1 is routed to the same pin on the second drive as logical address line 0 was on the first drive. The address jumper on the FDD cannot be completely ignored and for both drives to work the plug must be on logical drive 1 (DS1 usually).

If external units are to be fitted (assuming the FDC is suitable) they must have their own power supply. The control/data cable is connected to the back of the computer via a 37 way D connector on the FDC card and the pin specifications are given on Figure 6.5. As can be seen the external units are logical drives 2 and 3. Again, a setting may have to be made on the FDD depending on the form of addressing used as explained above.

In both the above cases terminating resistors in a small pack must be coupled **ONLY** to the last drive on the cable. This is normally a small IC package or by switch. Make sure this is accomplished as this may cause data to be corrupted on the control/data cable.

This is all that is necessary in fitting extra floppy drives. When the fitting is complete boot the machine up and after the A prompt put a disk in drive B and request a directory on drive B. There should be no problem, but if there is, carefully check the addressing on the disk drive.

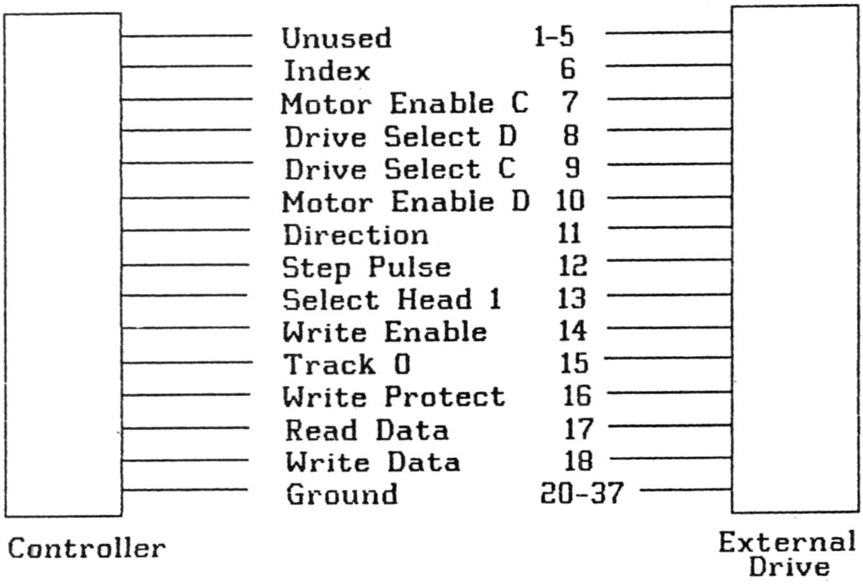

Controller		Signal	Pin		External Drive
		Unused	1-5		
		Index	6		
		Motor Enable C	7		
		Drive Select D	8		
		Drive Select C	9		
		Motor Enable D	10		
		Direction	11		
		Step Pulse	12		
		Select Head 1	13		
		Write Enable	14		
		Track 0	15		
		Write Protect	16		
		Read Data	17		
		Write Data	18		
		Ground	20-37		

Figure 6.5 External Cable Specification for Floppy Drives

With both Amstrad PCs (1512 and 1640), physically it is only possible to have two disk drives internally or one disk drive and one hard disk drive, anything over this amount must be external. In fitting a second disk drive a blanking plate must be removed and the FDD unit fitted mechanically as per instructions. Several suppliers quote floppy kits for the Amstrad together with fitting instructions.

Other Units

The new range of personal computers brought out by IBM have 3.5 inch disk drives, these computers are referred to as IBM PS/2 models. Several units have appeared to cope with interchange of information between various IBM type personal computers. Some of these are advertised by Plus 5 and allow a 3.5 inch unit to be attached to the old XT faithful so that the PC will read, write and format disks for the new range of machines. These units are either internal or external and supplied with a controller card, device driver and format software and power supply where necessary. There are also units for the reverse operation, i.e. model PS/2 to XT clone conversion.

The Hard Disk

This probably represents the most common storage upgrade that anyone will carry out. Unlike the floppy drives which have a fixed capacity, the hard disk can be obtained in various arrangements: 10 MBytes, 20 MBytes, 30 MBytes and upwards, it depends on what one wants to pay! Unlike the floppy disk, the hard disk is usually a permanent feature in a computer but there are a few that have a detachable hard disk cartridge. The hard disk comes in two basic sizes - 3.5 and 5.25 inches - but it is immaterial to the computer, it only sees it as a storage unit with a fixed method of storing information. The hard disk continuously rotates at 3600 rpm and so gives higher access speeds than a floppy unit. It should be noted here, however, that MS-DOS/PC-DOS up to and including version 3.2 can only cope with 32 MBytes maximum per disk. To overcome this the disk has to be "split" into two virtual drives each with a capacity under the 32 MByte limit, e.g. for a 40 MByte unit this can be split as 20 + 20, 32 + 8, 10 + 30 MBytes. Refer to the operating system manual for further advice and formatting arrangements.

With a hard disk unit there is nothing to be seen, unlike the floppy disk. The hard disk is in a metal container that does not permit the ingress of dust and is thus well protected. The hard disk is usually an aluminium disk coated with a magnetic medium held on by a binding agent. The medium is very similar to that used for audio tapes and floppy disks and is a ferric oxide compound. More recently some manufacturers such as Tandon (Western Digital Corporation have now acquired the Tandon hard disk division) have been using a thin film magnetic medium (e.g. pure metals or combination thereof) and plating it on to the disk . This latter method allows a higher data density on the disk as well as providing higher access speeds. Both sides of the disk are used, a typical disk being 10 MBytes, thus a 20 MByte unit is typically two 10 MByte disks in one container with the appropriate increase in read/write heads (see Figure 6.6). Another method of increasing storage capacity is the use of a different modulation method for the data e.g. RLL (run length limited) instead of the more normal MFM (modified frequency modulation).

The hard disk format layout is similar to that of the floppy disk but with increased numbers of sectors (typically 17) and cylinders or tracks (typically 615). These figures will vary somewhat with the type of drive, storage capacity and manufacturer. The reason it is called a cylinder is that if several disks are present, one above another on a common spindle, track N is in the same vertical position for all disks and the envelope is a cylinder. Figure 6.6 shows a diagrammatic layout of read/write heads and disks.

The method of formatting a hard disk varies somewhat from that for a floppy but the underlying principles are the same. Many suppliers will provide their product in a pre-formatted form but for others the procedure is as follows. First of all a primary format must be put on the disk (e.g. using DEBUG, G=C800:6 under MS-DOS). Following this, use FDISK - this allows partitioning of the disk. Having successfully done this then use FORMAT C:/s - this will finish the formatting of the disk and place the system files on the hard disk. The above is accurate for formatting drive C. This procedure should be well explained in the manual with the hard disk and controller card. When a hard disk has been formatted it is normally only capable of working with the type of controller it was formatted under. If the HDC card is changed for another type then re-formatting is likely to be necessary.

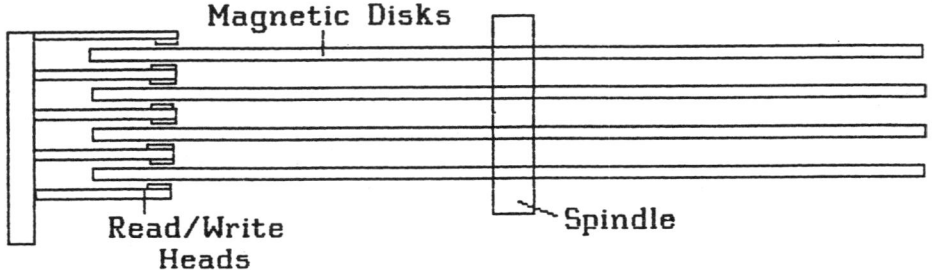

Figure 6.6 Diagrammatic Representation of Hard Disk Unit

The hard disk is controlled by a controller card (HDC) plugged into one of the expansion sockets and thus coupled to the system bus, DMA and interrupt circuits. There are now two approaches to choosing hard disk storage. It is possible to purchase units as follows:-

1. Separate hard disk and hard disk controller card
2. Hard disk attached to controller card (hard card)

The familiar interface standard in use for PCs is labelled ST506/412 and is an early standard and recognises a controller speed of 5 MHz and data rate of 625 kbps. There are however two new standards around: the Enhanced Small Device Interface (ESDI) and the Small Computer Systems Interface (SCSI). Both of these have clock speeds of 10 MHz and a data transfer rate of 900 kbps. The ESDI interface is used in a similar manner to the ST506/412 interface. The SCSI is a system level interface which in essence provides its own expansion bus to plug into. If buying hard disk and controller cards from separate sources make sure that they are compatible. The following is generally applicable to the ST506/412 interface which at present is the most common.

Separate Units

Here the hard disk drive is physically separate from the controller card and attaches somewhere inside the front of the computer case like a floppy disk drive. The earlier units were full height (3.25 inches or 83 mm) but all of the later units half height (1.62 inches or 42 mm). These units require three sets of connections - control, data and power. The associated controller cards can control two hard disks and Figure 6.7 shows a block diagram of a typical HDC card and note should be made of the ROM/EPROM. **NOTE** some hard disk controller boards cannot co-reside with another one in the same computer. When a hard disk access is required control is passed from the BIOS on the system board to a BIOS ROM on the hard disk controller and this then controls all I/O from the hard disk unit. This BIOS ROM is normally located at C8000H-C9FFFH (although CA000H-CBFFFH has also been seen mentioned) and is usually 8 kBytes. The HDC and HDD are controlled via I/O ports in the address range 0320H-032FH. Power for the hard disk drive itself and associated electronics comes direct from the internal computer power supply, but the HDC gets its power from the expansion bus. One hard disk controller card can handle two hard disk drives.

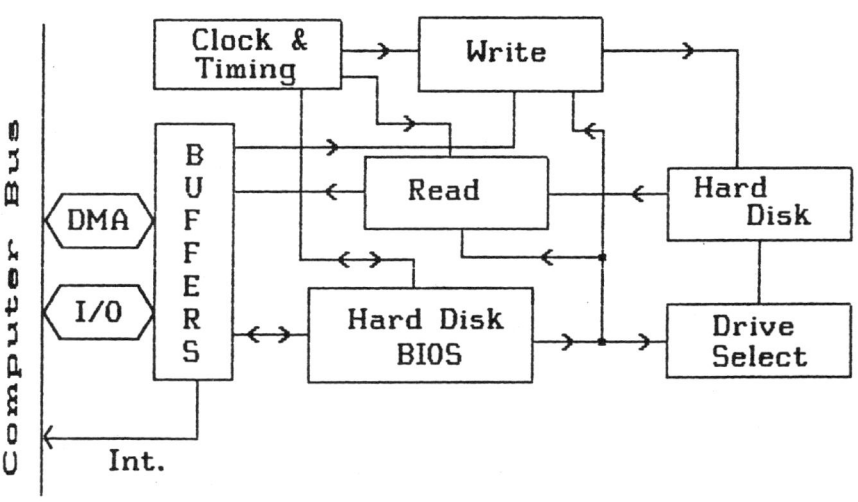

Figure 6.7 Block Diagram of Hard Disk

The Hard Card

In this arrangement the hard disk is physically attached to the controller card and the whole unit plugs into an expansion bus slot. A sketch of such a unit is shown on Figure 6.8. All power, control and data connections are via the expansion bus. In this case there is one control card per hard disk but the block diagram will be similar to that of Figure 6.7.

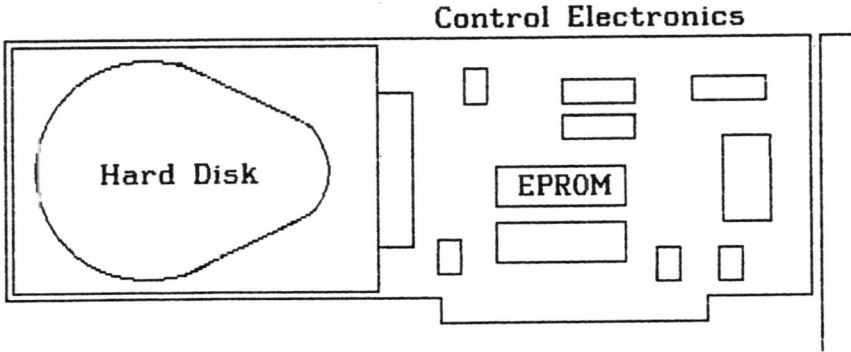

Figure 6.8 Typical Hard Card

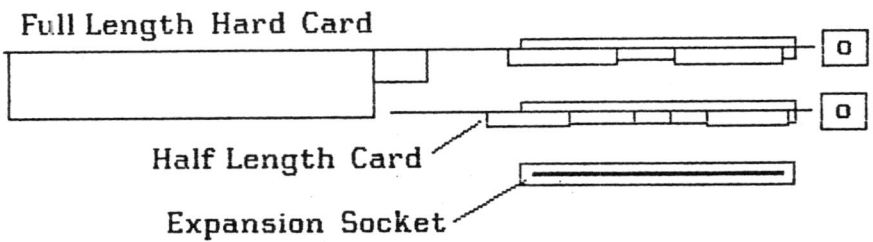

Figure 6.9 Installation of Hard Card and Adjacent Card(s)

In using the hard card approach one must make sure that sufficient room exists to accommodate it as some units take one and a half slots (see Figure 6. 9), the hard disk unit itself spilling into the space occupied by the adjacent full length board.

The operating system can cope with two hard disk units each up to the 32 MBytes maximum of storage capacity, and there is room in many of the compatibles to accommodate both of them (see later comments about the Amstrad). There are no motherboard switch settings for this storage device.

Data Transfer

Normal data transfer is carried out by direct memory address and controlled via DMA channel 3 and usually interrupt IRQ5. However, the setting up of the hard disk, status reports and physical attributes of the transfer is via I/O ports and the ranges 320H-323H and 324H-327H have been seen quoted.

The Physical Connections

Having explained how the hard disk drive interfaces to the computer generally, the installation must now be considered, and it is applicable to the common ST506/412 interface standard. The following explanation applies to an arrangement using a separate HDC and hard disk drive (see later for hard card). The hard disk drive should be screwed into the place reserved for it and a four pin power plug from the power supply plugged in (pins as for floppy disk drive). This plug can only be connected one way round. On the HD unit there will also be a jumper/switch setting for the disk drive number and this will normally be shipped as for a single drive installation (e.g. drive C). A terminating resistor pad will also be on the hard disk unit.

From the HDC board there are three cables attached to three connectors. There is a 34 way cable going to connector normally labelled J1 and this contains all of the control lines and forms a daisy chain arrangement, i.e. there are two connectors on it. For the first disk drive (normally C) use the first connector (or there may only be one). Then there is a separate 20 way cable for each of the drives from the HDC. J2 goes to the first drive and J3 the second (if fitted); these carry the data. Figure 6.10 shows the arrangement for the HDC and HDD whilst Figure 6.11 gives the pin designations for cables J1, J2 and J3.

When fitting the control and data cables make sure that they are terminated properly. If the cables are not terminated then there may be "ringing" on the cable causing distortion of the signals and possible malfunction. The terminations are normally in a small 14/16 pin integrated circuit package; they are merely resistors. If a daisy chain arrangement is used then the terminator must be on the drive nearest the end of the cable. In addition to the terminating resistors there is hard disk addressing to be considered. Hard disks can be addressed by means of jumpers on the hard disk unit or by a "twist" in the cable, i.e. 5 connections are transposed, just as for the floppy disk. The manual accompanying the hard disk unit should give details of any settings to be changed and/or checked.

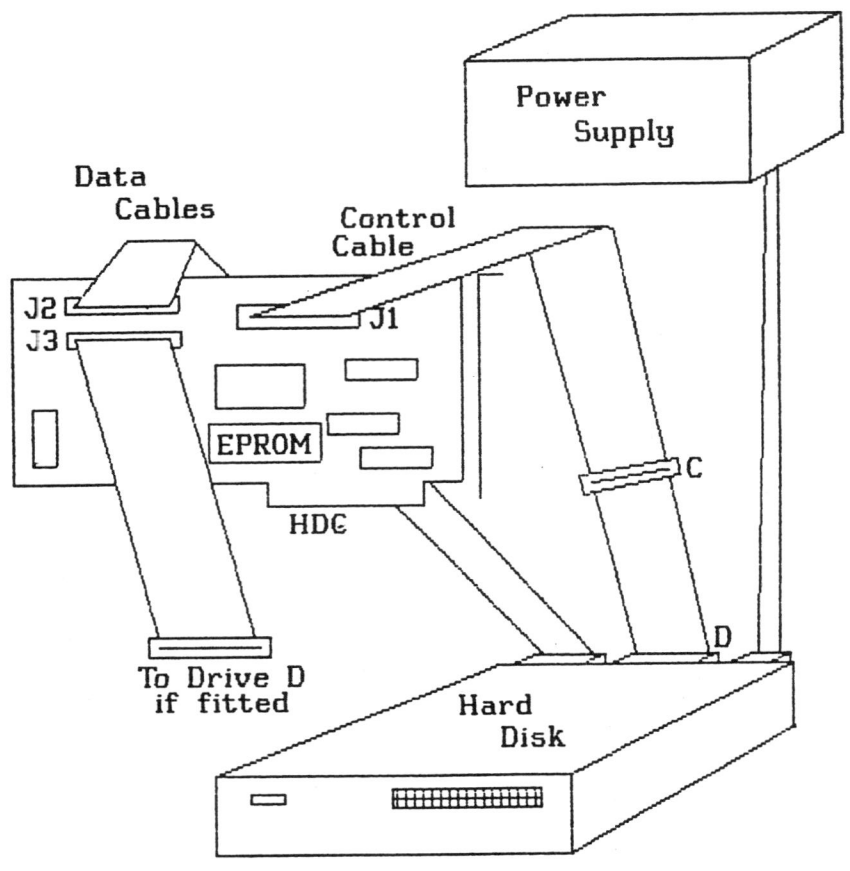

Figure 6.10 Connection of Hard Disk to HDC and Power Supply

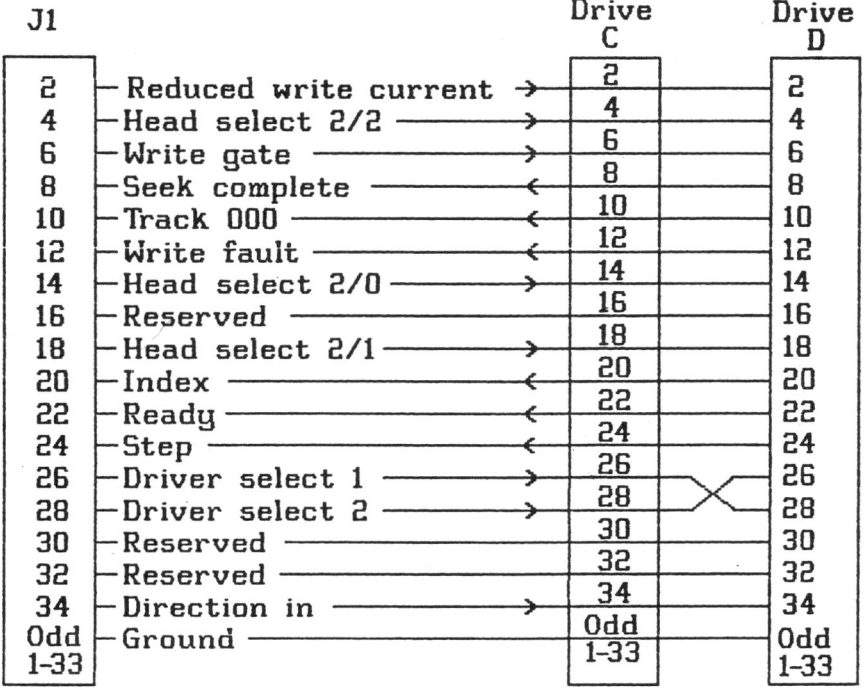

NOTE – addressing by twist in cable

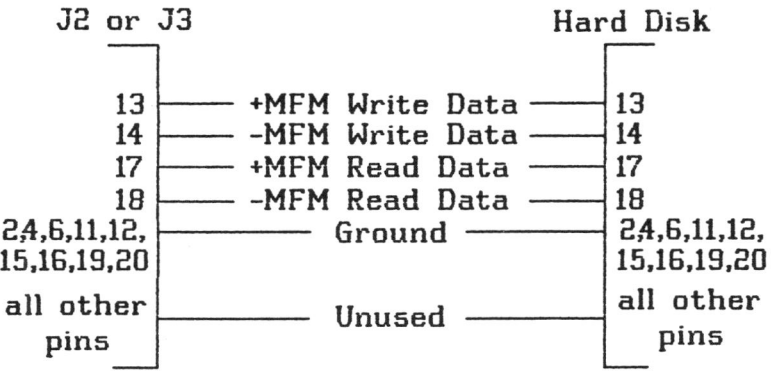

Figure 6.11 Hard Disk Connections

The hard card is much simpler to fit into the computer - just a plug-in job on the motherboard. However, before fitting some links or switches must be set to indicate if this is the only hard disk in the computer and the designation, i.e. drive C or drive D.

With the Amstrad an internal hard disk drive can be fitted but there are physical problems. If two disk drives are fitted and a
hard disk is also required then a hard card solution must be used or an external hard disk unit. If only one floppy disk drive is fitted then either a hard disk plus card is fitted or a hard card.

In the PC1512 the hard card or controller card will be fitted in the expansion area where there is a clip-off plastic lid. In the PC1640 a half length controller card can be fitted inside the main computer housing. The easiest solution is to fit a hard card. It is worthwhile asking the supplier if the units are compatible with the Amstrad machines - a minor problem has been reported with the Miniscribe Hardcard and this appears to involve heat dissipation when placed in the Amstrad machines.

Removable Cartridge Hard Disks

There are two units that come under this heading, the removable hard Winchester disk or the Bernoulli system. The Winchester system is basically a hard disk, but the read/write heads, instead of being lifted and parked when not in use, are retracted to allow the disk to be removed. The disk can therefore be removed to a secure place or it is possible for a different disk to be inserted. The interface is as for the hard disk units described above.

The Bernoulli box uses a removable cartridge about the size of a thin book. When the cartridge is put into the main unit air pressure is used to keep the storage medium from touching the read/write head.

Tape Streamers

As an alternative to the above and also as a storage media for backing up data from hard disks, a tape backup system has been developed. These units can either be internally fitted (if there is space) or external. The external type may have their own power supplies from the mains and there are numerous arrangements, depending on the manufacturer. The information is recorded on a 0.25 inch magnetic tape cartridge and can take from about 2 minutes up to 10 minutes to backup 10 MBytes of data file by file - depending on the interface arrangements and type of system. There are also some 0.5 inch tape units on the market.

If an external tape drive unit is used it is possible to connect it to various computers, providing they have the capability, and so will provide backup for more than one machine and hence be more cost effective.

These systems seem to fall into two categories:-

> 1) those that do not necessarily require additional add-on cards
> 2) those that must have an additional card.

Those in category 2) tend to be much faster in data transfer, more expensive but they also have larger memory capability. Both types require driver software and this is usually included in the package when purchased. Both types come in forms that can be internally fitted (if there is space) or externally fitted (within their own housing).

Type 1

These generally will try and use a spare driver from the floppy disk control card - either an internal spare connection on the daisy chain cable or the 37 way D connector for external drives (see earlier section on floppy disk control cards). If there is no spare floppy controller then an additional board must be used. Typical data transfer rates for this type of tape backup is 250 or 500 kBytes per second.

If a unit is to be fitted internally using an existing spare floppy control driver, then it will usually connect to drive B (see Figure 6.3 for a typical arrangement) and obtain its power from the internal power supply. If the unit is to be fitted externally and the floppy disk controller has a 37 way external connector then the tape drive will connect to this but it may have its own external power supply - again see Figure 6.3. If the unit is to be external and the floppy disk controller does not have a 37 way D type connector then a floppy tape adapter board is necessary in order to provide the external connection.

For the situation where a spare floppy driver is not available, then an additional interface card will be required. This card will slot into the expansion card and provide the equivalent of another floppy disk controller. It will also have connections on for either, or both, internal and external tape drive units. It is assumed that the fitting of the board into the expansion bus is carried out prior to re-routing cables. If an internal tape unit is fitted, the fitting is similar to that for floppy and individual Hard Cards.

Type 2

These units require an additional card that fits into the expansion bus irrespective of whether a spare floppy disk controller exists. They are often designated by the code QIC-xx, the QIC standing for quarter inch cartridge. It is also possible to get tape drives that interface via the SCSI standard interface as mentioned earlier in this chapter. The interface card requires up to two connectors on it - one for internal and one for external backup tape units (see Figure 6.12). Typical data transfer rates for these units are higher and 720 kBytes per second is fairly typical. Be careful, some manufacturers quote data transfer per second and some per minute!

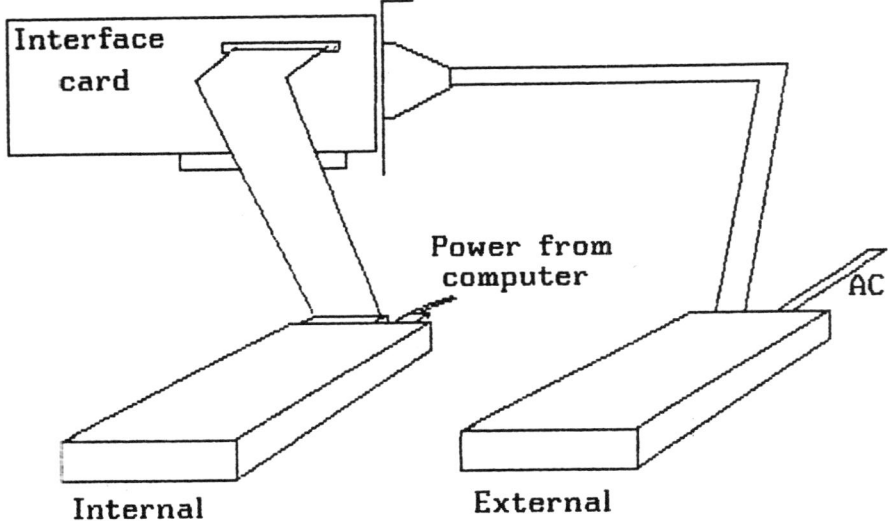

Interface card

Power from computer

AC

Internal

External

Figure 6.12 With Additional Mandatory Interface Card

This interface card is a typical PC add-on board and is fitted in the same way as other cards. There are some links/DIP switches which must be set and these determine the I/O address range to be used, the IRQ required (if used) and the DMA channel. Further information should be supplied in the accompanying manual. Plug in the appropriate cabling and attach to the tape backup unit.

Software

The software associated with driving these units is primarily designed to run from the hard disk and may need about 256 kBytes of RAM. The software supplied is menu driven and allows the user to set up for his/her application. First of all the software must be installed on the hard disk. A typical tape control program will provide the following facilities:-

> Backup to Tape
> Restore to Disk
> Tape Status
> Utilities
> Help
> Exit to DOS

These will again have sub-menus and typically allow complete or partial copying, tape formatting, memory available, erasing and verifying.

A new tape or one previously used with another system will need formatting. This marks out the tape into blocks and maps out blocks which are unusable. Formatting needs to be done only once but it is a slow procedure, typically in excess of one hour on a PC XT compatible. A directory is kept at the beginning of a tape and automatically updated.

Optical Storage

There are many changes going on in this area at the moment: prices are falling, ideals changing, and new products appearing almost daily. If one is considering buying some form of optical drive it would be best to browse through the latest periodicals and talk with a supplier. This section can only hope to give an insight into this interesting storage medium.

The optical disk is at present a choice really only for businesses that can justify it. The cost of these units is high at the moment but likely to fall as with any new innovation, but they may still then be a questionable acquisition. These units can hold a vast amount of information (500 to 2000 MBytes) and are mainly READ only, the data being put on during manufacture or a once write only operation. Some units are now just appearing on the market that are read and write with the ability to erase but the technology is still in its infancy. Optical storage is ideal for holding very large amounts of fixed information such as lists of books in print, dictionaries, encyclopaedias, parts catalogues, scientific abstracts, population census results and archived data.

The concept of these disks comes from the compact disk audio field and the data is recorded in similar style. The optical storage media fall into two camps: the CD-ROM which has its information placed on it during manufacture and the WORM (write once read many) disk. At present the CD-ROM is the more common and best developed system but the WORM is fast becoming a contender. However, they do offer slightly different characteristics and the use and type of information to be stored is determined by these.

CD-ROMS

This is probably the closest to the audio disk and has allowed much of the technology developed for that purpose to be used. It is a plastic disk 120 mm in diameter containing a reflective metallised layer. During manufacture, information is put onto this metallised layer in a long spiral track which has some 16000 turns per inch radially. The information is encoded onto the disk by means of small marks on the reflective layer and is then read in the drive unit by means of a laser beam which scans along the track. The current (1988) cost of the disk is of the order of £100 and the read unit is about £1000 and these prices will fall.

Figure 6.13 shows diagrammatically how the information is stored on the surface. The spiral is divided into sectors of constant length, the disk speed being controlled so that as the head goes from the outer spiral to the inner spiral it still takes the same amount of time to traverse a sector - this is known as constant linear velocity (CLV). This is where the disk is at variance with the audio form as this has a constant angular velocity (CAV). This changing in speed does mean that the electronics for the speed control of the disk rotation are quite sophisticated and hence reflected in the price. The number of sectors encountered in one revolution therefore changes with the radial position of the head and is about 20 sectors on the outer track to about 9 sectors on the innermost track.

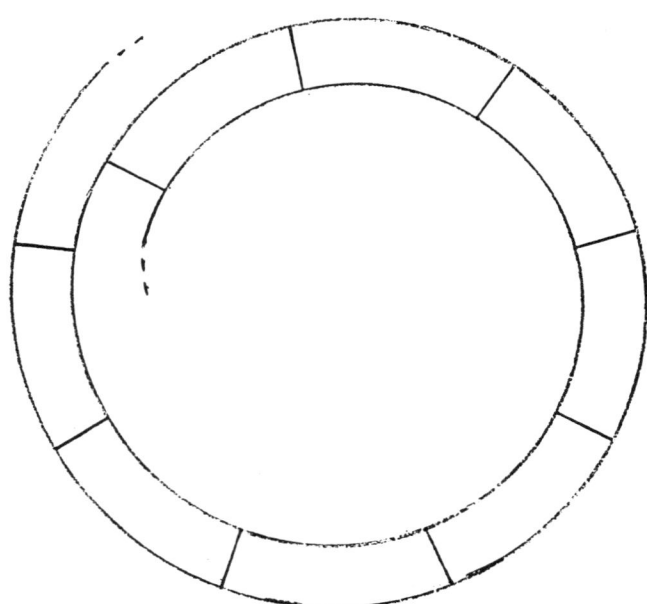

Figure 6.13 Optical Disk Storage Format (CLV)

The familiar track and sector addressing for the magnetic media cannot be translated to the optical form. The sector concept is fine but the track has no meaning because a spiral is being used. The method of overcoming this is to specify time from the beginning of the spiral and this approach does mean that optical disks do have a slower access time than their magnetic counterparts. A CD-ROM can hold some 270,000 sectors each containing 2 kBytes, giving a total of some 540 MBytes. One sector is the smallest addressable unit on the disk.

Agreed international standards now exist for the CD-ROM and this has led to firms like Microsoft providing software routines to cope with the difference between access for magnetic storage media and CD-ROM. There is an extension to MS-DOS to cater for optical media, each file merely being called by its name as for other disk forms and the optical disk drive being assumed to be drive D, for example.

WORMS

These disks allow the user to write to the disk once for each file, i.e. once stored it cannot be changed. This is obviously useful for archiving records, such as accounts, once they have been finalised. It therefore complements existing magnetic media and provides a permanent form of storage that is very hard to damage (unlike hard disks).

The worm disk itself is slightly different in structure to the CD-ROM, it is floppy disk size (5.25 inches or 133 mm) and consists of a metallic layer of Selenium Tellurium sandwiched between two layers of glass and mounted in a protective cartridge. When exposed to a small pin-prick of light from a low power laser, a small area of the metallic disk is evaporated, hence depositing data irreversibly onto the disk surface. The form of storage on the surface is on a spiral, as for the CD-ROM, but the management of this information is complex. Currently there is no agreed international standard for the WORM drive although attempts are being made. No software houses have yet provided a solution for this drive, but when buying one utilities are provided that interface with MS-DOS and allow it to be accessed with normal MD-DOS commands. When a file is written to disk then the catalogue must also be up-dated with information containing number of sectors and position. Also, because it is possible to provide additional information to any file this must somehow be appended so that the directory and file knows that additional information exists.

Connection to the PC

The majority of CD-ROM and WORM drives available can interface to the PC but check with the supplier to start with. The Optical Storage unit can either be installed as a full height internal unit or as an external unit. The interface is via a typical plug-in card, possibly using the SCSI interface (see earlier in the chapter under Hard Disks). This latter standard may well become the norm as it is increasingly being supported by Hard Disk manufacturers.

If the unit is internal then it connects to the add-on card with an internal ribbon cable. If the unit is external then it is via a typical screened multi-core cable with a D type connector. Figure 6.14 shows typical arrangements. There may be some DIP switch settings to make and these will determine the base address (e.g. between C0000H and D0000H) and the DMA channel. This should all be explained in the accompanying manual.

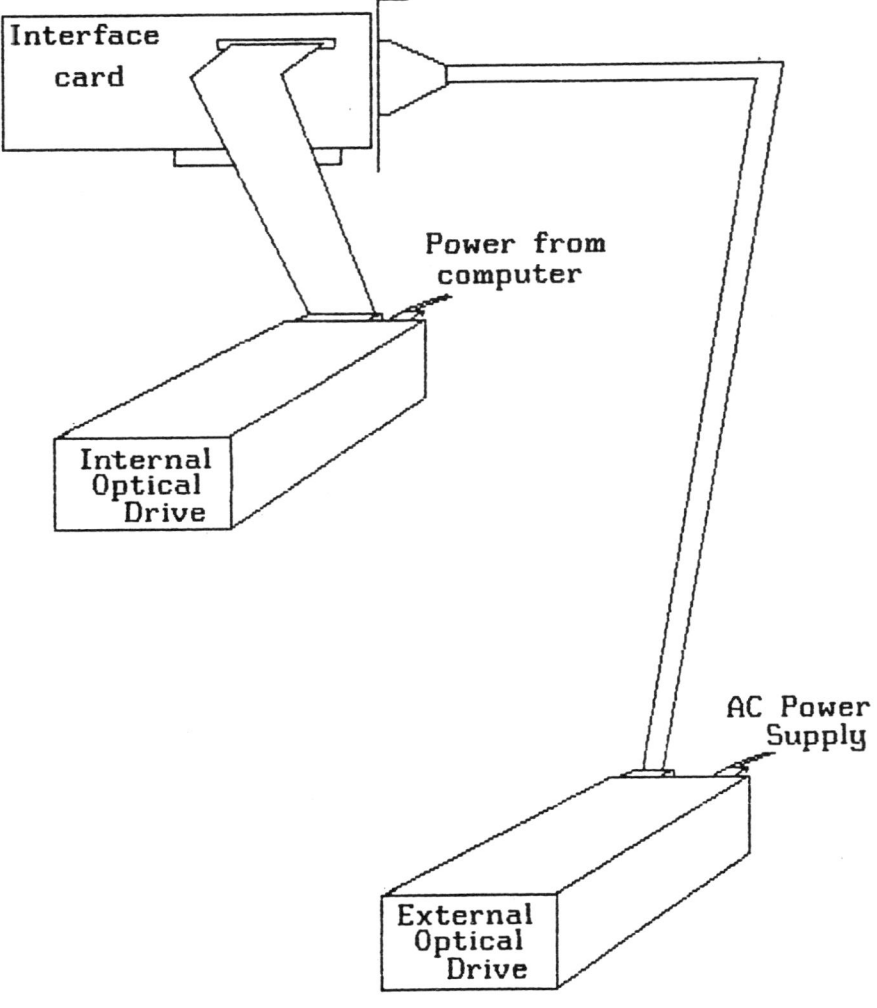

Figure 6.14 Connections for Typical Optical Drives

Suppliers

Ambair Systems - WORM drives
Cipher Data Products - tape backup
Computer Marketing - Plus hardcard
Core - hard disks, tape backup
CPU Peripherals - WORM, tape and hard disk drives, hardcards
Cristie Electronics - tape backup, hardcards, floppy drives
Ideal Hardware - hard disk controller card
Kudos Systems Ltd - tape backup, controller cards, hard disks
Logic 2000 - hardcards
Memory Corporation - tape backup
Micro Macro Distributors Ltd - tape backup systems
Mitsubishi - floppy and hard disk drives
Oxford Hard Disks - hard disks, hardcards, controller cards, tape drives, floppy drives
PC Relative - hardcards
Peripherals Connections - tape backup, hardcards, controller cards
Plus 5 - other size drives
Rapid Systems - cartridge Tape
Rodime - hard disks
Seagate - hard disk drives
Thame Systems - tape, hard and floppy drives, controller cards
Western Digital Corporation - hard disk drives, controller cards

7

MISCELLANEOUS ADD-ON UNITS

Introduction

There are some units that are difficult to place in any single chapter of this book. Alternatively, they could be included in other chapters as they do not warrant a chapter for themselves. Some of these units are very cheap whilst others are quite expensive; some units are only suitable for use with certain types of software whilst others are very much more universal in their application. These units are not necessarily boards plugging into an expansion slot but they all do represent add-ons and as such mention should be made of them and their suppliers. Some require to be attached via an RS232 serial link which is explained in Chapters 9 and 10.

Real Time Clock

This is probably the cheapest of the add-ons in this chapter. It can be a board in its own right (but more commonly is part of another add-on card with other options), an add-on unit for an integrated circuit socket or a small card that attaches to another device (slotless RTC). The advantage of these last two units is that they do not take up an expansion socket. Many compatibles, including the Amstrads, are already fitted with this option but some machines are not - including the original from IBM. In many machines it is part of an additional add-on card and in other machines such as the Amstrad and Opus II it is part of the motherboard.

Under MS-DOS or PC-DOS there is a TIME and DATE command and these are only accurate if the user enters the correct information when the computer is turned on each time. This information, as will be noted, is added alongside filenames on the disk and appears under the DIR command. It gives a useful check on when files are created. The real time clock will automatically update the TIME and DATE information when the computer is switched on, providing the correct software routines exist.

The real time clock is a battery powered unit so, once set, it continues to function even when the computer is switched off. A typical arrangement is shown in Figure 7.1. The battery is often a rechargeable nickel-cadmium type (which may give a life of some 5 years) but in some units it is of the non-rechargeable variety (e.g. Amstrad and OPUS). This latter type is usually of the Lithium (minimum 1 year life) or common zinc-carbon types. A crystal oscillator allows the clock chip to count time. On the expansion cards only there is a small trimmer capacitor to allow setting the accuracy. The clock provides the user with the same information as the operating system clock, viz:-

> seconds
> minutes
> hours
> day of the month
> day of the week
> month
> year (no leap year)

The information contained in the battery backed clock is independent of the system clock and small programs must be run in order to set the clock and read its information into the system clock. The information goes via various I/O ports plus the use of interrupts (usually IRQ2). The various clock add-on units are now dealt with separately.

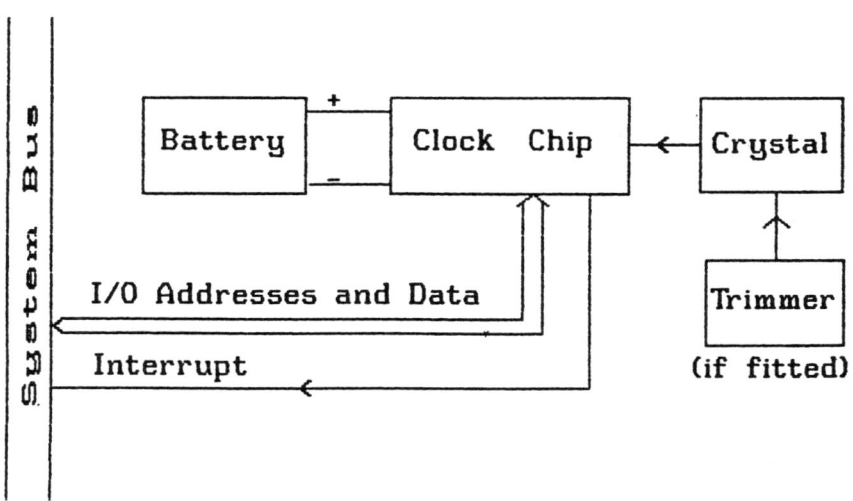

Figure 7:1 Typical Block Diagram of Real Time Clock Board

RTC on Expansion Card

This is the most common form for the RTC and it is easy to install the expansion card, it simply plugs into an expansion bus socket and there may or may not be jumpers/switches associated with the clock. On some boards it can be configured as either clock 1 or clock 2, but not both. The switches will determine the I/O addressing of the unit, mainly to avoid clashes with other allocations. If the battery is mounted on the PCB itself remember to remove any insulation on the battery terminals! With the clock board there should be a floppy disk with some programs on it, these allow:-

> setting of the real time clock
> passing the time and date information to the system clock
> and (possibly) a program to display time on the screen.

Having installed the clock card and turned the machine on, the first operation is to set the clock. The manual will tell you which program to run and then simply answer the questions. This transfers the date and time information to the clock chip. The next step of the operation is to ensure the system clock receives this information on booting up and is regularly updated during use of the computer. This is accomplished by putting a program from the disk supplied onto the disk containing the operating system. This must also be named in the AUTOEXEC.BAT file so that it is loaded on booting-up. Merely altering the date and time information with the operating system TIME and DATE commands does **NOT** update the battery backed clock. There may also be an additional program that allows display of the clock in one corner of the screen continuously. This is fine providing it occurs on a border, but certainly with graphic type programs it may appear as a mottled line on the screen and a line on the printed output. In these circumstances it is better to forego the clock display if provided.

As hinted earlier there are possible I/O addresses that may be used, those seen mentioned are:-

clock 1	340H-35FH
clock 2	2C0H-2DFH (default range) or
	240H-25FH

These appear to be *defacto* standards but are not necessarily to be relied upon. The range 2C0H-2DFH appears to be the most commonly mentioned and is arranged as shown in Table 7.1. The OPUS II manual states that it uses the 240H range whilst the Amstrad 1640 uses I/O port 070H for the RTC integrated circuit address and 071H for the RTC data.

Port Address	Function
2C0H	ounter, 1/10000 of second
2C1H	counter, 1/100 and 1/10 of second
2C2H	counter, seconds
2C3H	counter, minutes
2C4H	counter, hours
2C5H	counter, day of week
2C6H	counter, day of month
2C7H	counter, month
2C8H	RAM, upper nibble only
2C9H	RAM, last month storage
2CAH	RAM, year storage
2CBH	RAM, reserved
2CCH-2CFH	RAM, not used
2D0H	interrupt, status register
2D1H	interrupt, control register
2D2H	counter, reset
2D3H	RAM, reset
2D4H	status bit
2D5H	GO command
2D6H	standby interrupt
2D7H-2DEH	not used
2DFH	test mode

Table 7.1 Range of I/O Addresses

To reset the counter and RAM the following bit patterns are used:-

Data	Function
01	1/10000 of second
02	1/100 and 1/10 of second
04	seconds
08	minutes
10	hours
20	day of week
40	day of month
80	month

For the other ranges of I/O mentioned it is assumed that a similar sequence is followed.

Integrated Circuit Socket Type RTC

This is a fairly new development and was only seen by the author advertised from Pinna Electronics and marketed under the name Timekeeper. The clock is embedded in a 28 pin DIL socket and contains a CMOS chip, lithium battery and oscillator.

As the unit is in a 28 pin socket this means that in the PC design is must be accommodated in one of the ROM sockets lying typically between F4000H to FFFFFH. The RTC module fits into one of these sockets and allows the original integrated circuit to piggyback as shown on Figure 7.2. The advertisement states that it accepts any 28 pin bytewide ROM or volatile RAM. All of the pins pass directly through to the piggyback IC except pin 20 (CE) which is inhibited during the transfer of time information. This RTC module uses pins 1, 8(A2), 10(A0), 11(DI/O0), 20(CE) and 22(OE) for control. The unit is supplied with software on disk that performs the functions as for the expansion card above.

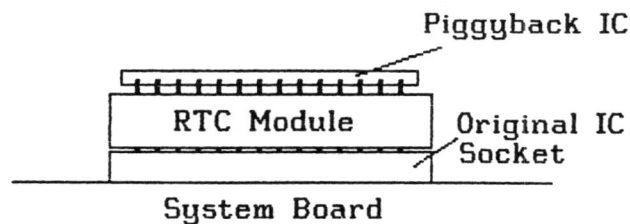

Figure 7.2 Piggyback Arrangement for RTC Module

Slotless Card RTC

This is a small card that appears to have just reached the British market and again is only single sourced by a firm called Bentley Computers. The model type is called dCLOCK-2.

This unit is a small PCB that plugs into the socket at the back of a floppy disk drive. The cable from the floppy disk drive adapter then plugs into this unit. The unit is claimed to have no effect on the disk drive and is completely transparent to the user. Obviously this unit can only be used if a floppy disk drive is attached.

The unit offers the same facilities as those described above and comes complete with driver software on disk that must be specified in the computer's CONFIG.SYS file. It must have MS-DOS 2.0 or later.

Speech Boards

This is one very interesting add-on unit which has applications in such varied areas as interactive learning, language tuition, telephone information, public address/information systems, security systems and last, but not least, in applications where disabilities such as blindness occur. Only one unit has been seen on the market and it is called Audiocard 300E and is marketed by STC Mercator. It is not a speech synthesis system with a moronic voice but it allows the recording of one's own voice, sound or music, digitally processed and stored in files on disk and then retrieved some time later by an application program. As only one has been found on the market then the following information is very much relevant to that particular unit. The manual appears to have plenty of detail and is easy to read.

The system gives up to 80 minutes of audio recording but requires 10 MBytes of permanent storage for the files. The file length and quality are dependent on the sampling rate used for the audio recording which is chosen from software. One does not, of course, have to use this full amount. The high quality audio recording and playback uses a CVSD (continuously variable slope delta modulation) coder/decoder IC and the unit is supported by a software package which has a driver for various programming languages such as Turbo PASCAL, BASIC, C and Assembler. It also allows interactive graphic/audio/text presentations.

Hardware Requirements

The board is half length and requires one vacant expansion slot. The minimum memory requirement is 256 kBytes and requires a contiguous block of 16 I/O addresses in the range 310H to 3FFH. Figure 2-14 (Chapter 2) gives a general map of the I/O addresses and this should be considered when selecting a range. A full table is given in the manual for selecting the I/O address range and placing the appropriate jumpers.

The interrupt and DMA channel also need to be selected and advice by means of tables is provided - Chapter 2 also gives details of the various interrupt and DMA channels used for various purposes. These must be chosen so that they do not conflict with other accessories added. Because a lot of memory is required it would appear that a hard disk is almost essential and hence only one free DMA channel is possibly available as well as only one interrupt. The standard settings for the unit are 350H-35FH, INT3 and DMA1 and some of the software drivers will only use these settings.

Fitting the board is the same as for any other add-on board and is the typical single screw fixing. A microphone and loudspeaker are provided with the unit and will give 2 W into a 4 ohm load. The microphone input sensitivity is 5-20 nₐV into 600 Ohms, there is a line input of 500 mV into a 50 kOhm load and a low level audio output at 500 mV and 50 kOhm. This expansion card and connections are shown diagrammatically in Figure 7.3.

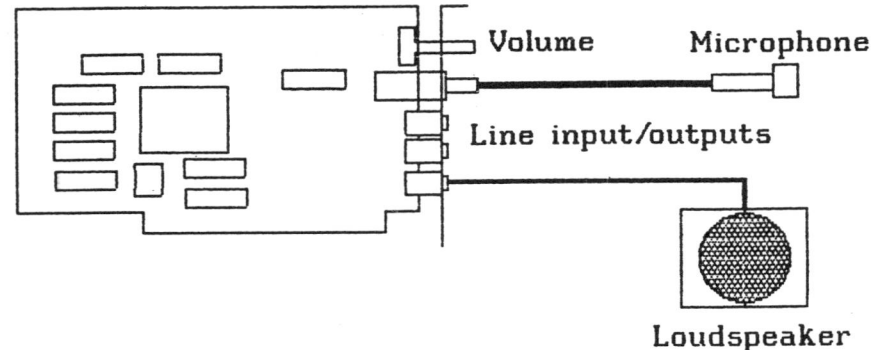

Figure 7.3 Speech Card Arrangements

Prototype Boards

These boards are provided to allow the users to develop their own applications. They are of full length and the boards plug directly into the computer expansion bus. On the board itself buses may be provided for the +12, +5, 0, -5 and -12 volt lines. There is also a specific area on some boards that is already layed out with pcb tracks for I/O address decoding and buffering of the system bus - normally referred to as the interface area. The nominal I/O address allocation for the prototype board is from 300H to 31FH but with anyone adept at electronics this can of course be altered in the interface circuits.

Some prototype boards may come with the typical end fixing metal plate which could be already punched for some form of D connector (25 or 37 way). Some cards may also come with the interface circuits already fitted and Amplicon provide an applications manual with their card. A typical prototype expansion card and its connections is shown diagrammatically in Figure 7.4.

All of the system connections are brought on to the card but it is up to the user to provide distribution on the prototype card. Typically wire-wrap techniques would be used for component interconnection (except possibly the interface area) and there is room for up to 60 wire-wrap DIL sockets on the board.

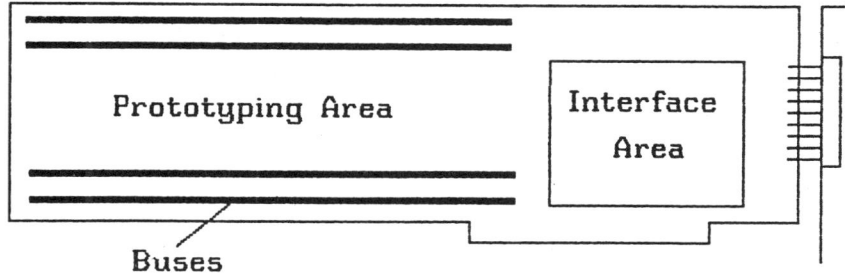

Buses

Figure 7.4 Layout of Typical Prototype Board

Eprom Programmers

As it is possible to develop software on the PC for a variety of applications it is logical that an EPROM should be capable of being programmed on the same host machine. To this end manufacturers/suppliers have on offer various units, some of which are mainly internal, others of which are completely external. Figure 7.5 shows the two options available and how the equipment inter-links. In Figure 7.5(a) most of the hardware for programming the EPROM is contained on an expansion card, the only item being external is the actual ZIF (zero insertion force) socket(s) for the EPROM(S). (A ZIF socket is a socket for an integrated circuit whereby the integrated circuit is put into the socket and the pins clamped onto its legs by an external lever.)

In option (b) most of the hardware is external to the PC, the unit being controlled and data being sent via an RS232 link (see Chapters 9 and 10). The models from the different manufacturers/suppliers seem to provide variations on a theme. Some can accept more than a single EPROM at a time; some may also be able to cope with PAL (programmable array logic), and some include the cost of the control software in the single price. Generally, the externally based units seem to cope with more types of EPROM than do the internally based units. Providing the software is available, the external units are more transportable between different computer systems.

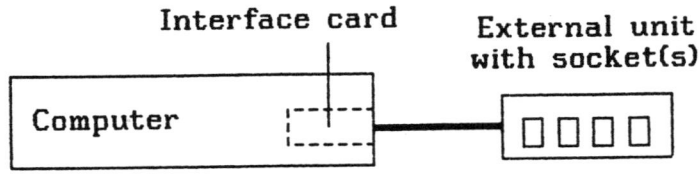

Figure 7.5 (a): EPROM Programmer using External Card

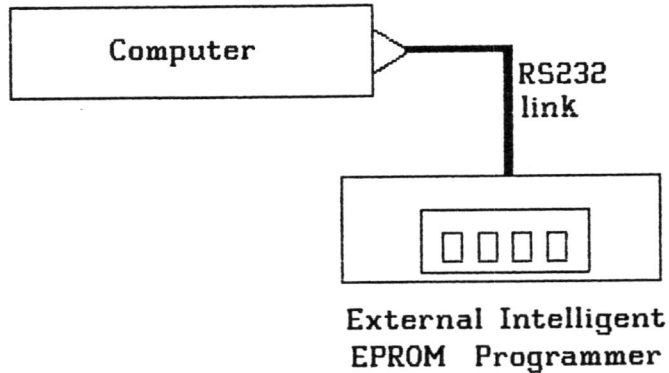

Figure 7.5 (b): External EPROM Programmer with RS232 Link

The software supplied and/or bought will provide most of the following facilities:-

    specify EPROM type
    quantity to program (only for multiple sockets)
    blank check EPROM
    specify start address in EPROM
    write and verify from RAM or disk file
    read EPROM to RAM or disk file
    copy EPROM

The EPROMs are generally of the 27xx family but there are software and adapter sockets that will allow the EPROMs contained within microprocessors to be programmed and read (e.g. 8048).

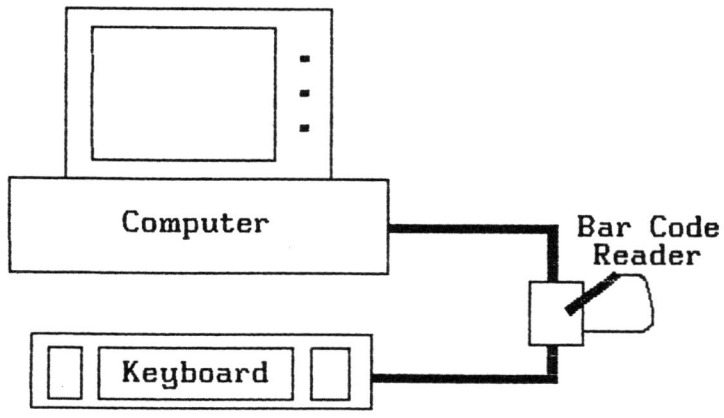

Figure 7.6 (a): Reader in Series with Keyboard

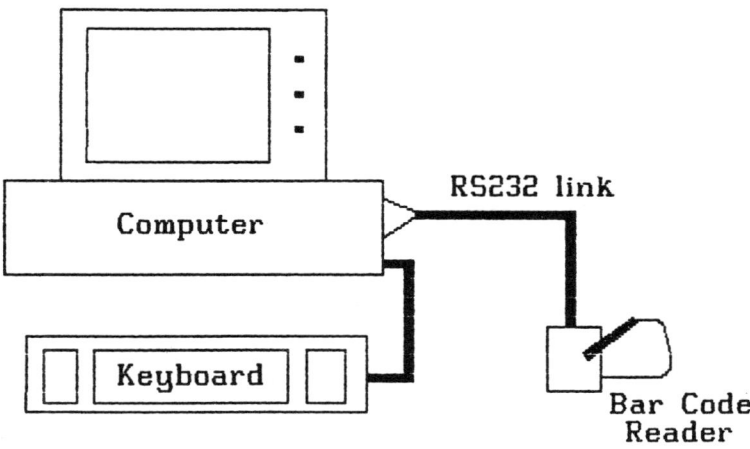

Figure 7.6 (b): Reader on RS232 Link

Bar Codes

There are two units of interest from firms mentioned in the suppliers and there appears to be two approaches for the user of the PC and compatible. The two variants are depicted in Figure 7.6 and the difference is the way the bar code reader interfaces to the computer. In the first case (a) the unit fits in series with the cabling from the keyboard to the PC and in the second (b), a possibly more universal approach, it couples to an RS232 port. Altek's devices function with printed barcodes whilst Datastripe appear to have models that can cope with both printed and magnetic media.

The unit that couples in line with the keyboard has incorporated a microprocessor and control logic. It will read, decode and verify the barcode and then pass this information to the computer. The computer in fact sees it as a keyboard input and can therefore easily interface with any software packages.

With the serial interface, similar electronics is incorporated in the interface box and the data is sent as ASCII characters to the serial port. A communications program is all that is needed to input this information but a specialised program may be available. It is possible to configure the RS232 link at the barcode end in order to suit various uses of the RS232 link (see Chapter 10).

The barcode readers can be supplied with the appropriate software packages plus (in one case) packages that will print out barcodes on popular centronic printers such as those from Epson. Barcode formats supported are EAN13, EAN8, UPC A, CODE 39 and Interleave 2 from 5 formats.

It is also possible to buy separate encoders for magnetically encoding cards. These units may interface by an RS232 port or via the keyboard connector with expansion card for power and interfacing.

Information Displays

These are moving message displays which can be driven from a PC and the only supplier found appears to be Control & Display Technology Ltd. A sketch of a typical display is shown in Figure 7.7 and the method of connection to the computer is via an RS232 serial link (possibly also a parallel output, RS422 and an RS485 for long line drives communicating with up to 16 stations). The units themselves are powered directly from the mains and the characters sent to them are in ASCII. Messages can be generated from within a word processor package as well as controlling characters for the movement of the display. The displays are from 0.6m to 1.5m long and use light emitting diodes, in red, green or amber.

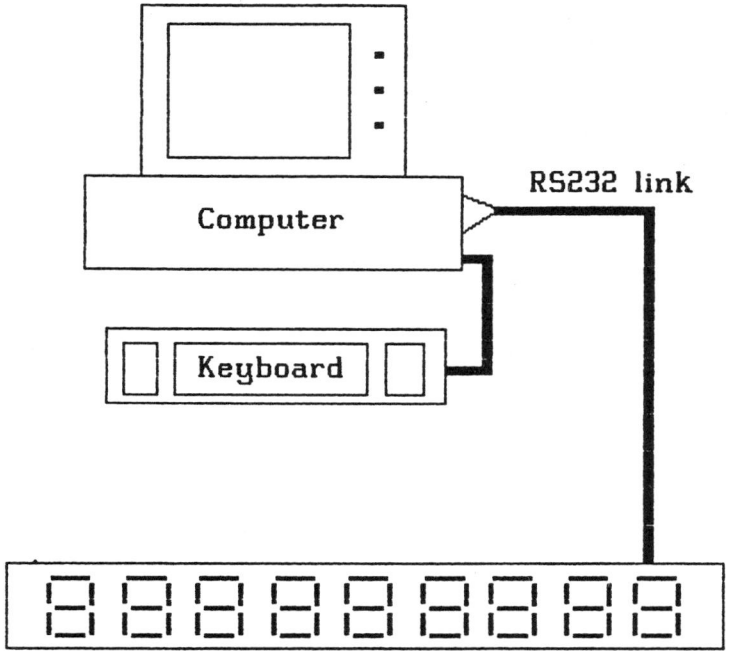

Figure 7.7 Typical Arrangement for Moving Information Display

Typical uses for these are floor/window displays, financial information, exhibition information points, transport terminals and display of technical information after processing by the computer, e.g. data logging.

Suppliers

Aditi Electronics - prototype card
Amplicon - various cards and prototype card, EPROM/PAL programmer
Altek Instruments Ltd - barcode equipment
Atomstyle - various expansion cards including real time clock

Bentley Computers - slotless RTC
Blue Chip Technology - prototype card
Citadel Products Ltd - expansion cards with real time clock
Continental Ltd - expansion cards with real,time clocks
Control & Display - information displays
Datastripe Ltd - barcode/magnetically encoded equipment
GP Industrial Electronics - EPROM programmers
Lloyd Research - EPROM programmers
Microprocessor Engineering - EPROM, PAL and EPLD programmers
MQP Electronics - EPROM programmers
Mutek - EPROM and PAL programmers
N.L. Ford and Associates - EPROM programmers
Pinna Electronics - DIL socket RTC
RS Components - prototype boards
Stag Electronic Design - EPROM programmers
Technomatic - various expansion cards including real time clock
Verospeed - prototype cards

8

IMAGE CAPTURE

Introduction

With the explosion in software packages for desk top publishing (DTP) and similar high quality output there is a growing demand for the inclusion of diagrams and pictures within the text. It is also desirable to be able to transmit images and text over a distance via services such as facsimile (see Chapter 12) as well as analysing images for medical diagnosis, component sizing and quality inspection. The main emphasis of this chapter is towards the publishing aspect.

Diagrams can be produced by some of the graphics packages such as GEM Paint, Autosketch, Autocad, TurboCad, DanCad, Generic Cad and PC Draw. More difficult is the inclusion of original pictures and diagrams within the text. As far as the DTP package and printer is concerned, this presents no problems. It is obtaining the image in the first place and getting it into a digital form suitable for storage on disk that is more difficult. The image may also be required for other purposes such as interactive learning, information services, sales demonstrations, and image comparison as well as for transmission by facsimile which is covered in Chapter 12.

The quality of the image on the paper is very much a function of the printer being used (e.g. dot-matrix or laser printer) and the quality of the screen image is dependent on the screen driver being used (e.g. Hercules, CGA, EGA, VGA). Having stated this, the method of obtaining the image is also very important as is the quality of the original document or image. In general the higher the definition required the higher is the equipment cost.

Figure 8.1 shows a typical block diagram of any of the image capture schemes. The analogue image is sampled by the optical device and digitiser which produces digital data corresponding to position on the image and the shade of grey seen (i.e. grey level). This is then in a form that is acceptable to a disk file, the software allowing manipulation of the image and its final storage. The number of samples per unit and levels will determine the definition and the various colour or grey levels. This in turn dictates the amount of storage required.

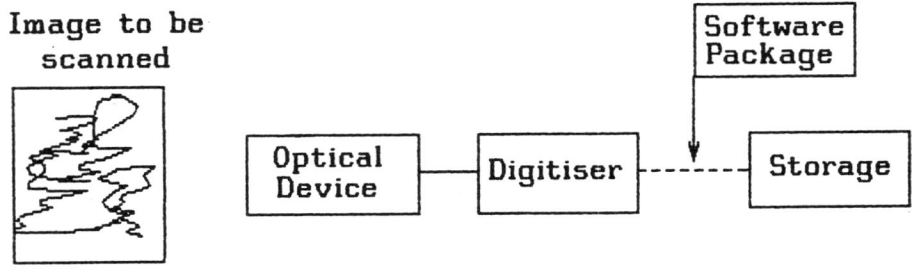

Figure 8.1 Typical Image Capture Arrangement

Graphic images can be stored in various formats depending on the source of the image. With a graphics package this is under the control of the software allowing the image to be created, but with the digitiser or scanner, because of how it operates, it can only provide information in one form. For the sake of completeness some of the common formats used for image storage are:-

Type and Package	Form
.PCX Format .. PC Paintbrush	Image
.GEM Format .. eg GEM Draw, GEM Graph	Line Art
.IMG Format .. GEM Paint	Image
.PIC Format .. Fontasy, GWBASIC, BASICA	Image
.SLD Format .. AutoCAD	Line Art
.DXF Drawing interchange format	
.TIF Format .. Aldus/Microsoft	Image
.EPS Format .. Postscript only	Line Art
Any scanner	Image

Line Art is stored as objects and vectors (mathematical expressions) whilst Image is stored as simple bits, 1's and 0's, relating to a screen dump in some form. Because image capture merely scans a line and samples it, it does not predict the picture, but can only store information as an Image. A useful little booklet on the various formats is obtainable free of charge from Electronic Studio Products provided an SAE is sent.

The equipment for image capture comes in three basic forms:-

1) That capable of accepting video signals (analogue and digital) such as produced by video cameras, video recorders and computers.

2) Fixed desk top scanners where the document is fed in and scanned automatically.

3) Hand held, where the scanner is moved across the document manually.

The last two types use similar principles and electronics and are dealt with together.

Video Type Image Capture

A typical arrangement for this source of image is shown on Figure 8.2. It is assumed that the image is obtained from a source that provides either a composite video signal or a digital signal such as RGB at TTL levels. This signal must contain information about the brightness as well as when to begin a new frame (frame or vertical synchronisation) and when to start a new line (line or horizontal synchronisation) - this is explained more fully in Chapter 5. In the UK and many European countries the TV system is known as PAL and gives 625 lines in 1/25 of a second and means that one line takes 64 us to scan irrespective of interlace type; this is likely to be the standard used by many video cameras. Other standards exist such as NTSC (TV in the USA) and industrial standards: the image capture system would therefore be ideal if it could cope with various standards.

In producing a digitised image the incoming video signal must be sampled so that each sample will relate to a pixel or group of pixels on the screen. Two standards appear to have emerged, splitting the line into 256 units and vertically into 256 units or for higher resolution 512x512. To sample at 256 units per line a sampling rate of at least 4 MHz must be used whilst the higher definition needs a rate of at least 8 MHz and this assumes a line duration of 64 us - this is a very fast sampling rate. It is the sampling rate that really divides this type of image capture into two areas, these are:-

1) The more expensive route - this allows an image to be captured in the time for one frame, e.g. 1/25 second. The advantage of this is that only a single frame is used and hence no movement is seen. This method is known as Real Time Capture.

2) The less expensive route - this is to digitise an image over a period of a few seconds. Here, the image must remain static as it takes many frames to build up the image slowly but allows dramatically less sampling rates.

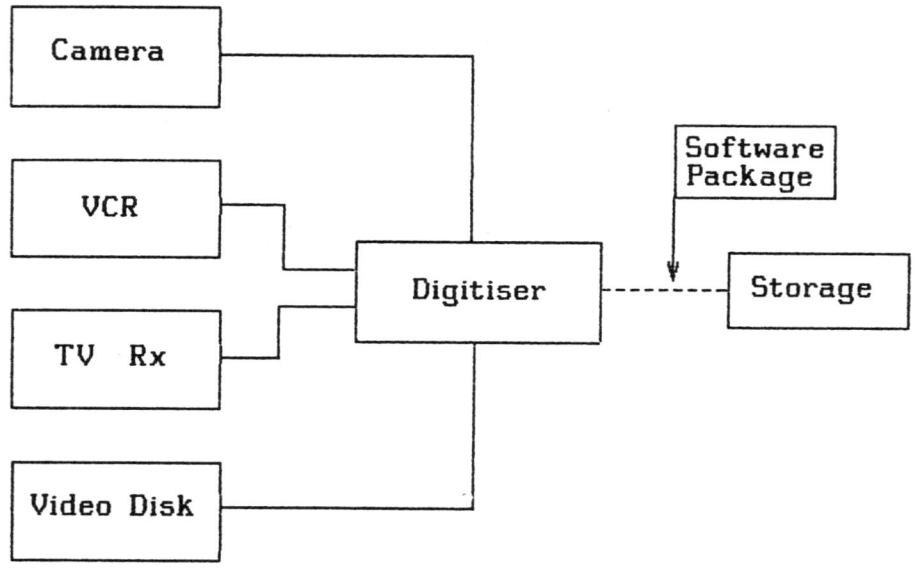

Figure 8.2 Video Image Capture using a Video Source

No. of Pixels	Grey Levels	Bits Needed	Memory for 1 image
256	2	1	8 kBytes
512	2	1	32 kBytes
256	255	8	64 kBytes
512	255	8	256 kBytes

Figure 8.3 Memory Replacement for Various Resolutions

When sampling the image each point is related to a pixel which can then be set to a level corresponding to the shade. For simple black or white only, then only one bit is required, e.g. 1 equates to white and 0 to black. In real life, however, we are used to shades and the eye can differentiate between about 64 grey levels. This relates to 6 bits as $2^6 = 64$. This is not too convenient as a computer usually works in multiples of 8 bits (i.e. bytes). Figure 8.3 gives the memory requirements for various combinations.

Expansion Cards

It is not possible to cover all conceivable combinations of equipment available for this form of video capture, and some units might even be in external housings. Figure 8.4 shows a block diagram of an expansion card suitable for the PC for video digitising, please remember that not all of the blocks may be available on every card.

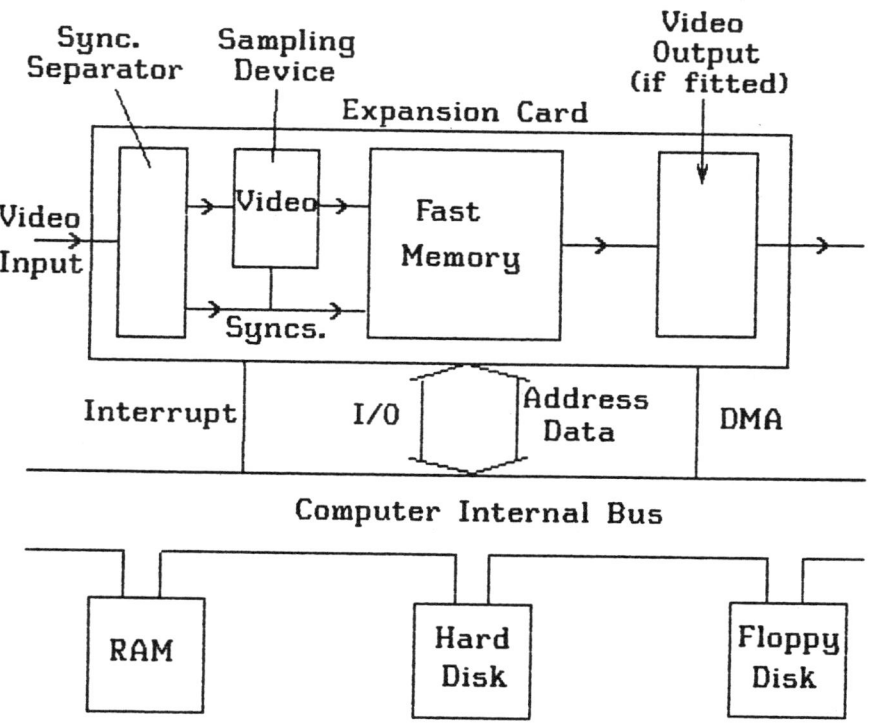

Figure 8.4 Possible Arrangement of Video Digitiser

The input video signal is sampled, and if analogue is then digitised; this data is then fed to fast RAM for interim storage. This RAM does NOT sit in the main memory map of the computer. Some expansion units now process this signal again so that an additional monitor can be use to examine the "captured" image. The monitor of the attached computer is used for running the software which will determine the outcome of the video image. To speed up image transfer to the storage devices many of the units use direct memory access (DMA) and so a free channel may be required - see Chapter 2 for the allocations. Input/output addresses are also necessary for setting the digitising card up and this may need to be set so as to avoid I/O conflicts. It is hoped that the supplier will have further details on this. The manual for "Computer Eyes" from Stem Computing is certainly very explicit about the board settings. Apart from these settings the fitting of the card is as for any expansion card, the unit backplate having the sockets for video input.

Software Available

In order to capture and manipulate images controlling software is required to run on the host PC. This is usually tailored to the system in use and may come bundled with the hardware - check with the chosen supplier. This can allow various operations on the captured image depending on complexity of the package. This can involve:-

    part of image selection and magnification
    enhance certain grey levels with colour,
    rotate, invert and reflect image
    store under different formats
    print image
    negative of image
    enhance contrast
    compare images

With running the software and capturing images there is a certain amount of RAM necessary and of the systems examined 384 kBytes would appear to be a minimum requirement.

Scanners

The units that come under this heading are very reminiscent of equipment built for facsimile transmission. They rely on a document being scanned by a light beam and the reflected signal being passed to a line of light sensors - this is shown diagrammatically in Figure 8.5. There are usually the equivalent of about 300 sensors per inch across the page and for an A4 page width this is about 2500. The light beam is gradually moved across the page so that the reflection is passed onto the sensors and about 300 samples are also taken per inch (cf. scanners as quoted 300 dots per inch). In addition to this horizontal movement there must also be relative longitudinal movement between the document and light beam/sensors. This is accomplished by either moving the document or moving the beam/sensors. A similar number of samples is also made longitudinally.

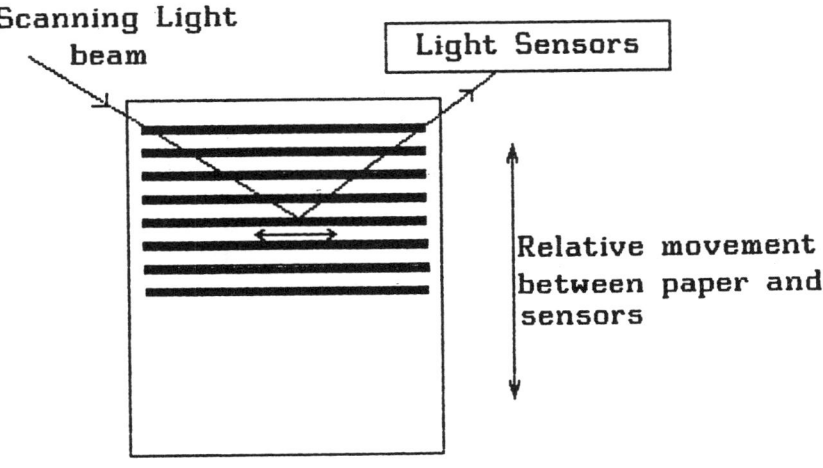

Figure 8.5 General Principals of Image Scanners

The quality of the final image depends on two factors:-

- the ability of the scanner to differentiate between grey tones and
- the resolution or number of samples taken per unit distance.

Very basic scanners will only give about 4 levels of grey whilst the more expensive types about 256 levels (the eye can detect over 64 grey levels!). The resolution again depends on the sample rate and typical scanners go from about 200 dots per inch to in excess of 600 - it all depends on how much one wants to pay. Scanners come in four basic forms and are further discussed below.

Roller (or Sheet Feed) Type

In this form a single page document to be scanned is moved past the light beam/sensors by means of a motor-driven friction roller. This represents the most common form of scanner and is the most moderately priced for the quality. The problem with this machine is that it can only cope with a single page document (i.e. it cannot be a page in a book) and has a maximum size.

Printer Scanner

This is really a subset of the above type. In this form a scanner head is attached to a printer head and the single page document fed into a printer friction roller. The printer head then moves under control across the document as it is fed through via the friction roller. This form merely tries to use existing mechanics to perform the movement as most people will have a printer.

Flat Bed Type

In this form the light beam /sensors are moved past the document just as in a typical photocopier. This allows both single pages and parts of books to be scanned but the increase in mechanical complexity means a corresponding increase in cost. This machine is capable of very high quality and a large document could be scanned into separate sheets.

Hand Scanners

These are the cheapest of the solutions but they give the poorest quality. Both types of document can be scanned but only in strips about 6cm wide. It also needs some form of rule or registration to allow the scan to be straight. The hand scanner does contain sensing devices that will detect if the scanner is stopped and so does not go on scanning the same line over and over again and thus fill the screen.

Scanners can also be very hungry in terms of the memory required for storage. A black and white only image requires much less memory than one involving many grey scales and of course it is also dependent on the size of the scanned image. These factors should be borne in mind when choosing equipment and considering what the end product is to be.

Connection to the PC

All of the units need some form of interface board and the way in which the information is transferred may be the deciding factor in the speed of operation. It is easy for an advertisement to say this only takes x seconds to scan, but the true time is for it to scan, process and pass to the host computer.

The connection from the scanner will generally be a high speed digital interface because of the amount of data that may need to be handled. This may be in a parallel or serial form using synchronous or asynchronous format (with some Canon equipment this is typically at 1 Mbps in burst form). There seems to be some variation in the facilities offered by the interface boards but they must all basically pass the digital data from the scanner to the hard disk unit. Some of the interface boards have a memory cache on them whilst others claim to function with extended memory (as described in Chapter 3).

Figure 8.6 shows the typical arrangements for connection of a scanner. The expansion card may well have DIP switches and/or links and these will determine:-

the I/O address used for setting the card parameters
if DMA is required and if so the channel number
if interrupts are required and if so the number.

Many of the expansion boards for the scanners use the Small Computer Systems Interface (SCSI) - briefly mentioned in Chapter 6).

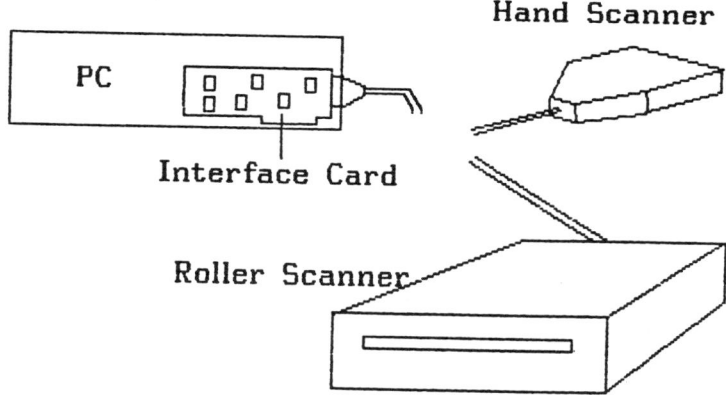

Figure 8.6 Connection of Scanners to the PC

Software

The scanners all have associated software that enables the scanner input to be put to hard disk. This may also enable the image to be stored in different forms, e.g. .TIF and .IMG formats, as well as performing various functions on the image. Typical of these programs is Gem Scan from Digital Research and Dest which is supplied with equipment from Formscan.

Optical Character Recognition (OCR)

This is mentioned here as it a form of image scanning and may use the same or similar equipment as mentioned in the previous section. In this arrangement a text image is scanned and the resulting bit image is processed in software in order to translate the image into text characters (i.e. alphabetic characters, numbers and punctuation marks). This has several applications: it allows text to be re-formatted so that it can be accepted by word-processing packages and also stored in a text form which is much more economical on storage space.

In OCR the character recognition software is at the heart of the translation process in trying to interpret characters. However, it does have shortcomings and depends on the software used. Typical limitations which exist at present may be that only a range of type fonts are recognised, it has difficulty with proportional spacing of letters, kerning, poorly formed or poorly printed characters. Some packages will only recognise a given size of printing and page alignment and if pages are askew this will hinder the process.

The software supplied, as mentioned, is the real heart of the process and it should also be able to automatically adapt to paper with varying contrasts and colour background, pitch, line spacing and skew.

Suppliers

APL Data Communications - image scanners and expansion board
Beyond Words - scanners, optical character recognition
Citadel Products Ltd - image scanners
Computers by Post - scanners and expansion board
Data Translation - image capture boards
Digitask - scanners and expansion board
Digithurst Ltd - video digitisers
Electronic Studio Products - video digitisers
Eltime Vision Systems - video digitisers
Formscan Ltd - image scanners and expansion board
Headway Computer Products - image scanners and expansion boards
Loughborough Sound Images - video digitisers and software
Stem Computing - video digitisers
Veren Computer Systems - image scanners
Westcoast - image scanners

DATA TRANSFER AND STANDARDS

Introduction

This chapter introduces the concepts of data transfer that are developed and examined in the following chapters. The transfer of data over either long or short distances is a growing area and is likely to affect our lives significantly in the future. The data may be text or pictures or a mixture, whatever it is, equipment is available and prices are dropping all the time. It is possible for the humble PC to be a part of this vast network.

Maybe the information is for far off places, maybe only to the next room or even the printer sitting on the table next to you. Maybe it is only for a single recipient or maybe it is for the world at large. Whatever the distance, various concepts and rules are applied, certain standards are adopted so that the information is easily decoded. Some of these concepts are now examined, those that are familiar with them may just like to skip through this chapter so that they know what has been discussed. For further reading on related topics refer to the bibliography.

Serial and Parallel

To start with, two basic concepts are examined - serial and parallel - which form the basis of all the transmission systems. The following discussion considers the transfer of a character which is represented by 7 binary digits (bits) but it could equally well be any number of bits, e.g. a standard teleprinter uses 5 data bits. The coding for each character will also be assumed to be ASCII (American Standard Code for Information Interchange) as this is the most common - a list of ASCII codes is given in Appendix A.

Figure 9.1 shows two units A and B that wish to communicate with each other; assume that A wishes initially to send a letter K (ASCII code 1001011). This can be done by sending one digit after another (serially) on a single pair of wires as in Figure 9.2 or it could be done by sending the seven bits on seven wires simultaneously - this is depicted in Figure 9.3.

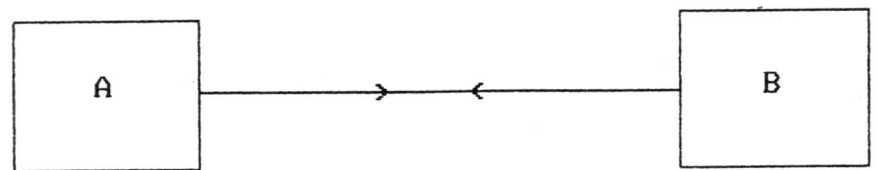

Figure 9.1 Communication Between Two Units

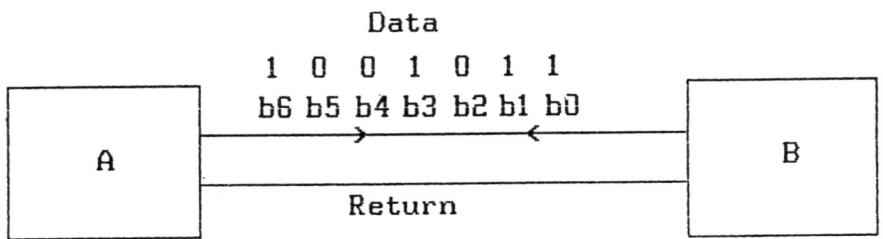

Figure 9.2 Serial Transmission of Data

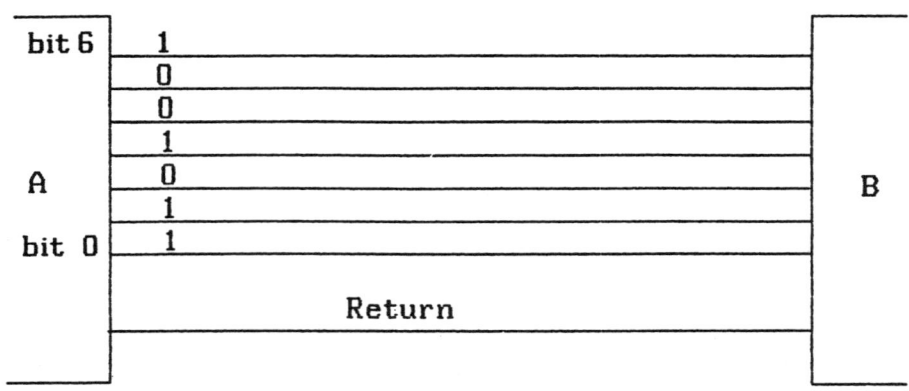

Figure 9.3 Typical Parallel Communications Arrangement

In any electrical system there must be a return path and hence the return wire marked on the diagrams. In the serial case B must know if bit 6 (b6) or bit 0 (b0) is to arrive first - assuming b6 is first then the beginnings of a standard have already started. In the case of parallel transmission a standard must make sure that the wiring is correct, i.e. bit 6 at A is transferred to bit 6 at B and so forth - again the beginnings of a standard. In both cases transmission can only occur in one direction at a time. As can be deduced, because parallel transmission passes all bits in parallel, then this is likely to be a faster form of data transmission than the serial arrangement, but 7 wires plus a return are needed. This obviously would not be practical if 7 telephone lines or 7 radio channels were required simultaneously and so, in these cases, a serial arrangement with possibly a slower rate at which data is passed may be more practical. These are some of the questions that must be considered in deciding whether a parallel or serial data transmission will be used. It is now easier to consider each of the types of transmission in turn.

Serial Data Transmission

The standards here cover bit rates, electrical characteristics and data formats and these are all discussed as the story unfolds. To start with unit B has no knowledge of when A will send the data. This can be overcome in two ways:-

- by sending a start message, or
- by passing a clock pulse for each data bit sent on a separate wire.

These methods are referred to as asynchronous or synchronous communications respectively.

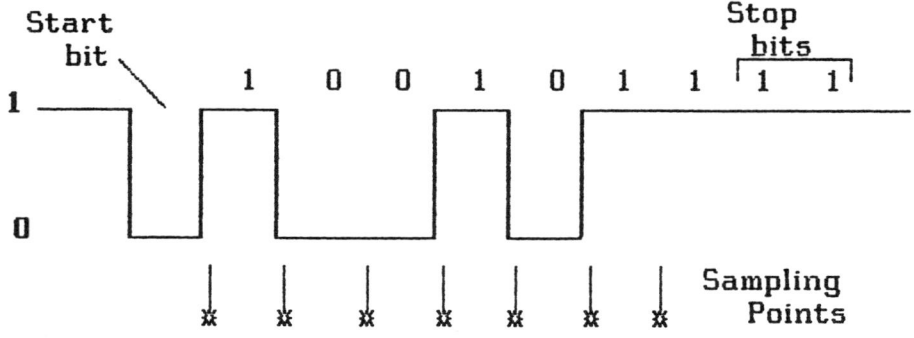

Figure 9.4 Asynchronous Serial Data Stream

The first method sends a start signal at the beginning of the data and possibly a stop signal at the end. For this method no extra wire is needed, but more information is sent on the same pair of wires; this is referred to as asynchronous communication. These start and stop bits are normally added to the data and a typical signal is shown in Figure 9.4, The receive station must also know approximately at what speed the data will come. The line will normally sit at a logic 1 and the start bit is recognised as a 1 to 0 transition. On recognising this the receive station decides when to sample the incoming data in order to retrieve the information sent. The receiving equipment must know how many start, data and stop bits to expect, so that when it has received so many characters it can strip off the start and stop bits and be left with just the data.

The only problem now is if interference has caused an error in the bit pattern. One simple way to try and detect this is to include a parity bit. A parity bit is a binary digit included between the end of data and before the stop bit, typically making the data up to 8 bits. The terms odd and even parity are used and this depends on the standard used and how the value of the parity bit (1 or 0) is determined. In even parity, the number of bits at "1" are counted in the data; if they are an even number the parity is set at 0, if odd, it is set at 1. In odd parity the reverse is used.

The group of digits to be sent can be assembled using software, stored in a memory location and then sent out a bit at a time at a predetermined speed. More often this is accomplished in hardware and there are integrated circuits available that can be pre-programmed with the number of start/stop bits, number of data bits and type of parity. The format of the data may be hard-wired, or in a more flexible approach, the IC contains registers that are preset using software. The data is then passed to the IC, it assembles all the start/stop and parity bits around the data and transmits it according to the data rate set. The setting up of registers by software for start/stop, parity and number of data bits gives a very flexible approach as obviously the format of the data sent is easily changed and a single IC can cope with a variety of formats.

In synchronous serial communications a clock signal is sent which is dependent on the data rate. In Figure 9.5 this is shown set at half the data rate and represents only one way of carrying out the operation (in this case a transition occurs at each data bit). In the idle state both data and clock lines sit at logic 1. When the receiver sees a transition from 1 to 0 it prepares to sample the incoming data on each of the following clock transitions, i.e. 1 to 0 and 0 to 1. At X (Figure 9.5) a parity bit could be added if required. In synchronous serial communication there is no overhead of start and stop bits and only 7 bits are required instead of the 10 bits in the asynchronous case where start/stop bits are used.

As in most arrangements there are variations on a theme but these examples serve to show the differences between the two serial cases. Asynchronous communications are commonly used up to about 9600 bps (bits per second) with synchronous communications starting from about 2400 bps, there is thus quite an overlap area. Synchronous serial communication is the more reliable serial form for high speed data transfer.

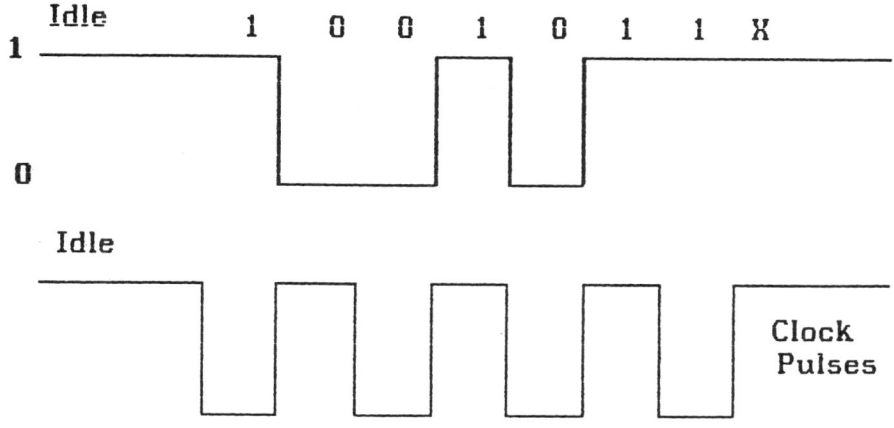

Figure 9.5 Synchronous Data Stream

There are various common data rates used with the PC for asynchronous communication and those supported by MS-DOS are given below:

110,150,300,600,1200,2400,4800,9600 and 19200 (MS-DOS 3.3) Baud.

The unit, the Baud, has been introduced here. This is the number of bits sent per second (i.e. the total including start/stop and parity) and not the number of characters. When modulation methods become more complex it is better to use bits per second. Although the above data rates are mentioned it is possible to obtain others by addressing the RS232 I/O board directly.

The basic clock frequency is derived from a crystal oscillator and the typical ICs used in the PC design for serial communications (eg 8250) can be programmed by software for the various data rates.

Having discussed the format for the data to be sent, the next step is how the data is physically sent, i.e. voltages and currents. Two standards exist here, the 20 mA current loop stemming from the early teleprinters using electromagnets and RS232 (or its derivatives RS422, RS423, etc.) using voltage levels. It is easy to convert from one standard to the other using simple electronic interface circuits.

20mA Current Loop

This is an old standard deriving from post office telegraphy methods using teleprinters and it relied on sending a 20 mA current to energise a small electromagnet. It is normally used for fairly slow data rates but can be used up to about 9600 bps on short circuits. It is usually less susceptible to noise than voltage signals on longer routes. One standard is:- if 20 mA flows in a circuit then a logic 1 is assumed, if less than 4 mA then a logic 0 assumed. The hardware is low-cost at the interface between the computer/terminal and line.

This standard is not very common and is more likely to be found in industrial applications rather than office applications.

RS232C (V24) Standards

These standards not only define voltage levels to be used but also additional control lines, line lengths and pin numbers on plugs and sockets. It was a standard set up by the Electrical Industries Association (EIA) in the USA and has become an almost universal standard for serial data communications throughout the world. It has its international counterpart, defined by CCITT Recommendation V24 (signal definitions) and V28 (electrical parameters). RS232C has a complex technical definition but essentially is for line lengths up to 50 feet (15 m) at a maximum data rate of 20 kbps. Figure 9.6 shows the voltage levels encountered. Line lengths greater than 15 metres can be used providing the line capacitance is kept to a minimum and certainly less than 2500pF.

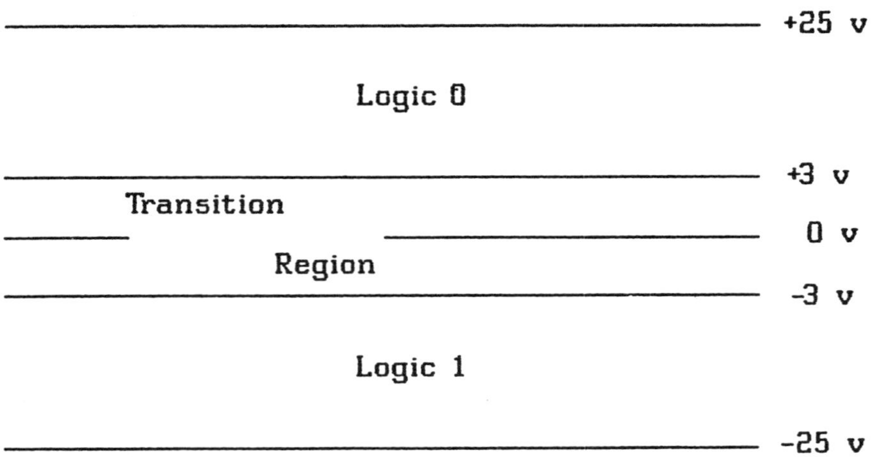

```
                                                    ────────  +25 v


              Logic 0


                                                    ────────  +3 v
        Transition
   ─────────              ────────────────────────  0 v
              Region
   ─────────────────────────────────────────────   -3 v


              Logic 1


   ─────────────────────────────────────────────   -25 v
```

Figure 9.6 Voltage Levels in RS232C Communications

The RS232C standard defines additional control lines (handshakes) as well as defining the equipment at either end. It is in these areas that many of the confusions arise so it is worth spending a little time trying to understand the fundamentals. The full specification defines a 25 pin connector (typically a D type) and all of the lines. In most computer applications only certain lines are used and only these will be discussed further. The equipment at either end is named. At the master or controlling end it is a Data Terminal Equipment (DTE) and at the remote end a Data Communication Equipment (DCE). The problem arises when, for example, the equipment at both ends is a computer and then the question is who controls whom as each may have to run a communications package. When writing a table of the various pin functions it may be easier to think of inputs and outputs. It is hoped that the documentation accompanying any serial communications device to be attached to the computer will be explicit as to connection details.

As already mentioned the RS232 definition includes specification of items such as plugs and sockets. The definition is illustrated in Figure 9.7 and shows where the plugs and sockets are located. The plug/socket is normally defined for the 25 way D type connector, but in certain circumstances due to space limitations, other D connectors such as 15 and 9 way devices are used. Not all manufacturers adhere to the strict definition and this is the beginning of where problems arise. It is possible to make and/or buy gender changers for the plugs and sockets and many firms supply these - it is a matter of looking in various catalogues or visiting the nearest suitable shop. The component suppliers tend to be cheapest for buying plugs, sockets, wire and ready made up cables. In all the advertisements and manuals examined for plug-in serial boards, the DTE standard is adhered to.

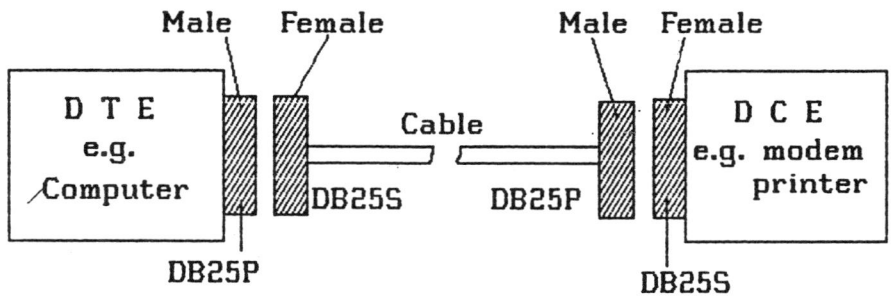

Figure 9.7 RS232C Plug and Socket Definitions

Figure 9.8 gives the definition of the commonly used pins in RS232C (V24) and the following is a discussion of the various abbreviations used for each of the pins and the meaning it has for the appropriate set of equipment. Please note that when equipment uses RS232 links it may not use all of the pins. It is fairly common for pins 1 and 7 to be tied together. Pin connections are for 25 way plug and socket. Both 15 and 9 way D type connectors are used (see Chapter 10). Consult the appropriate manual for the pin connections, they may not follow any standard pattern!

CCITT	RS232C	Pin	Meaning	DTE		DCE
103	TxD	2	Transmit Data	0	$\longrightarrow$	I
104	RxD	3	Receive Data	I	$\longleftarrow$	0
105	RTS	4	Request to send	0	$\longrightarrow$	I
106	CTS	5	Clear to send	I	$\longleftarrow$	0
107	DSR	6	Data set ready	I	$\longleftarrow$	0
109	DCD	8	Data Carrier Det.	I	$\longleftarrow$	0
108/2	DTR	20	Data Term. Rdy	0	$\longrightarrow$	I
125	RI	22	Ring Indicator	I	$\longleftarrow$	0
101		1	Chassis Gnd		————	
102		7	Signal Gnd		————	

Figure 9.8 RS232C Pin Definitions

The commonly used pins are now described more fully.

Pin 1, Chassis Ground: Connects metal frame of DTE and DCE together electrically. Connected to screen of connecting lead.

Pin 2, Transmit Data (TxD): Transmit data line from DTE to DCE. DTE should be logic 1 or low between data transmissions. RS232C also requires RTS, CTS, DSR and DTR to go to logic 0 (high) before transmission is allowed. (NB DSR and DTR may not be used in simple communications).

Pin 3, Receive Data (RxD): Receive data, from DCE to DTE. This line held at logic 1 (low) when DCD is low. Also in a half-duplex system (see page 136) it must also be low when RTS is high, logic 0.

Pin 4, Request to Send: Signal generated by DTE to indicate it wants to transmit data. Normally in logic 1 (low) condition. When it goes high it expects DCE to respond with CTS going high and DTE will then transmit to DCE. If RTS returns low it should not become active again until DCE turns CTS low.

Pin 5, Clear to Send (CTS): Generated by DCE.

Pin 6, Data Set Ready (DSR): Generated by the DTE. It indicates that the DTE has performed any other tasks as necessary and it is now in an active condition - i.e. ready for communications.

Pin 7, Signal Ground: Common return and reference line for the signal paths. Usually at 0 v and sometimes connected to pin 1.

Pin 8, Data Carrier Detect (DCD): Generated by the DCE to indicate that it is receiving a signal from its own communication channel that appears valid.

Pin 20, Data Terminal Ready (DTR): This signal is generated by the DTE. When it goes high (logic 0) it indicates to the DTE that the communication link should be maintained. If it goes low then the DCE should abort the communication channel after the completion of the data transfer in progress.

Pin 22, Ring Indicator: Signal generated by the DCE when (if for example it is a modem) an incoming ringing tone is detected. It goes high on receipt of this signal, otherwise it remains low.

The control of passing information is executed by "handshaking", i.e. each unit informs the other when it is permissible to send and when not to. This handshaking can be accomplished by both hardware and software. Using the extra control lines in a full RS232 communication, this is a hardware solution, and the following is the sequence of events, assuming the DTE initiates the communication.

    1) send DTR
    2) expects to receive DCD and DSR
    3) send RTS
    4) expects CTS
    5) sends data
    6) Go to 3 until data transmission is ended.

Items 1 and 2 occur at the beginning of the communication, with RTS and CTS controlling the flow of information when the link has been established.

If the DCE initiates a communication then RI will occur first (if it is used) and then the sequence is:-

    1) DCD goes high
    2) CTS goes high
    3) Check RTS is high
    4) transmits data on RxD
    5) Go to 3 until data transmission is ended.

As mentioned earlier not all of the handshaking may be used; an absolute minimum system might use only ground, RxD and TxD. More common is Ground, RTS,CTS,RxD and TxD. In communications over telephone lines, hardware handshaking is not possible and a software method must be used - see Chapter 12.

The biggest problem with RS232 connections is whether equipment is DTE or DCE and if manufacturers have adhered to correct definitions. The pin connections always seem to be the biggest problem and to help overcome this some suppliers provide in-line units with links/switches. These allow the user to experiment with the various cross connections. Also, there are units made which have LED indicators that light up to show which line is active, again a useful tool in trying to sort out a link. Units are also available that have both of these facilities. Another useful arrangement is a pair of DB25 connectors back to back with the pins wired pin for pin except that pins 2 and 3 are transposed as are pins 4 and 5. This may help get two units working together that are wired as either DTEs or DCEs. See Chapter 10 for further discussions.

RS232 Drivers and Receivers

The most universal ICs for receiving and driving cable for RS232C are the ubiquitous 1488(75188) and 1489(75189). The 1488 line driver is typically powered with +/-12v in a computer and driven from TTL logic (+5v). The external line therefore has typically +/-12V swing. The 1489 line receiver is powered from a +/- 12v line but can accept input voltages of +/-30V maximum. It has typical TTL output voltages for interfacing to the computer circuitry. Figure 9.9 shows the pin connections for these devices.

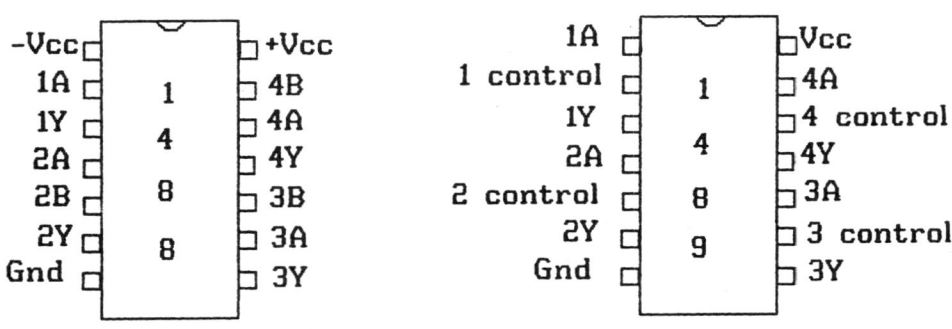

Figure 9.9 The Ubiquitous 1488/1489 RS232C Line ICs

RS232 <--> 20 mA Loop Conversions

It is a fairly easy matter to convert from one of these standards to the other and Figure 9.10 shows various circuits for achieving this.

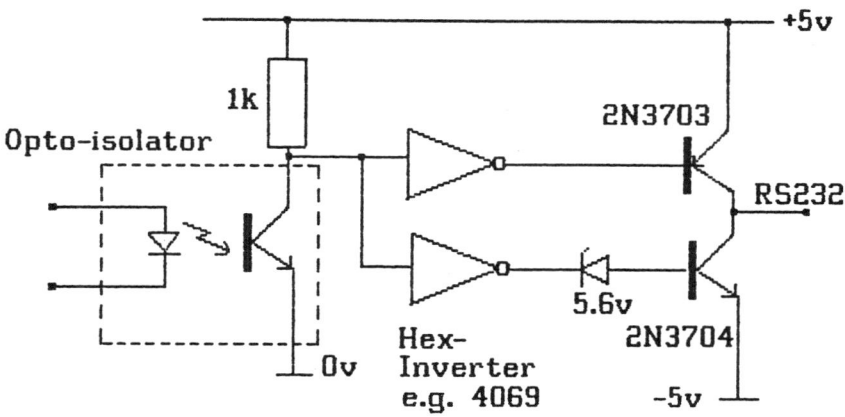

Figure 9.10 (a) Current Loop to RS232

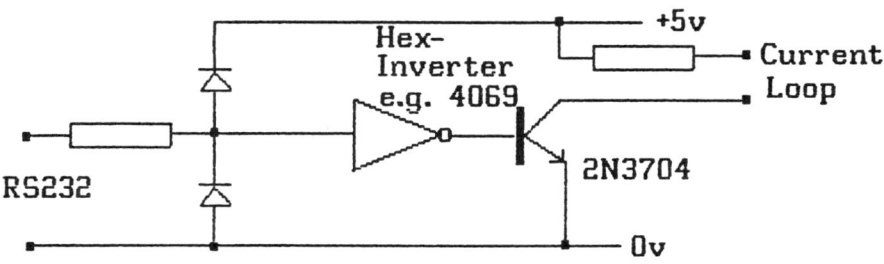

Figure 9.10 (b) RS232 to Current Loop

RS422 Standard

RS422A (CCITT V11 and X27) specifies differential balanced circuits, line length of 4000 ft (1219 m) at rates up to 100 kbps or 40 feet (12 m) up to 10 Mbps. The voltage levels here are: logic 0 between +2 and +6 volts, logic 1 between -2 and -6 volts. The connector is specified as a 37 way D type. Due to the circuits being balanced, this standard is NOT inter-operable with RS232C.

RS423 Standard

RS423A (CCITT V10 and X26) defines parameters using unbalanced bipolar circuits, line lengths of 4000 ft (1219 m) at 3 kbps or 40 ft (12 m) at 300 kbps. A logic 0 is defined between +4 and +6 volts, whilst a logic 1 is between -4 and -6 volts. Generally RS232C will accept signals from this standard although in the strict definition this standard requires a 37 way D type connector. This is the standard the BBC Computer uses. It is generally a better specification for long serial lines than RS232C.

RS449 Standard

This is another standard and specifies a maximum data rate of 2Mbps on a line length of 667 ft (213 m). The original 25 way D connector is replaced by a 37 and a 9 way D connector. The first connector specifies a Category 1 or main circuit and the 9 way a Category 2 or secondary circuit.

Parallel Data Transmissions

In parallel communications no one standard has emerged as with the serial case and there are several standards, each developed for its own particular sphere of use, e.g. Centronics for printer connections, IEEE488 for control of equipment and VME for control between boards in a multiprocessor environment. The connections to the expansion socket in the PC is a parallel communication.

Figure 9.3 shows the absolute basics of parallel communication but units A and B have no idea which way the data is flowing. Assuming A and B can both send data to each other, then certain additional control lines are needed. A must send a signal to B saying "are you ready to receive" and B must reply with a signal saying "send now". If B was to send to A then there must be a set of lines for control in that direction. For true two way communication then a minimum of 4 more wires is needed as shown in Figure 9.11. If only a one way communication is required, e.g. A to B, then two of the control lines can be dispensed with. This situation might be akin to B being a printer and A being the computer. The computer would then simply ask the printer if it is ready and the printer would request data to be sent, it would then use this data and the sequence would be repeated. In reality there are more control lines - see the following section on the Centronics Parallel Connection.

Building on this, it may be necessary for A to have several devices attached. Now A must be able to address which device it needs. This could be approached in two ways. Additional wires could be added that carry the address information - this of course must be sent before data appears and so correct sequencing of ready and send lines must occur. Alternatively, the data lines could be used to carry address information with the addition of another control line that denotes if the lines D0-D7 are carrying addresses or data - this comes under the heading of multiplexing. In the case of parallel data transfer the signals are represented on the lines as voltages, e.g. 0v denotes a logic 0 and a positive voltage a logic 1. The convention $\overline{RDY}$ may be encountered, this denotes that this signal is active when low, just RDY would denote active when high.

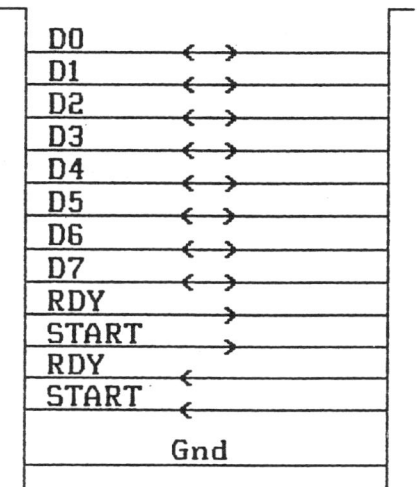

Figure 9.11 Typical Parallel Communications

Centronics Parallel Interface

This is essentially a parallel specification for communication with printers. There is no reason, however, why it should not be used for other communications provided the sequence of signals on the pins are followed. On the back of the PC it is typically a 25 way D type socket whilst on the printer it is an IEEE488/Centronics connector (50 way connector on Epson printers). In some applications it may be a Centronics Connector at both ends. Figure 9.12 gives the pin connections and signal codes.

The following is a description of the signals:-

> **STROBE:** Active when Low. Indicates to attached device that data on data lines is valid.
>
> **D0-D7:** Eight data lines, high for logic 1.
>
> **ACKNLG:** When low indicates printer has received data and ready for next.

BUSY: When High indicates printer not ready to receive data, when Low indicates ready to receive data.

PE: Signal line from printer, when High indicates printer is out of paper.

SLCT: When high indicates printer is in selected state. May be wired permanently high in the printer.

AUTO FEED XT: When Low indicates to printer to feed one line after printing a line. Can be fixed permanently Low by DIP switch in printer.

ERROR: Active Low. Indicates error condition has occurred, e.g. out of paper, gone off line.

INIT: When Low resets printer to initial state and clears printer buffer. Normally sits High.

SLCT IN: Data entry to printer only possible when Low. May be set permanently Low by DIP switch in printer.

Code	Definition	Computer	Pin		Printer	Pin
STROBE	Data lines Valid	Output	1	-->	Input	1
D0	Data, bit 0	Output	2	-->	Input	2
D1	Data, bit 1	Output	3	-->	Input	3
D2	Data, bit 2	Output	4	-->	Input	4
D3	Data, bit 3	Output	5	-->	Input	5
D4	Data, bit 4	Output	6	-->	Input	6
D5	Data, bit 5	Output	7	-->	Input	7
D6	Data, bit 6	Output	8	-->	Input	8
D7	Data, bit 7	Output	9	-->	Input	9
ACK	Data accepted	Input	10	<--	Output	10
BUSY	Printer busy	Input	11	<--	Output	11
PE	Paper out	Input	12	<--	Output	12
SLCT	Printer selc'td	Input	13	<--	Output	13
AUTOFD	Feed one line	Output	14	-->	Input	14
ERROR	Printer error	Input	15	<--	Output	32
INIT	Init. Printer	Output	16	-->	Input	31
SLCT IN		Output	17	-->	Input	36
GND			18-25	----		16,19-30,33

Figure 9.12 Typical Centronics Connections on PC

132

A basic communication can manage with just $\overline{\text{STROBE}}$, D0-D7, $\overline{\text{ACK}}$ and/or BUSY. However, it is logical to include such items as out of paper, printer error and off-line should be detected so that the communication can cease. Signal levels are 0 to +5 V, i.e. TTL levels. Common output ICs are the 74LS244, whilst input could be a 74LS240.

IEEE488 Parallel Bus

This is a parallel bus coping with distances up to 20 metres. It was conceived by Hewlett Packard and is sometimes referred to as HPIB (Hewlett Packard Interface Bus) or GPIB (General Purpose Interface Bus). It can control up to 15 devices and the data rate can be as high as 1 MBaud. It was designed for connecting systems together such as computers, voltmeters, power supplies, frequency generators and other instrumentaion. It is therefore relevant if the PC is to be used in such industrial applications as automatic testing. Much instrumentation that is manufactured today has the option of an IEEE488 parallel bus for this purpose. There are 24 bus lines and the connectors are the IEEE488, the same as for the Centronics parallel connection. Figure 9.13 gives the pin connections and the basic definitions.

The lines are defined and grouped in the following manner:-

8 data bus lines (DIO1-DIO8)

> **Data Lines (DIO1-8):** Data input/output lines. DIO8 is the MSB. For commands only 7 bits are used, whereas for data and address 8 bits are used.

3 data byte transfer control or handshake lines (DAV,NRFD,NDAC)

> **Data Valid (DAV):** Active High and indicates data on data bus is valid and used by any device on the bus.

> **Not Ready for Data (NRFD):** When Low it indicates that receiving devices are not ready.

> **Not Data Accepted (NDAC):** Will be pulled High if receiving devices have accepted data. If Low indicates that data has not been accepted.

5 general interface management lines (EOI,IFC,SRQ,ATN,REN)

> **End or Identity (EOI):** This has two functions. Can indicate the last byte of data when many bytes are being transferred but also in conjunction with ATN can cause a polling sequence to be initiated.

> **Interface Clear (IFC):** When High causes the system to reset to a known starting condition.

Service Request (SRQ): If this line goes high it indicates a device needs attention. It is like an interrupt.

Attention (ATN): If High denotes data on I/O lines is an address or command. When Low it indicates data. This line is cleared by the controlling device.

Remote Enable (REN): When Low all devices attached to the bus should be in local mode. When High it enables remote operation of any device on the bus.

There are several ground lines corresponding to different pins and these are also defined in Figure 9.13.

Code	Definition	Computer Pin	Instrument
DIO1	Data line 1	1	<------------->
DIO2	Data line 2	2	<------------->
DIO3	Data line 3	3	<------------->
DIO4	Data line 4	4	<------------->
EOI	End or Identity	5	<------------->
DAV	Data valid	6	<------------->
NRFD	Not ready for data	7	<------------
NDAC	Not data accepted	8	<------------
IFC	Interface clear	9	<------------
SRQ	Service request	10	<------------
ATN	Attention	11	<------------->
SHIELD	Shield	12	------------
DIO5	Data line 5	13	<------------->
DIO6	Data line 6	14	<------------->
DIO7	Data line 7	15	<------------->
DIO8	Data line 8 (MSB)	16	<------------->
REN	Remote Enable	17	------------
GND(6)	Gnd for pin 6	18	------------
GND(7)	Gnd for pin 7	19	------------
GND(8)	Gnd for pin 8	20	------------
GND(9)	Gnd for pin 9	21	------------
GND(10)	Gnd for pin 10	22	------------
GND(11)	Gnd for pin 11	23	------------
GND(logic)	Gnd for pins 5 & 17-24		------------

Figure 9.13 IEEE488 Connections

The RS232 and Centronics links have only connected two devices but the IEEE488 can cope with 15 devices. Some form of addressing is therefore required and it is the first approach made so far in this book towards a network. Since the system has no address or complete control bus, the data bus is used to perform all of these functions. The mode of operation can get quite complex and it is left for the enquiring reader to turn to Chapter 13 where a little more information is provided or refer to other texts if a much more detailed explanation is required (see Appendix 6). It is hoped that if an application is to be used it will be already set up for a user, otherwise one may get involved in the realms of electronic engineering. The signals are generally TTL compatible.

Frequency Encoding

Reverting again to serial transmission, the binary 1s and 0s may be converted to a tone frequency. There are various standards for this, e.g. Bell, CCITT, but here only the principles are considered.

Assuming A wishes to communicate with B as in Figure 9.2, then a logic 0 may be sent as a burst of frequency f0 and a logic 1 as frequency f1. The encoded signal for 1001011 would be as shown in Figure 9.14 (slightly exaggerated in scale). B could then reply in similar fashion when the lines are clear. This type of communication where only one station can transmit at a time is classified according to the capabilities of the equipment at either end and can either be simplex or half-duplex. The differences between these two may seem to be splitting hairs but it is an internationally accepted difference.

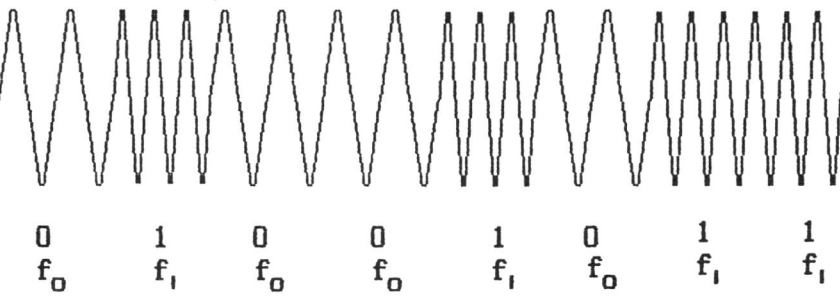

$$0 \quad 1 \quad 0 \quad 0 \quad 1 \quad 0 \quad 1 \quad 1$$
$$f_0 \quad f_1 \quad f_0 \quad f_0 \quad f_1 \quad f_0 \quad f_1 \quad f_1$$

Figure 9.14 Frequency Encoding

SIMPLEX .. Two-way data transmission possible, but only carried out one way at a time.

HALF-DUPLEX .. Two-way simultaneous data transmission possible but terminal equipment limits operation to one-way at a time.

A more elegant arrangement is to allow two way data transmission simultaneously by using two frequency pairs, i.e. f0 and f1 in direction A to B and frequencies f2 and f3 in direction B to A. This is known as DUPLEX or FULL-DUPLEX operation.

DUPLEX .. Data transmission in two directions simultaneously.

In the above example the encoding of binary 1s and 0s into a frequency tone is known as **MO**dulation and the reverse procedure of frequency to binary digits is termed **DEM**odulation. The piece of equipment capable of performing this is known as a MODEM and a block diagram of a basic modem is shown in Figure 9.15. Logic signals from a computer (for example) are received, encoded into frequencies and sent via a combiner to the communication channel. On the receive side the signals are received from the communication channel, decoded from frequencies back to logic signals and sent to the computer. A data rate generator is also required as this will determine how fast the data is sent and received on the communication link. There is a more detailed discussion of modems in Chapter 12.

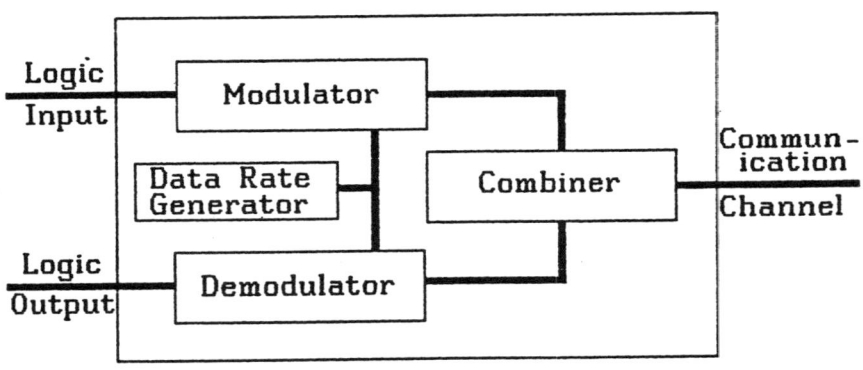

Figure 9.15 Block Diagram of Basic Modem

10

PC RS232 AND PARALLEL LINKS

Introduction

This chapter is concerned with basic data transfer/communications to or from the PC to a single unit using mainly an RS232 or parallel link but without the use of modems (see Chapter 12). The applications can be diverse in nature but they use similar principles in the data transfer. For other direct connections to the PC with analogue and digital signals please see chapter 13. It is assumed that the reader is familiar with or has read the information in the previous chapter. For further information please refer to the Bibliography - the book by Ian Cullimore is a useful text which gives many practical examples.

The items to be considered are:-

parallel communications	serial communications
PC to PC communications	PC to BBC computer
PC to PCW	printer buffers
line drivers	serial mouse
bus mouse	

It is hoped that these items will provide the reader with a firm footing so that other applications can be developed that are of immediate use. It is not possible to cover all the many applications and would be unwise to do so as some uses are very technically detailed and demanding. It is possible to write one's own controlling software but wherever possible a source of software has been mentioned. This book is also no substitute for reading and understanding the manuals accompanying any add-on cards being purchased and following the advice they offer. Unfortunately the English in some is poor and probably represents a mere literal translation from the original language! A good supplier should always be able to give a sound after-sales backup and be willing to answer technical queries. If they are not willing to do this then buy from someone who will! It may be slightly more expensive initially but it will be recouped in the long run.

Before delving into any one of the applications it is worthwhile taking a look at the relationship between the I/O channels and the computer bus and how information is transferred. This will hopefully provide a good basis for further investigations.

System Board to Input/Output

With all I/O the information is sent to and from the system board and this section examines this relationship and the I/O and memory maps concerned.

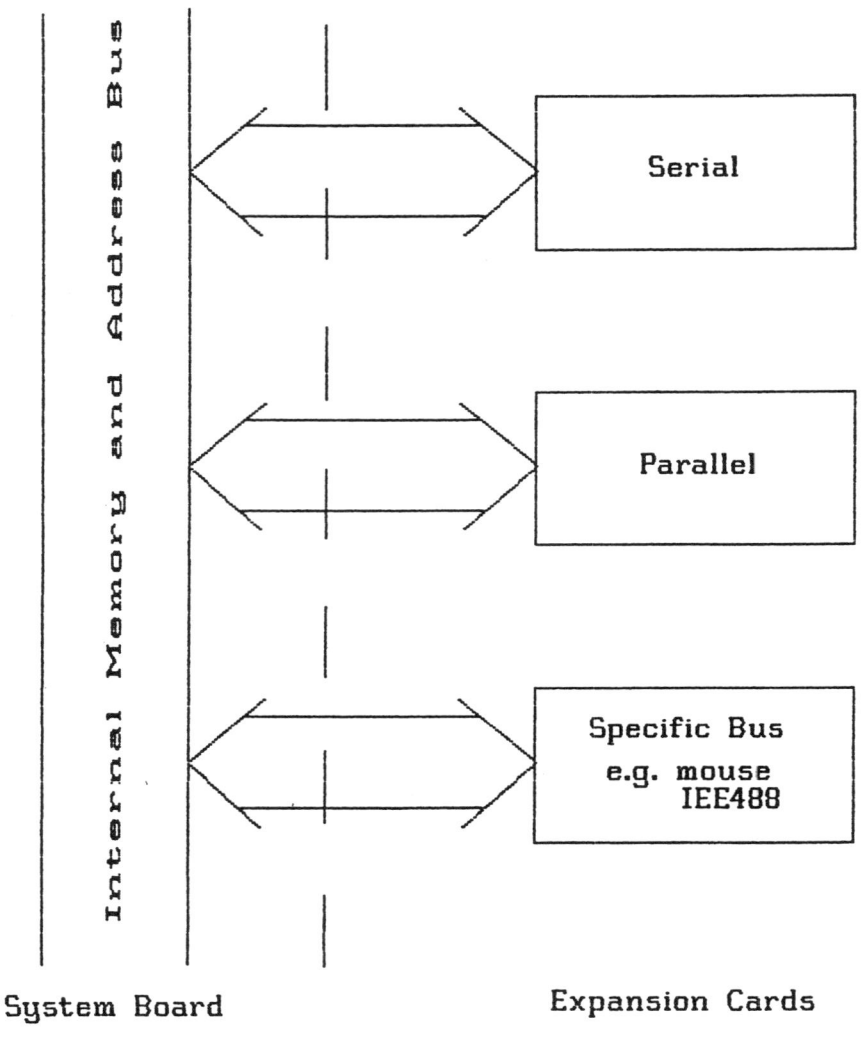

Figure 10.1 Expansion/System Board Interface

Outgoing information is processed by the computer, sent via the parallel internal buses and appears on the expansion sockets. Into these sockets are added the appropriate add-on card(s) in order to take the communication into the external or real world. The outputs to the real world are the standard RS232 serial link, centronics parallel link or more specific links such as for a bus mouse or the instrumentation bus IEEE488. Some of these have already been explained in the previous chapter and the IEEE488 link is dealt with more fully in Chapter 13. The add-on board will convert to the appropriate output format but how does a board know it is being asked to perform an I/O function ? Figure 10.1 shows diagrammatically the relationship between the the system bus and the expansion cards.

Serial I/O

This is probably the most common communication port used and it employs the ubiquitous RS232 or a close alternative. The MS-DOS/PC-DOS operating system up to and including version 3.2 only supports two ports, named COM1 and COM2, but several manufacturers of add- on boards provide more of these by using spare I/O ports, and addresses and software can be bought, written or modified to cater for these. MS-DOS 3.3 handles four COM ports and these can easily be accessed via the MODE command. The majority of users will not have version 3.3 and so the emphasis is on situations where only COM1 and COM2 are fully defined.

The I/O addresses for COM1 and COM2 are as defined in Table 10.1

COM1	COM2	Description
03F8H	02F8H	Tx/Rx buffer
03F8H	02F8H	Division latch LSB
03F9H	02F9H	Division latch MSB
03F9H	02F9H	Interrupt Enable Reg.
03FAH	02FAH	Interrupt ID Register
03FBH	02FBH	Line Control Register
03FCH	02FCH	Modem Control Reg.
03FDH	02FDH	Line status register
03FEH	02FEH	Modem status register

Table 10.1 I/O Addresses for COM1 and COM2

It will be noted that some of the I/O addresses have a dual purpose but this causes no problem, as for example one cannot transmit and receive at the same time! The division latch is set up at the beginning of a transmission and is the code for the data rate being used (110, 150, 300, 600, 1200, 2400, 4800 or 9600 baud). The Tx/Rx buffers have an obvious use and are bi-directional.

For those who are interested, the various registers mentioned above are split as follows.

Division Latch -

The values held in these two memory locations are dependent on the Baud rate required. The 8250 communication chip functions with a crystal oscillator of 1.843200 MHz. The number held in the divisor latch is determined from the formula:-

$$\text{Divisor number} = 18432000/(16 \times \text{Baud rate})$$

Interrupt Enable Register -

0	received data interrupt (enabled=1)
1	Tx hold reg. empty interrupt (enabled=1)
2	Rx line status interrupt (enabled=1)
3	modem status interrupt (enabled=1)
4-7	not used (=0)

Interrupt ID register -

Bit	Function
0	interrupt pending (=0)
1	interrupt ID bit 0
2	interrupt ID bit 1
3-7	not used (=0)

Modem Control Register -

Bit	Function
0	DTR (data terminal ready)
1	RTS (request to send)
2	out1
3	out2
4	loop
5-7	not used (=0)

Line status register -

Bit	Function
0	data ready
1	overrun error
2	parity error
3	framing error
4	break interrupt
5	Tx hold register empty
6	Tx empty
7	not used (=0)

Modem Status Register -

Bit	Function
0	Delta CTS (clear to send)
1	Delta DSR (data set ready)
2	trailing edge of RI (ring indicator)
3	Delta DCD (data carrier detect)
4	CTS
5	DSR
6	RI
7	DCD

The receive buffer is a register that holds the incoming character until read by the computer whilst the transmit holding register is a buffer that holds the outgoing character until read by the output device.

Figure 10.2 shows a typical block diagram for a serial card - the main chip is of the 8250 variety and made by several manufacturers. Some boards may have a facility whereby the voltage level can be converted to a 20 mA current loop (as mentioned in Chapter 9) or alternatively variations of the RS232 link such as RS422 and RS423. These will normally be determined by link or switch settings.

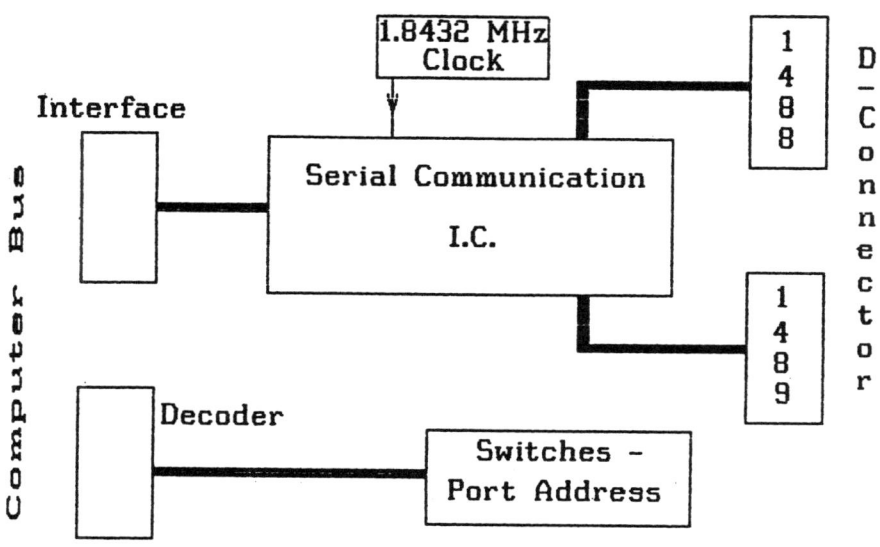

Figure 10.2 Block Diagram of Serial I/O Card

Multiple Serial I/O

Many firms now offer expansion boards with multiple channels. Typically this ranges from 2 to 8 ports, there being a mechanical limit due to the number of connectors required. In fact for systems greater than two, the connectors are on flying leads or an external distribution panel. There is no standard for additional serial ports but one possibility is 03F0H-03F7H for COM3 and 02F0H-02F7H for COM4 with additional channels occupying spare I/O addresses. In addition to this, an IRQ line must be allocated to cater for these additions - see Chapter 2. It must be stressed - read the accompanying manual very thoroughly if the standard arrangement of 2 COM ports is to be exceeded. As the number of serial channels increases it becomes important to keep a very accurate check of their allocation in order to minimise clashes with other facilities. (NOTE if 03F0H to 03F7H is used there may be a clash with addressing for the floppy disk drive adapter - see Chapter 6).

The multiple I/O boards come in two forms: the non-intelligent and intelligent types. With the non-intelligent type each RS232 port has its own specific I/O address and provides an interrupt into the PC. As the number of serial ports increases this inevitably must slow down the host computer with the various servicing requests. In the intelligent type they are all accessed via one I/O port but the unit has dual ported RAM and its own microprocessor. The unit's microprocessor handles all of the serial ports, interrupts and so forth before passing information to the host computer - i.e. it takes some of the workload. Information is processed and presented to the host computer via dual ported RAM, i.e. memory that can be switched into the host computer memory bank or used by the unit's own microprocessor. The intelligent types can therefore handle more data throughput as well as higher communication speeds if the expansion board is fitted with a 16450 integrated circuit instead of the staid 8250.

To increase the number of serial channels still further it is permissible to use several of the boards, the determining factor being either the driver software or I/O allocations available.

Parallel I/O

Most of the time one of these ports will be tied up as a printer output port but there is no reason why it should not be used as a general I/O port with the appropriate driver software. The operating system is quoted as supporting three parallel ports labelled LPT1, LPT2 and LPT3. The story, however, is a little more complex. If a graphics card with a combined parallel printer port is installed this is always LPT1 and any other parallel port(s) must be LPT2 or LPT3. If no graphics/printer card is installed then the parallel ports can be defined as LPT1 or LPT2 or LPT3 depending on the card - see the manual. The I/O map then is as follows:-

LPT1*	LPT2*	LPT3*	Description
03BCH	0378H	0278H	Data Register - i/o
03BDH	0379H	0279H	Printer status port
03BEH	037AH	027AH	Printer control port

The data register is an 8 bit register and contains incoming or outgoing information. Although the other ports are labelled Printer they can be used for other I/O providing the correct pins and data direction are observed as defined by the centronics parallel interface connections. They are further defined as follows.

Data Register -

Bit	Description	Centronics pin	I/O
0	D0	2	I/O
1	D1	3	I/O
2	D2	4	I/O
3	D3	5	I/O
4	D4	6	I/O
5	D5	7	I/O
6	D6	8	I/O
7	D7	9	I/O

Printer status port -

Bit	Description	Centronics pin	I/O
0	not used I		
1	not used I used in Amstrad for other purposes		
2	not used I		
3	Error	15	I
4	Select	13	I
5	Paper out	12	I
6	Data accepted	10	I
7	Busy	11	I

Printer Control Port -

Bit	Description	Centronics pin	I/O
0	Strobe	1	O
1	Auto feed	14	O
2	Initialise	16	O
3	Select In	17	O
4	Interrupt enable (IRQ7) n/a		n/a
5	not used I		
6	not used I used in Amstrad for other purposes		
7	not used I		

A block diagram of a typical parallel control port is shown in Figure 10.3. The output IC is usually a 74LS374 or similar and can source just over 2 mA and sink 24 mA.

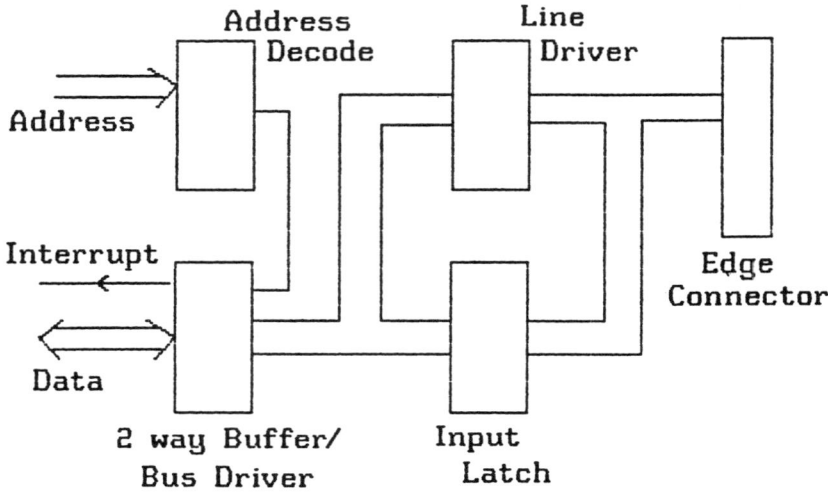

Figure 10.3 General Arrangement for Parallel I/O

If installing another printer card to drive another printer or parallel device please remember to set the jumpers/DIP switches correctly on the new board so that I/O conflicts do not arise. Under the later versions of MS-DOS it is possible to re-direct output via software, i.e. send data for LPT1 to LPT2 instead.

Parallel Connections

These in general cause little problem as they follow the standard Centronics interface but one will always get the rogue connection - why manufacturers will not adhere to some form of standard is incomprehensible. There is no reason why one should not wire the cable and plugs oneself but be very careful not to get any solder bridges between pins - the pin positions are numbered in some way and the plugs/sockets cannot be reversed. This cable can be prone to cause interference to radio equipment and should be made from high quality shielded cable with the braid well bonded to a good ground. Also, to minimise interference, internal twisted pairs in the cable could be used. When running an application program make sure that the correct printer driver program is selected. When using **PRINT** and **TYPE filename >PRN** under MS-

DOS or one of the programming languages a Centronics parallel interface is assumed. Within the printer there may be some DIP switches and the setting of these may need altering. Typically these are:-

Paper out detector - can be set to allow signal to computer when paper has run out or to continue.

SLCT IN signal - can allow computer to control selection or it can be set in a fixed condition in the printer.

AUTO FEED XT - this can allow an automatic line feed on carriage return or not.

If on printing a document an extra line feed is encountered then try the alternative setting for AUTO LINE FEED. Do this with the printer OFF. There may be printers with additional settings - please refer to the printer manual for advice.

Serial Connections

These devices are likely to cause the most problem. The pitfalls can be divided into two categories:-

Data rate/baud rate - These must be set on the computer and attached device before any attempt at communication. The parameters to set are data rate, parity and number of start/stop bits.

The serial link - RS232 normally but depends on what the attached device is configured as, i.e. DTE or DCE (it should ideally be DCE). Also, not all of the RS232 lines are necessarily used and the computer must sometimes be 'fooled' into thinking that they are.

The first item can hopefully be solved fairly easily by reading the relevant manuals, noting the desired transmission format and setting the DIP switches appropriately. The setting of the computer must then correspond to this, either via the MODE command under MS-DOS or in the serial device driver program.

The second item - the serial link - can be much more of a problem. What is explained here is also relevant to ALL other applications using the RS232 communication link. Chapter 9 discusses the RS232 link and presents what is the ideal case for the computer - external device link (see Figures 9-7 and 9-8). Whole books have been written about this area and in this chapter it is only possible to scratch the surface. The accompanying manual with any piece of apparatus may also be able to assist as well as the manual on the serial I/O board. The RS232 problem can be sub-divided into the case where the correct DCE/DTE arrangement is used but not all electrical connections are used, and the case where the printer or apparatus is of the same designation as the computer, i.e. DTE/DTE or DCE/DCE.

A very useful device in trying to establish the link is a "wiring box" or "break-out box". These are available from several sources and the cost varies according to the degree of sophistication of the unit. (A basic break-out box is fairly easy to make and is shown diagrammatically in Figure 10.4.), It is connected somewhere in the serial cable and allow various pins to be connected across individually until the correct configuration is found. This should be done on a methodical basis and the results noted at each stage. Also helpful is a high impedance voltmeter or oscilloscope that can measure the voltage levels.

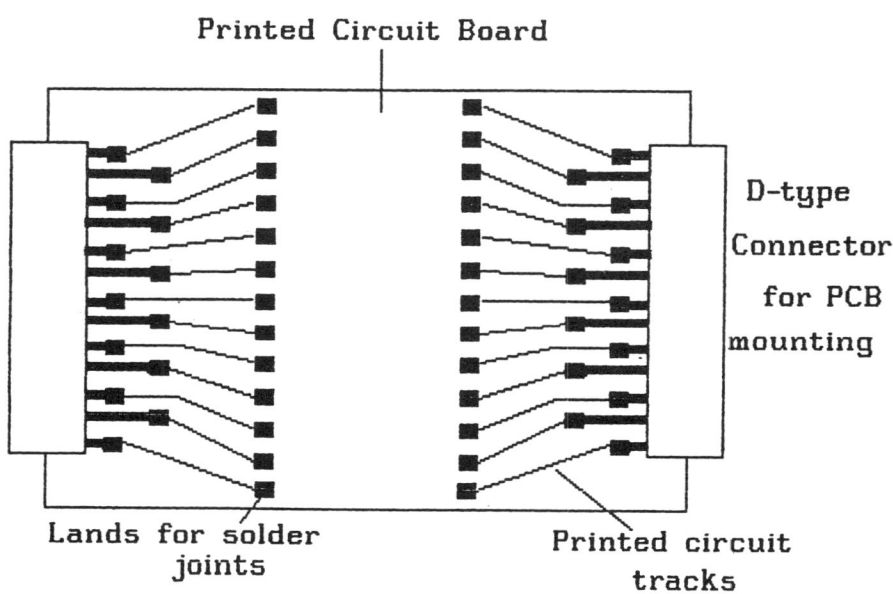

Figure 10.4 Wiring for RS232 "Break-out" Box (not all pins shown)

A slightly more expensive device for examining where there are signals is a "tester box". This contains LEDs to indicate the presence of signals on certain important lines and also the polarity, i.e. one colour LED for positive and another colour for negative. These are more complex and costly to make than the break-out box.

In addition to this a "loop-back" tester is useful for testing the RS232 port itself. It may be needed with some diagnostic routines that are supplied with certain machines. The typical wiring for such a unit is shown in Figure 10.5. It allows the computer to "send" to itself, so that the signal output can be read back in and a check made. These are very easy to make with a single plug and some soldering or alternatively they can easily be produced from a break-out box.

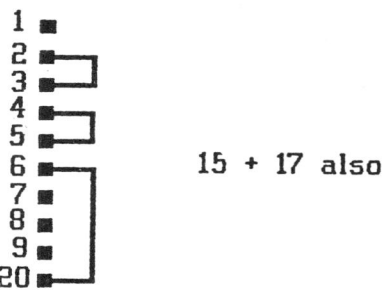

15 + 17 also

Figure 10.5 Wiring for "loop-back" Tester

DTE/DCE Arrangement

Providing all the pins from the computer are used correctly there should be no problem with this arrangement. A diagram for it is shown in Figure 10.6.

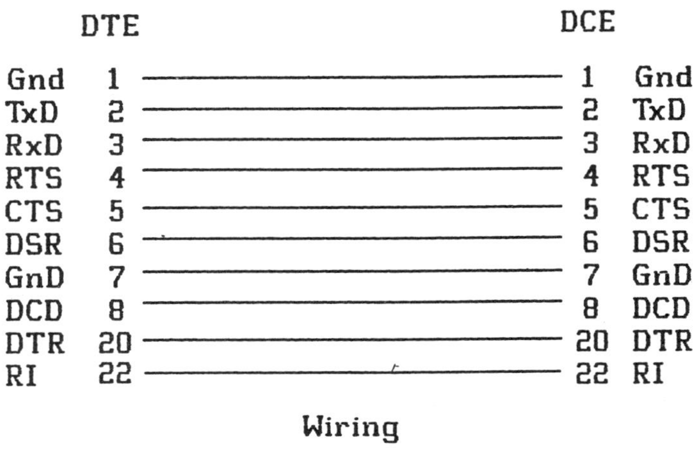

```
        DTE                                    DCE

Gnd     1  ──────────────────────────────  1   Gnd
TxD     2  ──────────────────────────────  2   TxD
RxD     3  ──────────────────────────────  3   RxD
RTS     4  ──────────────────────────────  4   RTS
CTS     5  ──────────────────────────────  5   CTS
DSR     6  ──────────────────────────────  6   DSR
GnD     7  ──────────────────────────────  7   GnD
DCD     8  ──────────────────────────────  8   DCD
DTR    20  ────────────────────────────── 20   DTR
RI     22  ────────────────────────────── 22   RI
```

                              Wiring

Figure 10.6 Full RS232 Implementation

What happens if not all pins are needed or used at either end ? The RS232 link can be made with just TxD, RxD and a ground ,but does not cater for hardware handshaking. It is suitable for a link where only a small flow of data occurs and is acted upon immediately without waiting for equipment to respond. It is possible to use software control of data, e.g. Xon/Xoff. Figure 10.7 shows the typical connections. What should happen to RTS,CTS,DSR,DCD,DTR and RI in this case ? This depends on the drive program and the DTE. Figure 10.7 shows possible connections dotted in case they are needed.

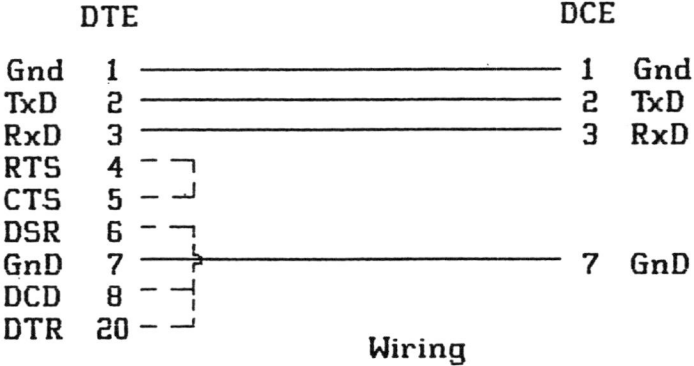

Figure 10.8 Simplest Possible RS232 Connection

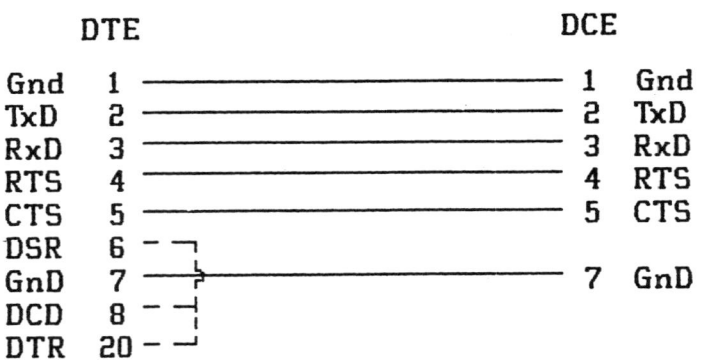

Figure 10.8 Minimum Solution Using Hardware Handshaking

What may be regarded as a minimum configuration using hardware handshaking is given in Figure 10.8 and probably represents a fairly common arrangement. Data flow is thus controlled by RTS/CTS with the possible permanent wiring of DSR,DCR and DTR at the computer, giving a permanent READY condition. The IBM/Amstrad/clone is normally satisfied with this arrangement.

Occasionally a serial I/O board will be encountered that only has a 9 pin connector for the RS232 link. This is not a standard connector for this type of link but is common as a second COM connector on some serial boards and on some IBM AT models and compatibles. Figure 10.9 gives a typical set of connections but it is always advisable to check in the manual as a different arrangement is sometimes quoted.

AT Computer 9 pin
D Connector

Gnd	5
TxD	3
RxD	2
RTS	7
CTS	8
DSR	6
RI	9
DCD	1
DTR	4

Figure 10.9 Possible Connections for 9 pin D Connector for RS232

DTE/DTE Arrangement

This is the case where most problems arise and it will occur where two computers are wired together for communications. The conflict arises because of the expected data flow direction on the various pins. Both sides of the link must be "tricked" into thinking they are receiving the correct sequence of signals. The break-out or wiring box will be most useful for sorting out the links here. The absolute simplest link without any hardware handshaking is given in Figure 10.10 but it may not work if responses are also expected on RTS,CTS,DSR,DCR and DTR.

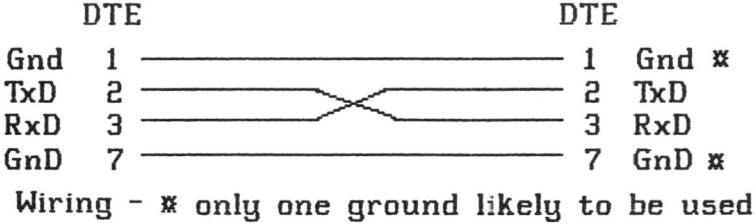

Figure 10.10 Simplest Connections for DTE - DTE Link

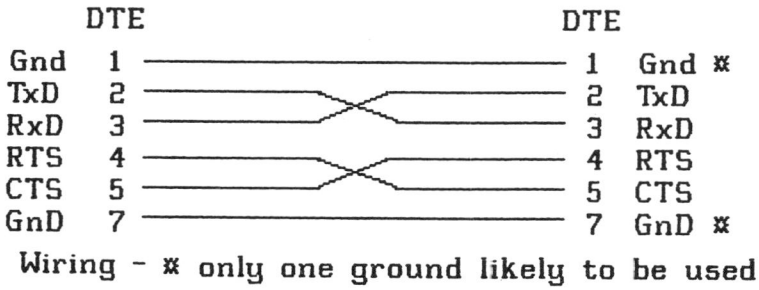

Figure 10.11 Simplest DTE - DTE with Hardware Handshaking

In order to establish a simple hardware handshaking arrangement it is possible to wire up the equipment/cables with RTS and CTS crossed as in Figure 10.11. This arrangement is satisfactory providing that the receiving DTE does not object to its RTS/CTS signals appearing in reverse order. If it does it will not work. The problem with connecting two DTEs with hardware handshake is the correct sequencing of signals. If at this stage there is no communication try connecting DSR and DTR as in Figure 10.12. As a final solution, it is worth trying the arrangements shown on Figure 10.13. Here each end responds to some of its own signals. This last arrangement is also referred to as a "null-modem" and wires 11 and 12 on either side may also be crossed over.

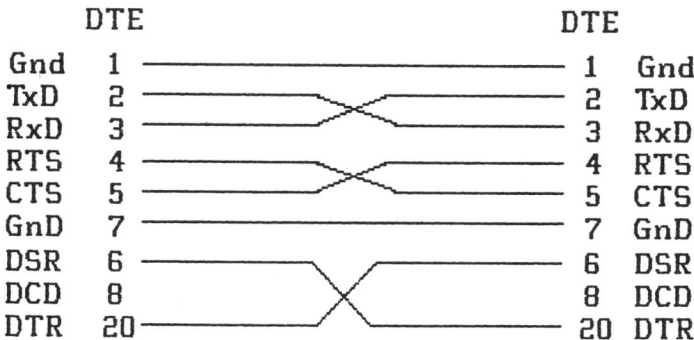

```
     DTE                              DTE
Gnd  1 ─────────────────────────── 1  Gnd
TxD  2 ──────────────╲ ╱────────── 2  TxD
RxD  3 ───────────────╳─────────── 3  RxD
RTS  4 ──────────────╱ ╲────────── 4  RTS
CTS  5 ──────────────╲ ╱────────── 5  CTS
GnD  7 ──────────────────────────  7  GnD
DSR  6 ─────────────────────────── 6  DSR
DCD  8 ──────────────╲ ╱────────── 8  DCD
DTR 20 ───────────────╳─────────── 20 DTR
```

Figure 10.12 Another DTE - DTE Possibility

```
     DTE                              DTE
Gnd  1 ─────────────────────────── 1  Gnd
TxD  2 ──────────────╲ ╱────────── 2  TxD
RxD  3 ───────────────╳─────────── 3  RxD
RTS  4 ──────────────╱ ╲────────── 4  RTS
CTS  5 ──────────────╲ ╱────────── 5  CTS
GnD  7 ──────────────────────────  7  GnD
DSR  6 ─┐                       ┌─ 6  DSR
DCD  8 ─┤                       ├─ 8  DCD
DTR 20 ─┘                       └─ 20 DTR
```

Figure 10.13 Yet Another DTE - DTE Possibility

Computer to Computer Communication

Occasionally it is necessary to make one computer "talk" to another, something that may be useful in transferring or downloading files without going through a magnetic media. It is also very useful for transferring text and data files between computers that have disks of different sizes and formats. If each has a different kind of microprocessor the chances that a program will run satisfactorily are very remote.

These are particular cases of a DTE to DTE communication link and it will be assumed that some form of communication program is to be used for controlling the flow of data. The first problem, and the most time consuming item, will be getting the actual wiring of the cable between the two serial ports correct.

PC to PC Communications

The suggested arrangement for PC to PC communications is Figure 10.12. The second problem is the communication program. It is necessary to set up the following parameters at both ends of the link correctly:-

serial port used	number of data bits
data rate	number of stop bits
number of parity bits	protocol being used

Having accomplished this it is then a matter of following the program instructions to obtain the data transfer. If only 7 data bits are specified then it is only possible to transfer data using hexadecimal coding from 00H to 7FH (i.e. the typical ASCII character codes). If the complete range from 00H to FFH is required then 8 data bits are needed. This, however, can then cause some problems as some of the codes from 80H to FFH may be used for control purposes. It is best to check with the software manual for the options available. Typical examples of such programs are Procomm and PC-Talk from the public domain or Xtalk and Chit- chat from the commercial domain.

PC <> Amstrad PCW Communications

This represents a typical upgrade route for users and possibly allows thenm to still stay within the Amstrad family if they so desire. The PCW is a good word processing machine but unfortunately it does not have an RS232 serial communication port as standard and uses a different size floppy disk and format. Suggested connections for this arrangement are shown in Figure 10.13.

PC <> BBC Computer Communications

This is a fairly common case, especially as each type of computer will not read another's disks (unless some of the costly later options are used for the BBC Master and Archimedes) . Thus it represents a typical upgrade route that someone may make. The BBC computer is ostensibly an RS423 link, with the low signal being 0 V and not a negative voltage. It only uses TxD, RxD, CTS and RTS whereas the PC is a full implementation of the RS232 format. Providing not too high a baud rate is used then the connections given in Figure 10.14 will suffice, crossing the RTS and CTS lines would not allow data transfer at all.

Again it is assumed that communication programs are available for both machines, for the PC as described above and for the BBC typically Commstar, Communicator or Terminal. The various parameters must be set up as above and then data transfer can take place. This arrangement has not caused any undue problems except for an annoying additional carriage return. The link has only been tried for ASCII characters 00H to 7FH. As the word- processing programs on each machine are somewhat dissimilar, it is not possible to transfer them with their control codes as well. First of all the text file should be made into straight ASCII format ("spooled" in some programs) before file transfer commences.

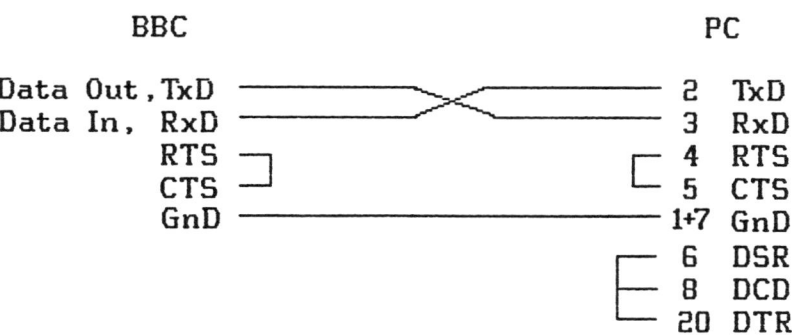

BBC   **PC**

Data Out, TxD ─────────╳───────── 2 TxD
Data In, RxD ─────────╳───────── 3 RxD
          RTS ┐   ┌ 4 RTS
          CTS ┘   └ 5 CTS
          GnD ──────────────── 1+7 GnD
                          ┌ 6 DSR
                          ├ 8 DCD
                          └ 20 DTR

Figure 10.14 RS232 Connections for PC <> BBC Computer Link

Printer Buffers

Printing long documents, especially with graphics, usually ties the computer up for long periods when one could be getting on with another job on the machine. The reason for this is that the computer RAM and disk hold the information and it is passed to the printer only as the printer can cope with it. The printer may be limited to holding 2 kBytes in its buffer and so does not alleviate the problem.

A solution to this is to have an external memory store that can accept all of the information to be printed from the host computer. In doing this the computer thinks it has finished its job and so allows other functions to happen, e.g. typing in another document or programming. Several firms have produced buffers for this purpose and Figure 10.15 shows how they are attached. These units come in varying memory capacities and this is of course reflected in the asking price. A typical unexpanded unit comes with 64 kBytes of memory and copes with parallel in to parallel out or similar with serial connections. (A typical page may consist of 60 lines with 65 characters per line. This equates to 3900 bytes without any control characters. 64 kBytes is something like 16 pages of text and about 256 pages requires 1 MByte. It is difficult to provide any estimate for graphics as it depends on pixel sizes used.) Slightly up-market units will cope with parallel and serial inputs and give cross connections out if desired as shown on Figure 10.16.

There are also some units which can be fitted with various protocol options to allow interfacing to devices with data protocols different from those the host computer can cope with. All the units examined by the author had the capability of memory being extended to 1 MByte. This is very useful in business applications where CAD plots are required that can take several hours to print out. There are also units that allow multiple units to be connected to input and output and these are mentioned in Chapter 11. In many units there is also the ability to pause for paper changes between sheets (as on the host computer), to print a document more than once, and show a visual indication of how full the buffer is.

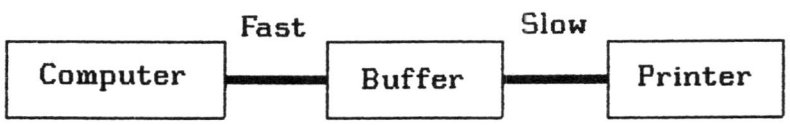

Figure 10.15 Typical Buffer Connection

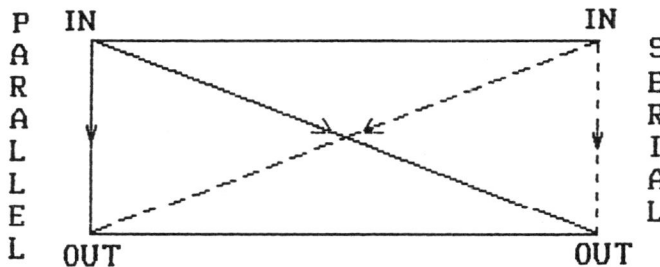

Figure 10.16 Facilities Offered by some Buffers

Line Drivers

The RS232 serial and Centronics links do have a limitation in length of cable that can be attached. The inductance, resistance and capacitance of the cabling eventually cause rounding of the edges of the rectangular pulses sent as well as attenuation of the amplitude. This becomes worse the longer the cable and the distance from the sender, and the receiving equipment finds it more difficult to decode the signals accurately.

In order to increase the distances on the cable it is possible to insert units that will increase the distance that can be transmitted. These may take various forms and are often referred to as line drivers. Some are discussed here but the use of modems and telephone lines is discussed in Chapter 12. For the enquiring reader a look through a communications catalogue is quite enlightening.

Line Boosters

These are the simplest of the devices and involve electronics that will receive and reshape the incoming signal and then re- transmit it in a form almost identical to that received. They require an external power supply and can typically double the distance. They are available for V.24/RS232 and Centronic links.

Centronics-Serial

To minimise the cabling and if it cannot be accomplished at the computer it is possible to purchase parallel to serial converters that are capable of driving lines of up to 1200 m using RS422 or RS423 standards. These units do require mains power and one is required at either end. They can also be used for driving a serial device from a parallel data source.

An additional device that does not really fit into any heading is an external box from Aditi. This is labelled PSI box and allows conversion from RS232 to Parallel and IEE488.

Fibre Optics

This is using fairly up-to-date technology and it provides a communications medium that is also not prone to picking up electrical interference *en route*. A signal must be transformed into a serial form and then converted to light energy. It is then passed down a fibre optic cable giving transmission distances of the order of 1 - 4 km depending on type and model.

These units come in two forms: that which plugs externally into the D type connector on a serial port, and the board that plugs into an expansion socket. In the external unit it derives its power from either a pin on the D connector or a small external power supply, whilst the internal device takes power from the computer bus. The internal unit is seen by the computer as a COM port and so is addressed as COM1 or COM2 which is switch selectable. In both units connection is made to the optical fibre by standard SMA connectors. A brief mention is also made in Chapter 14 concerning this transmission medium.

The Mouse

This is a very popular device which users want to attach and is very common in CAD applications. However, there is no reason why it should not be used in more mundane applications, but do not get one just for the sake of it. Several suppliers will provide a mouse in the total package when a computer is purchased. The mouse by itself is no use but must be provided with a driver program. This allows movements of the mouse to be detected and translated into cursor movements on the screen as well as recognising which of the mouse buttons has been depressed. Some suites of programs such as GEM provided by Amstrad have an in-built mouse driver routine, but more common is the provision of a mouse driver program on a disk when the mouse is purchased.

The mouse comes in two basic forms, dependent on the way it is attached to the computer. These are called serial and bus mice. However, as far as the operator is concerned there is no apparent difference. The mouse driver program must be run before the mouse is activated and in some application programs there is a facility in naming the program in a configure file. Otherwise the application program may need to be "informed" that a mouse is connected. Many business type programs are not initially mouse compatible but on the disk with some of the mice are driver routines that allow them to be incorporated into their use.

One form of mouse consists essentially of a roller ball that comes into contact with a surface - see Figure 10.17. As the mouse is moved across a surface the ball rotates and pulses in the sensors. This connection can be either optical or mechanical or a combination of these. The sensors in fact count pulses in an X and a Y direction as well as determining forward and reverse motion of the roller ball. These pulses are then shaped by the electronics into a form that can be processed by the host computer. Signals from the buttons on the mouse are also passed to the computer.

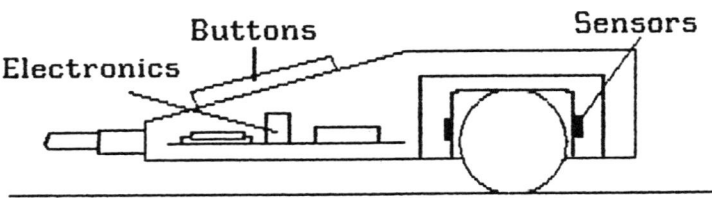

Figure 10.17 Typical Construction of Mouse

Another form of optical mouse must be used on a special pad with a lined pattern on a reflective surface. This mouse has a small light transmitter underneath plus a receiver. As the mouse moves over the surface it counts the crossing of the lines in order to determine its position.

Both of the above mice are coupled to the computer by a cable and couples as explained below. One variation is a mouse without a cable (cordless) that uses an infra-red link to communicate with the computer marketed by Numonics. The infra-red unit couples to the computer via a serial port and allows a space separation from the mouse of up to 1.2 m. This unit will work on any surface.

The Serial Mouse

This simply plugs into one of the asynchronous serial ports with a 25 way D connector and in setting up the driver routine, the port used must be specified, e.g. COM1 or COM2. The driver routine then converts the incoming pulse and direction information into screen cursor movements and the button presses into keyboard equivalent signals.

The Bus Mouse

This requires an additional add-on card to attach it to the computer system which plugs into one of the expansion slots and so communicates directly with the computer system bus. The previously mentioned signals are now dealt with directly on the computer bus but with the same effects as above.

Suppliers

Altek Microcomponents Ltd - various serial and parallel I/O cards
Atomstyle - various serial and parallel I/O cards
Brigden Technology - buffers, line boosters
Citadel Products Ltd - various parallel and serial I/O cards
Data Design Techniques Ltd - multiple RS232 I/O boards
Electro + Graphic Products - cables, connectors
Datalines - cables, connectors
HK Systems - multiple RS232 I/O boards
Logitech - mouse
Maplin - components, cables, plugs and sockets
Memorex - cables, connectors, buffers
Nighthawk Electronics Ltd - buffers, cables
NTS - mouse
Numonics - infra-red mouse
Ringdale Peripherals - buffers, cables
RS Components - components, cables, plugs and sockets
Technomatic - mouse, cables, plugs and sockets
Trend Datalink Ltd - computer cables, plugs, sockets, buffers

11

SHARED RESOURCES

Introduction

This chapter examines the option of being able to share expensive devices between two or more computers, or one computer being shared between several external devices. It does not embrace the concept of local area networks (LANs) which are discussed in Chapter 14. With shared resources it may be up to a user to physically change between two peripheral devices by means of a switch or it may be sensed electronically and accomplished automatically. The changeover between two devices is NOT accomplished from the computer keyboard.

If one computer is to share just two output devices then this arrangement is possible with expansion cards. This is the option of dual RS232 ports (COM ports) or dual parallel ports (LPT:x ports) or a combination of both. The user can normally switch between outputs via the application software in use, or re-direct output from the operating system.

Some items of equipment represent a large capital outlay to many small organisations, especially if the equipment is wanted for two or more PCs. In many instances the equipment is only used say 5% of the time (how often do you access your hard disk ?) and sits idle otherwise. Therefore, if the same piece of equipment is wanted for two PCs it seems logical that it could be shared. It is often inconvenient to have to carry the unit between the two PCs and plug it in again, and to overcome this problem various manufacturers/suppliers market devices that allow the extra unit to be switched between, for example, at least two PCs.

Devices for which sharing might be considered are:-

      laser printers
      daisy wheel printers
      dot matrix printers
      memory back-up (e.g hard disk and tape)
      modems
      plotters
      VDUs/monitors

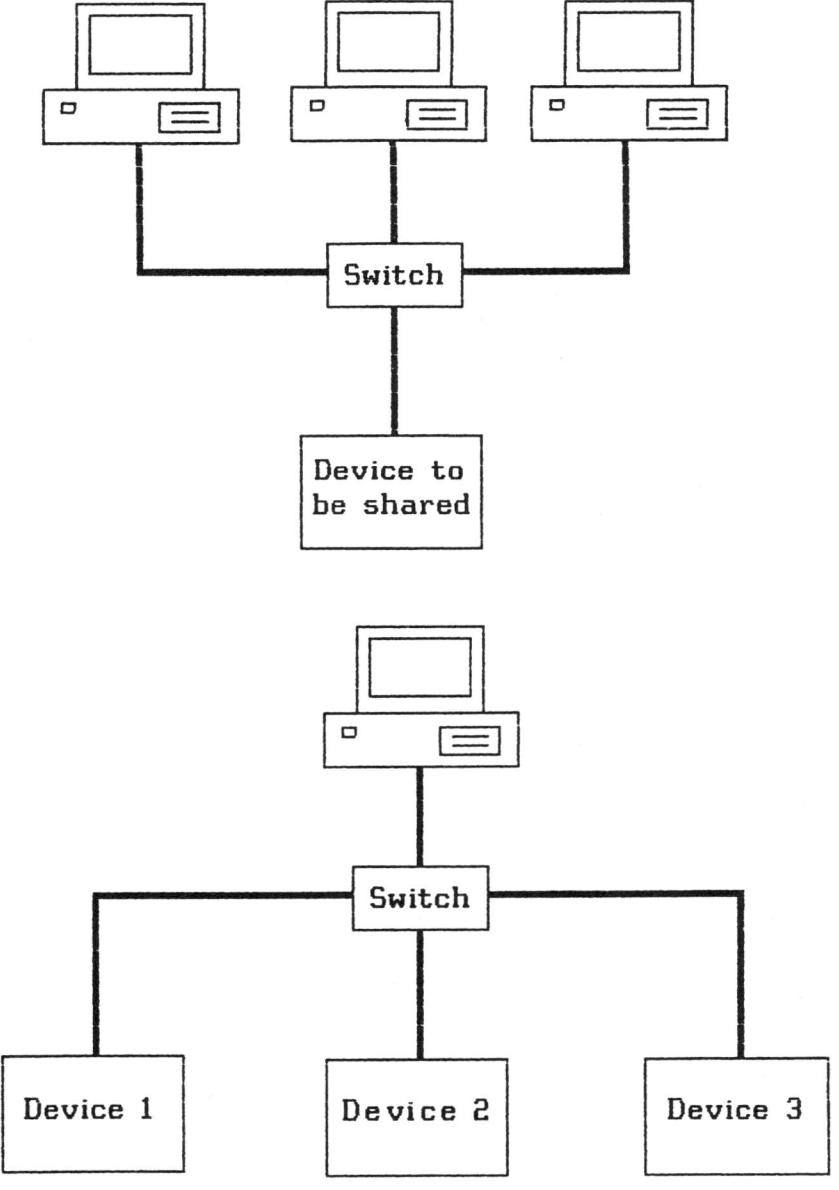

Figure 11.1 Typical Arrangement for Sharing Resources

These devices are generally limited by the use of an RS232 or parallel centronics link and two simple shared links are shown in Figure 11.1. Figure 11.2 is the simplest arrangement of a cross- over where two PCs can switch between two shared devices.

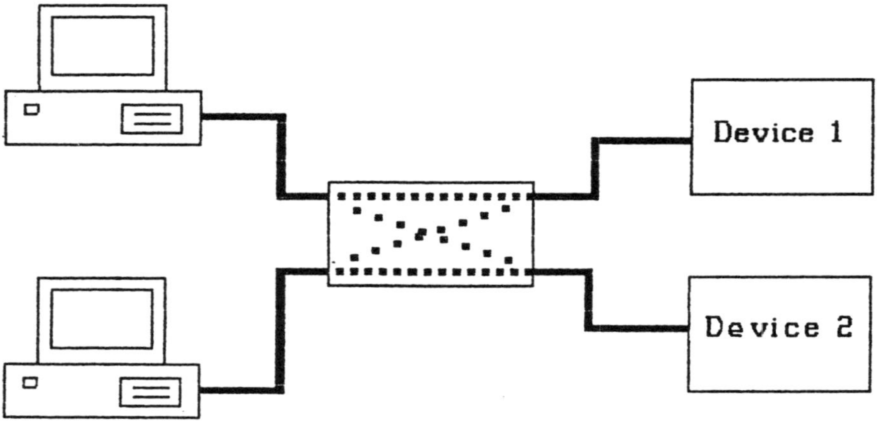

Figure 11.2 Simplest Cross-over Arrangement

There is also the possibility of the PC being used by at least two users, i.e. shared, and this is dealt with in a section at the end of this chapter.

PCs Sharing Peripheral Devices

This probably represents the most common sharing arrangement considered in a small firm and hence is dealt with first.

Placing of the Shared Device

This may or may not pose physical problems. If two PCs are in the same room then hopefully a suitable position can be found which is convenient to keep equipment AND STAFF happy. If the PCs are not close to each other, or a device is to be shared that people consider noisy, then obviously an alternative location has to be sought. Do not decide to put it in some draughty and damp old corridor where there is considerable dust; choose a place that you would also put the PC itself. It is convenient to have storage facilities for items such as paper and ribbons if the unit is a printer. The length of cable run from a shared device to the computer must also be kept reasonably short (typically less than 5 metres) but there are ways to increase this which are discussed briefly in Chapter 10.

Next there is the placement of the switch itself (if required) and it is suggested that this is near the shared device. A good reason for this is that to use the shared device one is forced near the equipment and one can also see if it is in use or almost ready to be used by someone else or has been left in a mess by another user. Certainly someone should be made responsible for the shared unit, otherwise no one will care for it !

The Switch

The switch units divide into two categories: the purely mechanical switch and the electronic switch. The division also can be between those that do not require power and those that do require power. Both of these items may have some influence on the choice of unit. The units may also be able to offer different types of plug/socket on input and output as well as gender changing for the connectors.

Both types offer the possibility of using the devices in series as shown in Figure 11.3 so that the total number of lines can be increased if required. It should always be checked, certainly with RS232 links, if all the pins are connected through because if not this may pose limitations on the use of some external devices such as modems.

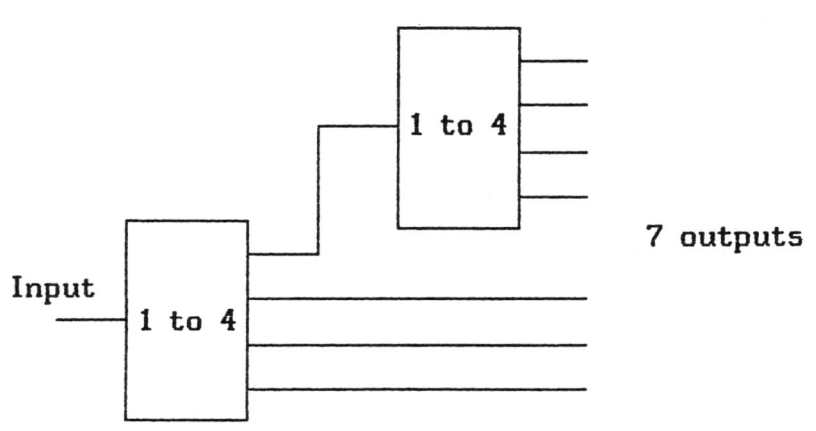

Figure 11.3 Expansion of Outputs with Cascaded Sharers

Mechanical Switch Units

These represent the simplest units available and also the cheaper units; they consist essentially of multi-way electro-mechanical switches. These units are not restricted to just digital signals but can pass analogue signals as well such as composite video, and all of the through connections are bi-directional. They also include units that can be easily made by a technician with good soldering skills, but the economics of making and buying a finished unit will depend on whether labour costs are considered important.

Units are available with D type connectors, Centronics/IEEE488 connectors as well as typical coaxial types such as BNC and twin-ax. Figure 11.4 shows a switch arrangement using a four pole change-over switch for a simple RS232 connection using straight through ground connections. This arrangement can be extended for the various possibilities. The switches could be of the push type or wafer variety but they should have good quality contacts and be suitable for low level signals. It is also preferable for the switch to be mounted in an earthed metal box to minimise radio interference. For BNC type connections the wiring is considerably reduced, whereas for a full centronics 36 way or IEEE488 connection the wiring is considerably increased.

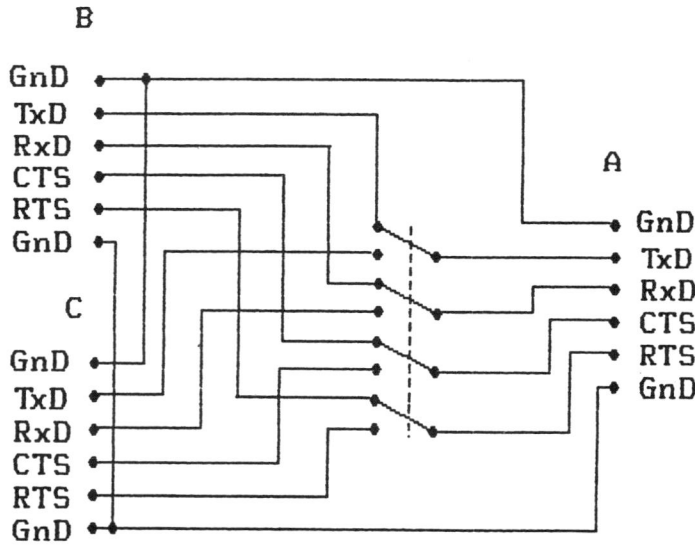

Figure 11.4 Typical Switching for Simple RS232 Link

Electronic Switch Units

The units that come under this category can provide an extensive selection of additional facilities as well as providing the basic switching function. However, of the units seen advertised, they all only carry digital signals. Typical of this range of switches are:-

straight switching between ports - manual
straight switching between ports - automatic
parallel to serial conversion
buffering for printers, serial or parallel
additional line driving capacity.

The straight switching, but manual units, require the user to press a switch to determine the input and output ports to be connected, whilst the automatic units sense an input and connect it to the output if it is clear, if not it holds it with a BUSY signal until the output is clear. Some units will also produce an automatic line feed (LF) before switching over to another input. In addition, some of the units will allow more expansion sockets to be added as they consist of small plug in modules - it may be worth considering this factor in the initial choice of a sharing device. Some of the electronic sharing devices can also be set up by software when the computer is booted up and can thus give, for example, an order of priority to the connections available.

The serial-parallel conversion is normally in addition to other switching facilities as is the buffering and additional line driving capabilities. (See Chapter 10 for more on buffers.) They will allow the length of cabling to be increased but the line drivers may curtail the bi-directional capabilities of the individual lines if care is not exercised.

Limitations

There are generally few limitations imposed by this form of device sharer. It should be mentioned however that if a different device is to be used make sure that the correct driver program has been selected for the new device, the device sharers cannot do that job for you !

Several Terminals Sharing a Single PC

This is on the verge of multi-user systems but represents a simplified form - it almost represents a small local area network. The systems seen advertised all come from Savtec and are labelled PCSHARE (2 users) or PCSHARE Plus (up to 9 users). In addition to sharing the single computing unit the terminals also have access to the peripherals such as printers and they allow electronic mail transfer between terminals providing the software exists.

No additions are required to the operating system but an interface board must be added to the host machine and the video monitors used must be only TTL driven, i.e. NOT analogue video signals. The advertisement states that different programs can be run independently on each terminal but for applications requiring large amounts of memory then there is an additional memory sharing board available. A typical arrangement for a two user system is shown in Figure 11.5 and the system comes with about 15 metres of cable. It would appear that this system is fine unless both terminals become very hungry on CPU time for their programs and then the whole system may become unacceptably slow.

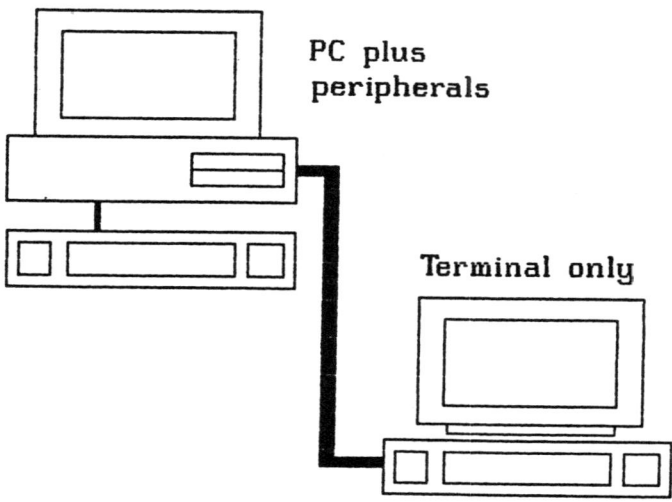

PC plus
peripherals

Terminal only

Figure 11.5 PCSHARE for Two Terminals

Display Multiplexers

It is possible for one computer to drive several monitors with the same or different images. This might be of use in circumstances involving public information displays, banking displays and advertising. There appear to be two approaches to this option: an external add-on or on internal add-on.

The external add-on will cope with varying forms of video signal, composite or TTL levels but these signals cannot be mixed. The units supplied are either one form or the other and contain electronics to buffer the PC so that its video output is not overloaded. The units available couple onto the existing video output from the PC and provide similar multiple outlets with 4 or 6 outputs being typical. These units cope with EGA, CGA and monochrome displays and distances which vary, according to type, up to 150m.

The other form is the internal expansion board that allows additional facilities. Typical of these units is EMAC from Europa Systems. This board is full length, occupies one slot and uses I/O port addresses 272H to 278H. It provides 4 standard TTL level outputs only (all colour). On-board switches select EGA or CGA modes and its input is from the 32 way features connector on the EGA board. With this board it is possible to store two different screens for each channel for display selection under program control.

Suppliers

Brigden Technology Ltd - mechanical and electronic switches
Case Communications Ltd - mechanical and electronic switches
Connexions (UK) Ltd - cables, mechanical and electronic sharers
Europa Ltd - display multiplexers
Maplin - cable, switches
Memorex - cable, mechanical and electronic switches
Nighthawk Electronics - mechanical and electronic switches
Ringdale Peripherals - mechanical and electronic switches
RS Components - cable, switches
Savtec - PC sharing
STC Electronic Services - cable, switches
Trend Datalink Ltd - mechanical and electronic switches

12

COMMUNICATION OVER TELEPHONE LINES

Introduction

This chapter examines various forms of communication which are possible over telephone lines, both those operated by national companies (e.g. BT, Mercury, City of Hull) and private lines (i.e. lines within factories and buildings not necessarily conforming to BT specifications and not connected to them). The forms of communication considered are telex, data communication and facsimile (FAX) although it may be argued that there is considerable overlap. Operation over the public telephone networks (PSTN) requires the equipment connected to have passed certain rigorous tests so that it will not cause malfunction of the network into which it is connected, and possibly cause danger to those working on the equipment (often referred to as BABT Approval). There are also certain national and international standards for data transfer and these are discussed fully where appropriate. The equipment to be used with the PC can either be an external unit or an internal unit where it will take up one of the expansion slots. In most cases software must be used with the additional equipment both to set up the parameters for data transmission, to dial the correct digits and for the transfer of data and any necessary protocol and terminal emulation. Where possible, mention is made of available software packages or packages that contain communication options.

The last item in this chapter may be of great relevance to companies as it allows dialling from the PC itself as well as performing accounting functions on the telephone calls made.

National Land-line Networks

Although the wording Land-line is used, with present technology at some parts on a route signals can be by fibre optics, microwaves or satellites. There are two old established land-line networks in existence with data networks providing a powerful third force. Of the older networks one is the familiar telephone network with its associated exchanges and international connections and the other is the telex network with its own exchanges and connections into international circuits. The telephone network normally assumes a range of frequencies from 300 - 3400 Hz plus additional signals such as ringing tones. The telex network uses a +/- 80v signalling system for many of the older installations plus a newer overlaying system using tones plus additional facilities such as SPC (Stored Program Control). The data rate used for telex is 50 baud.

In addition to these, there are high quality public, private and leased lines for users requiring higher data rates in their communications and these routes usually just link the main towns and cities. Typical examples are:-

Private Circuits

      KeyLine   analogue for low speed data
      KiloStream   data up to 64 kbps
      MegaStream   high speed data, e.g. 2 Mbps

Public Circuits

      Public Data Network (PDN)   X25 Dataline
                                    X28 Dial-up
                                    X28 Dataline

Possibly the backbone of digital services will be provided by ISDN (Integrated Services Digital Network), a digital trunk network. Access to it will be by IDA (Integrated Digital Access) for the customer. This is mentioned further in Chapter 15.

With many services there may also be the possibility of either 2 or 4 wire working. In the 2 wire system (e.g. the typical telephone), information is passed in both directions on the same wires; in a four wire system one pair is used in one direction and the other pair in the opposite direction.

Telex

This derives from an old form of information transmission using electro-mechanical devices. Its precursor was Morse code using hand operation of devices. Morse was suitable for slow information rates but used variable length coding. The teleprinter code was developed by Baudot and Murray and the familiar 5 bit code known as International No.2 code was established. It become a world wide standard over land-lines and used a 50 Baud speed. It was a standard that used the so-called 20 mA current loop to drive electro-magnets and involved start and stop bits recognised by electro-mechanical means. With the development of electronics and computers the functions provided by the electro-mechanical machines can be simulated by newer technology. Information was originally encoded onto paper tape so that time was not wasted during transmission periods and the information likewise could be stored on paper tape at the receiving end.

With computers and modern technology the information can be stored on magnetic disks or put into RAM prior to transmission.

With teleprinters the number to be contacted is obtained by a separate dial sent over its own lines to telex exchanges.The information is then sent over the land-line as a voltage shift or as a tone pair (SCVF or Single Channel Voice Frequency), the communication being only simplex. Figure 12.1 shows the typical arrangement. Instead of talking about ones and zeros, it has been more normal in telex terminology to mention marks and spaces which correspond to logic 1 and logic 0 respectively. This again is due to its roots being in electro-mechanical technology.

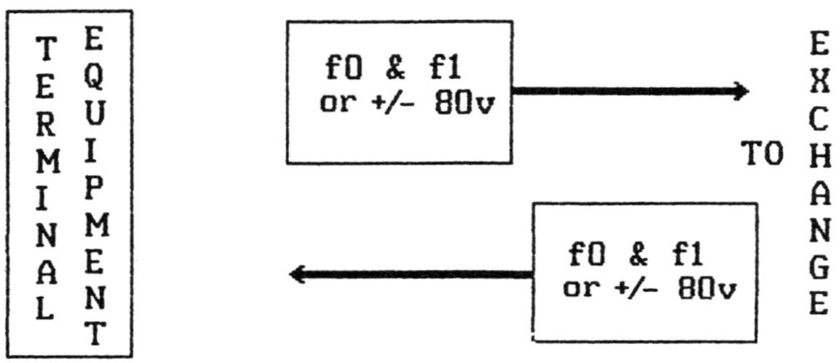

Figure 12.1 Typical Telex Arrangement

Equipment Available

Apart from the standard equipment provided by the large telecommunication organisations. There is one telex unit that can be connected externally to a PC, it is produced by Dowty. Another internal unit is produced by Communicate and both units have BABT approval.

The external unit (Microtelex) has the appearance of a typical modem (which it is) and connects to the PC using an RS232 link. It comes complete with a software package which provides the following facilities:-

> runs in background mode
> will accept ASCII files from wordprocessors
> has automatic message store
> stores up to 500 frequently dialled numbers
> automatic re-try
> management/logging facilities.

As far as the PC is concerned it requires as a minimum:-

    64 kBytes RAM
    twin 360 kByte floppy disks
    RS232 interface
    printer port & printer
    clock/calendar card
    video display.

The other unit which is labelled as Procom 20 is a full length expansion board with its own processor and 64 kBytes of associated RAM plus the SCVF modem. The facilities provided are very similar to the above package as are the basic requirements except that the advertising literature suggests a minimum of 256 kByte of system RAM.

Before the buyer rushes out to buy a telex unit it should be borne in mind that it does require the provision of a telex line by BT or another organisation. An alternative to the true telex line is the use of services such as One to One or Telecom Gold. Not only do these provide electronic mail facilities and so forth using standard telephone lines but they also provide access into the Telex Network. The equipment required by these services is the same as for standard data communications as discussed in the following section.

Data Communications

Although telex is a form of data communication it was included separately due to its origins, its own network and low data speed. However, as with some forms of telex, the use of a modem is required and it is here that different standards are encountered which are explained a little later. As can be seen from Figure 12.2, the modem is connected to the computer with various manufacturers providing the option whereby the modem can be plugged directly into the system board rather than having an external unit.

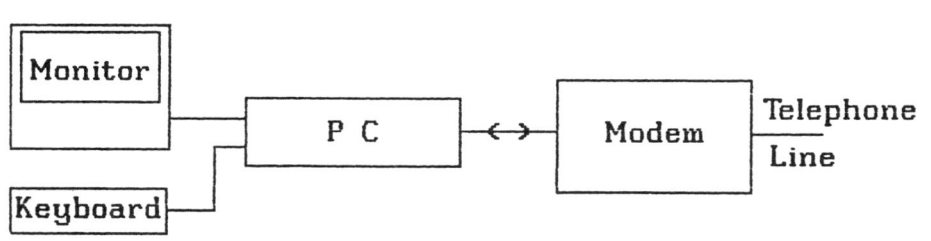

Figure 12.2 Modem Connection for Data Communications

The modems for data communications are more complex than those used for telex. Many modems are multi-standard (i.e. data rates) and so this has to be selected and, as with the previous usage, a telephone number still needs to be dialled. In addition to this the number of data bits may need to be specified as does the number of stop bit(s) and also whether parity (odd or even) is being used or not. This is not the end as it is possible to use transmission protocols with better error detection than parity and some may even provide error-correction. This may require that the transmitted data has to be split into blocks as it is sent and error detection be performed before the next block of data is sent.

Data Transmission Standards

There is quite an array of data transmission standards world- wide, two noticeable blocks being Europe using CCITT standards and the USA using Bell standards. Although some of the data standards are interoperable, others are not. This means that on international circuits some form of translation has to take place. In many instances the data rate is the same but it is the frequency and tone pairs that are different. However, as far as the end users are concerned they can carry on a transmission without any hindrance. In this book the CCITT standards are mentioned, some are explained further in the following sections (in order of complexity) and shown in Table 12.1 or summarised in Appendix 2. In Appendix 3 some of the Bell System parameters are given along with Bell/CCITT compatibility.

The ideal is for the data transmission to fit into a single voice frequency telephone circuit (i.e. 300-3400 kHz) so that standard telephone circuits can be used. At slow data rates, up to about 1200 bps, this is fairly easy to do with simple methods of modulation (e.g. frequency shift keying - FSK). As the data rates rise then this is more difficult but it is still possible to fit the transmission into approximately the same audio bandwidth using more complex modulation methods (e.g. differential phase shift keying - DPSK and Quadrature Amplitude Modulation - QAM). Thus, after a certain point it is technically not feasible and special telephone links must be used that can carry high speed data. These of course have a cost penalty for their provision. Even at 2400 bps, full duplex, some telephone lines may cause undue problems and BT may be willing to fit suitable equalising equipment. At the higher data rates of 1200 and 2400 bps the data transmission will be more vulnerable to poor and noisy telephone lines.

CCITT V.21 Standard

This is the standard for typical low speed data transmission. it specifies data rates up to 300 bps. The frequency pairs used for calling and answering are different and are shown in Figure 12.3.

As the call and answer frequency tone pairs are different then full duplex data transmission is possible. The modulation is FSK, asynchronous so that start stop and possibly parity bits must be included in the data stream. Although it is stated that the data rate can be up to 300 bps, the data rate normally used is 300 bps and standardised for use on the public telephone switched network (PSTN).

CCITT Standard	Speed bps Forward	Reverse	Modulation	Frequency Hz
V21	0-300		FSK Async	Originate 980 (1) 1180 (0) Answer 1650 (1) 1850 (0)
V22	1200		DPSK Async & Sync	Modes I/II Originate 1200 Answer 2400
	600(F)			Originate 1200 Answer 2400
V22bis	2400		QAM Async & Sync	Originate 1200 Answer 2400
V23	1200	75	FSK Async	Forward 1300 (1) 2100 (0) Reverse 390 (1) 450 (0)
	600(F)	75		Forward 1300 (1) 1700 (0)
V26*	2400		4DPSK Sync Async	Carrier 1800
V.26bis*	2400 1200 (F)		As V.26 2DPSK	As V.26
V.27*	4800		8DPSK	As V.26
V.27bis*	4800 2400 (F)		As V.27 As V.26	As V.27 As V.26
V.29*	9600 7200 (F) 4800 (F)		QAM sync	Carrier 1700

FSK = frequency shift keying   DPSK = differential FSK
QAM = quadrature amplitude modulation   F = fallback speed

* usually half-duplex on 2 wire PSTN, duplex on 4 wire systems

Table 12.1 Some Modem Transmission Standards

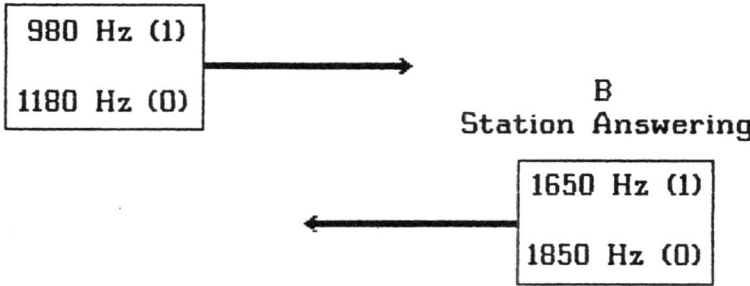

Figure 12.3 Modem Frequency Arrangement for V.21

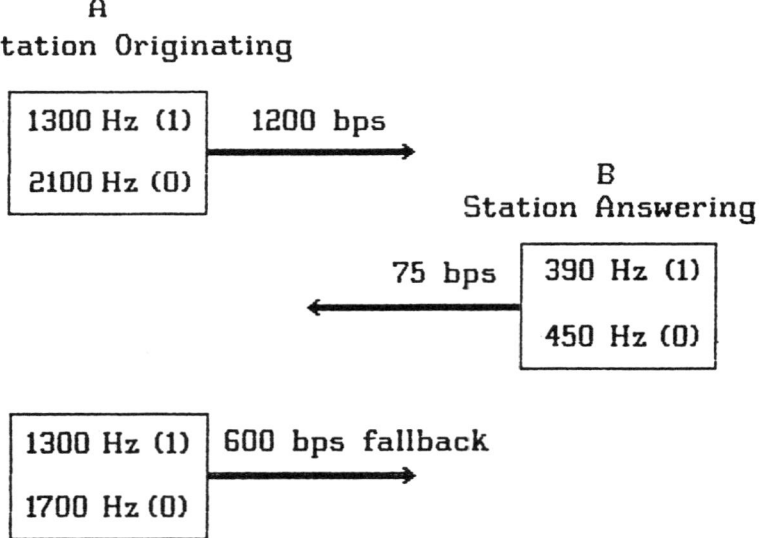

Figure 12.4 Modem Frequency Arrangement for V.23

CCITT V.23 Standard

This standard again is only asynchronous and uses frequency shift keying. It uses different data rates in one direction from those in the other. The standard is usually 1200 bps in one direction with only 75 bps in the opposite direction. It has a fallback speed for use on noisy transmission circuits of 600 bps but still uses 75 bps in the other direction. The 600bps transmission uses a different tone pair to the 1200 bps transmission. The 75 bps transmission always uses the same tone pair. Shown diagrammatically in Figure 12.4.

Many modems give the option of which way round the 1200/75 or 75/1200 bps is used. It is economic for the station passing the greater amount of data to use 1200 bps. Not all modems will support the 600 bps standard yet in some it is automatic if the error rate is outside an acceptable limit. The 1200/75 or *vice versa* is full duplex working as is 600/75. Some modems allow a 1200/1200 bps working but only in half-duplex mode. The V.23 standard also allows an echo-suppressor disabling tone of 2100 Hz.

CCITT V.22 Standard

This is the first of the standards to be specified for both synchronous or asynchronous over standard telephone lines. It does in fact have five possible operating strategies, these are shown in Table 12.2

Mode	Standard
I	1200 bps, synchronous
II	1200 bps, asynchronous
III	600 bps, synchronous
IV	600 bps, asynchronous
V	1200 and 0-300 bps asynchronous

Table 12.2 CCITT V.22 Standard Operating Strategies

To keep the transmission bandwidth within a normal telephone channel differential phase shift keying (DPSK) is used. Here the digital information is contained within the phase changes of the tones used. The calling station employs a tone of 1200 Hz, and that replying will use 2400 Hz. This of course permits full duplex operation. Normal use is on the 1200 bps standard with 600 bps use as the fallback standard on noisy channels. This is not always accommodated in modems. Option V does not appear to be catered for. Whenever there is an answering station on line (2400 Hz) the modem transmits a 1800 Hz guard tone at all times in order to suppress in-band telephone signalling. Modems can be supplied in various versions and these are designated A, B and C by the V.22 standard.

A .... synchronous only
B .... A plus asynchronous
C .... B plus mode V

CCITT V.22 bis Standard

This standard allows the use of 2400 bps with originate and answer frequencies as for V22. To keep the bandwidth sufficiently narrow for the PSTN lines and to be able to use full-duplex, a modulation known as Quadrature Amplitude Modulation (QAM) is used. This is the fastest of the data rates at the moment for use on the PSTN with full-duplex.

Data Protocols

Data is normally sent using 7-bit ASCII coding and this allows the definition of 128 characters and control codes (hex codes 00H - 7FH) - see Appendix 1. However, to cater for sending data, machine code programs, BASIC programs that are tokenised and the extended IBM character set, it is sometimes necessary to use an extended character set using 8 bits giving up to 256 characters and control codes (i.e. 00H to FFH in hexadecimal). The data can be sent in either a continuous stream or in blocks of a given size. There is some advantage in splitting the data into manageable block sizes, so that if re-transmission is required the whole set of data does not have to be repeated. It also allows the receiving station to interject.

Due to noise (both natural and man made) on telephone lines, corruption of data can occur. Hence, if it is important to avoid errors, some additional form of error detection and/or correction coding must be used as the familiar parity bit is not sufficient to cope with this. There are several ways a block of data can be checked and encoded for error detection/correction. One simple way is to add up all the character codes in the data and form a checksum. This is then transmitted along with the data. At the receiving end this checksum is recalculated and compared with the value sent. If they agree it is assumed no error is present. Another method is the cyclic redundancy check (CRC). This is more complex than the checksum method but provides a much more rigorous test for errors.

The block size, the way in which the error check is performed, how a correctly received block of data is acknowledged, how a re- transmission is requested and so forth is called the protocol. Obviously in a transmission both ends of the link must be using the same protocol. In addition, and especially with transmission systems using error correction, the term ARQ (Automatic Repeat on Request) may be encountered. In these types of system all information passing between the two points in the network is checked for errors - even logging on information. There are different systems in use on either side of the Atlantic. There have been differences on either side of the Atlantic over error correcting coding but a system designated MNP (Microcom Networking Protocol) has become very common in the USA and because of the products sold, common here also. In Europe LAP-B or D (Link Access Protocols) had been used on ISDN and the CCITT have now made recommendation V42 as the standard. This is a compromise specifying LAP-M (Link Access Protocols for Modems) with MNP as a secondary error coding.

A brief description of some of the more common protocols ensues.

RTS/CTS

This is a hardware handshake as defined by the RS232C definitions. It provides control over each byte of data sent if the control lines are implemented. More details were given in Chapter 9 in the discussion on the RS232C standard.

Xon/Xoff

This method allows the data to be split into manageable block sizes and controlled by a software handshake. It also requires fewer control lines to be connected. When as much data as the receiving station can handle has been received, it sends a pause signal to the computer. Two ASCII control codes are used for this method of control - DC1 (device control 1 or Xon) and DC3 (device control 3 or Xoff). The computer will send on the TxD line and as soon as the receive unit cannot cope will send a 13H (DC3) on the RxD line. When it is ready to accept information again then an 11H (DC1) is sent on RxD and data should recommence on the TxD line.

Xmodem

This is a very early system and is sometimes known by its developer's name Ward Christensen. It is very common and is supported by most communication software packages. It uses a 128 byte block and checksum for error detection. It requires the use of 8 bit data (no parity bit) in order to cope with binary file transfer. There is also a variant of this that uses CRC instead of checksums, this is again common and some software packages can adjust to either mode and the block size is identical. On an error occurring it will try ten times to get the information across.

Ymodem

This is based on Xmodem described above. It will support 1 kByte and 128 Byte blocks and includes CRC error checking.

Zmodem

This again is based on Xmodem but is somewhat more sophisticated. It supports longer blocks, typically 256 Bytes at up to 2400 Baud and 1024 Byte blocks above this speed.

Kermit

This was originally developed at Columbia University. It has two modes of operation: 1) both ends using 8-bit data and 2) when one or both machines use 7-bit data. By special encoding it can cope with 7 to 8 bit transfers and *vice versa*.

CET Telesoftware

This was a protocol specially produced by the Council for Educational Technology. It was designed to give easy transfer of program files from viewdata systems systems such as Prestel and Micronet. Most UK viewdata terminals support this as well as the viewdata systems themselves. This is nominally a 7 bit data system.

Many of these methods of data transfer are in the public domain and it is possible to find fuller descriptions of them on many bulletin boards. In some cases the definitions run to many pages. Variants of the above also occur such as Xmodem-CRC, Xmodem-1k, Ymodem-g, WXmodem and Super Kermit.

The PC to Modem Connection

As the name implies this section deals with connection of the modem to the PC. It examines both internal and external modems and how the PC sees them in its memory and I/O map, how the modem is controlled (e.g. Hayes control characters), how the link is controlled (communications program) and terminal emulation. Note: the concept of a modem was given at the end of Chapter 9.

A section at the end of this chapter gives a summary of many of the modems available and the standards provided. This list cannot be exhaustive and is merely representative of what is on the market. Omission of a particular make merely indicates that no information was sent when requested. Some modems are now badge-engineered and these will not have been included in the list. Again, it should be emphasised that only BABT approved equipment should be connected to a telephone circuit that is attached directly or indirectly (e.g. via switchboard) to the PSTN. If private wires exist within a building or site then the equipment does not need to be approved, however, it should not generate radio interference.

BABT approval is an expensive procedure at present and this in part is responsible for the high cost of modems in this country. The other problem, which seems endemic to other walks of life also, is that of the £1 = $1 syndrome. This is especially true if equipment is of American origin. The moral, if buying a modem, is to decide what facilities are required and then to shop around and haggle if the case is warranted - see what software can be thrown in with the package if necessary.

The following applies to both approved and non-approved modems: it is up to you the customer to make sure that equipment is approved for connection to the PSTN, if in doubt look for the green approval insignia and/or ask for the BABT approval number. What will be necessary is for the telephone line at your premises to have the modem type of plug and socket. Another item that may be of importance is the REN (ring equivalence number) of the modem. This is a measure of the loading on the telephone line for the ringing circuit. A typical telephone has a REN = 1 and a normal telephone line will handle a total of 4 units before the ringing may be impaired. Be careful if you have a single telephone line with several extensions, especially as some modems have a REN = 3.

The modems all come with an instruction booklet, the physical quality of which varies somewhat. The contents are also variable, from what almost appears to be a reference manual to a step by step approach to one's first telephone contact. Before purchasing a modem try and get a look at the accompanying manuals - it could save a lot of wasted time. The manuals seen by the author (Dowty, Dataflex and Miracle) all seem adequate.

Manual or Intelligent Modems

First of all, modems can be classified under this heading. A manual modem is controlled directly by hardware, e.g. fixed setting or switches, the number has to be dialled via a normal telephone dial and then switched over when communication has been established. Although the flow of data is under software control, the line is under operator control via switches, usually on the front panel of the modem.

The intelligent type, as might be expected, is more costly but is controlled by software in the computer and in the modem. It can dial numbers passed to it from the host computer or stored internally, change standards according to control codes and some can even sense incoming data rate and set themselves accordingly. The tendency is for modems to be of the intelligent or semi- intelligent type.

External Modem

This is where the modem is a unit external to the PC itself and is also self powered. Figure 12.5 gives the basic connection details and definitions. The advantage of an external modem is that it can be connected to other computers if changes are made. The disadvantage is that it clutters up more space on an already crowded desk or shelf !

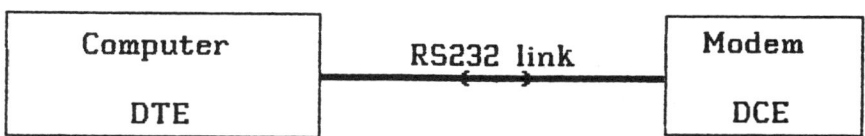

Figure 12.5 Typical PC/External Modem Link

The connection from the computer is a standard serial RS232 link. The computer therefore accesses the modem as if it were a communication port, e.g. COM1 or COM2 (COM3 or COM4 only with special software or MS-DOS 3.3). The RS232 link is set to a rate determined by the computer (e.g. MS-DOS MODE command) or from within a communications software package. The link to the modem is usually identical to the transmission on the telephone line but the PC has no 75 bps setting nor can it operate split data rate working. In this case the modem will adjust to receive 1200 bps from the computer and send at 75 bps. On receive at 75 bps it will have to send to the DTE at 1200 bps. If the modem is of the intelligent variety there may be additional wires used in the RS232 link, these possibly are:-

Pin 23 Data signalling rate (output to DTE)

The external modem comes in two forms:-

acoustic type
direct connection

With the acoustic type the telephone handset is placed in a cradle on the unit. With a direct connection it is via a BT 600 series modular plug/socket - plug type 431A - direct to the telephone line. This is for either PSTN or leased lines, the difference being in the pins used on the 6 way plug; the systems are not interoperable. On the standard telephone two-wire lines only asynchronous communication is normally possible.

There are usually various indicators and switches on the modem, some of these could be:-

Indicators -
AA	-	auto answer
DCD	-	data carrier detect
TxD	-	transmit data
RxD	-	receive data
RTS	-	request to send
PWR	-	power, ON/OFF
TEST	-	test routine
CTS	-	clear to send
RI	-	ring indicator
DTR	-	data terminal ready

Switches -
ON/OFF
TEST
ANSWER/ORIGINATE
DATA/TELEPHONE
AUTO/MANUAL

One external modem seen here of note is the Trailblazer from Dowty or its suppliers. This is a modem for very fast links - up to 18000 bps - that adapts to the quality of the

PSTN line. It does provide a duplex link and the speed drops back in less than 100 bps decrements until the communication link is reliable. This modem splits the signal up amongst a multitude of carriers spaced 7.8 Hz apart with dynamically adaptive multi-carrier quadrature amplitude modulation (DAM QAM). If all else fails, or if required, this modem will function on V21, V22, V22 bis and V23 standards.

Internal Modem

Many suppliers also provide the option of a modem card that fits into one of the expansion slots. This needs no external power source, it takes all its power requirements from the expansion bus socket, and is fitted as all other expansion cards are. The modem cards vary from full length to half length. The unit is still treated as a serial communications port and may be addressed via COM1 or COM2. Some software may permit a COM3 and COM4 option but this must set up its own I/O addressing unless MS-DOS 3.3 is used. The DIP switches normally provided on these internal modems are for selecting which COM port it is. Most of the comments for the external modem also apply as these are limitations of the PC itself but as these units are all internal they must be of the intelligent type and have no visible switches or indicators.

I/O and Memory Allocation

As already mentioned MS-DOS 3.2 and earlier will only support two serial communication ports. As the modems use standard serial port arrangements the memory allocation is as discussed in Chapter 10.

Control Programs

Under this heading two forms of control program must be considered, that for controlling the modem itself and that for controlling the communication link as well.

Modem Control

The intelligent type of modem must have commands passed to it via software. They usually will have some in-built default settings but of course these will not suit all applications. A very common and almost *de facto* standard is that referred to as Hayes. This was developed by Hayes Microcomputer Products Inc, Georgia, USA. However, this has had to be modified to cater for the UK usage but is supported by most modem manufacturers. When using some software communication packages, especially those of USA origin, be wary - not all commands can be used. A summary of some of the Hayes commands is given in Appendix 4.

The Hayes command set is not particularly friendly and for this reason most of the communication packages mentioned below provide some form of menu driven approach to these commands. The command set will determine such parameters as:-

number to be dialled	whether automatic re-try
immediate answer or not	delay in answering
re-execute last command	duplex or half duplex
synchronous or asynchronous	pulse or DTMF dialling
PSTN or private	local echo or not
number of rings before disconnect	
reset	

Communication Software

This concerns the program that controls the communication link as well as the modem. The program will need to specify the above parameters as well as the data protocol being used, the number of data and parity bits, terminal emulation and so forth. There may also be the ability to accept data from various other software packages so that it can be sent over the link. This software will also usually allow file access for transmit and receive, call- logging, ASCII/binary file transfer, control of the COM port, printer control and various other options.

In reading documentation on various communication software packages one will come across Terminal Emulation. Before the PC was popular various mainframe computer manufacturers developed their own communication terminals and these had various functions assigned to various control keys. These, unfortunately, as is so typical in many installations, do not follow any common principle. Hence, to allow the PC keyboard to simulate these other variations and to help operators familiar with them, many programs will assign functions to various of the PC keys as per the terminal being emulated. Typical names one will come across are:-

IBM 3101	DEC VT52
DEC VT100	Televideo 900
Lear Siegler ADM 3/5	Heath/Zenith 19
ANSI mode	

The last is the most widely used and is defined by the American National Standards Institute. It is almost identical to DEC VT100.

The programs available are either from the public domain sector or commercial. A selection is:-

Public Domain	Commercial
Procomm	Datatalk
PC talk III	Crosstalk IV
Qmodem	GemComm
Boyan	Mirror II
Telix	Sage Chit chat

Facsimile (or FAX)

This is commonly abbreviated to FAX and concerns the electrical transmission of documents. The documents can be text, graphics or a mixture - there is no restriction. It allows an original document to be scanned and sent to a remote location and *vice versa*. Although the system is not restricted to telephone or land-line communications, it is assumed to be so for this book. Figure 12.6 shows the typical arrangement on a telephone line. Unlike telex, this is the standard telephone network and the lines can be equally used for voice or FAX. A normal telephone number is used and it is assumed a FAX machine will be coupled at the other end. When the connection is made, the transmitting unit will send a signal; the far-end receiving unit recognises it and puts itself into a condition for receiving an image.

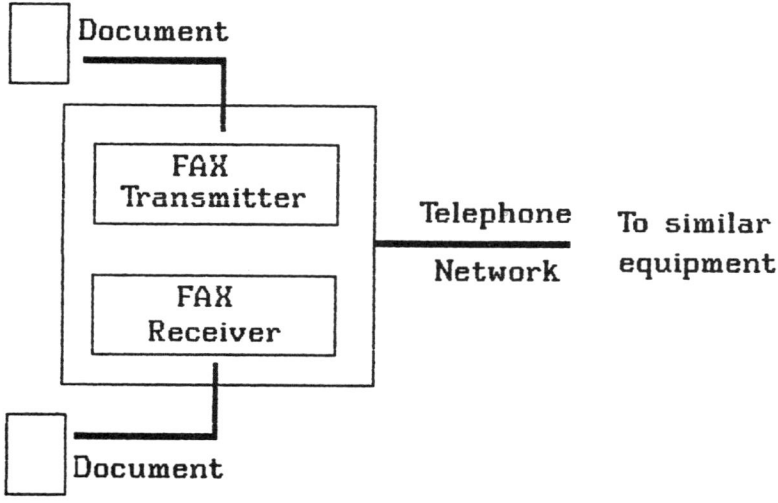

Figure 12.6 Typical Arrangement for FAX

The original system employed frequencies between two outer limits representing black (1300 Hz)and white (2100 Hz). This method was known as Group 1 and took about 6 minutes to transmit an A4 page. This was improved upon by another analogue method which reduced the transmission time by about 50% giving a similar reduction in the time to produce a page (Group 2). These analogue standards are being replaced by a digital method known as Group 3 which stems from about 1980 and is promoted by CCITT. A further standard - Group 4 - is on the way and will give enhanced definition but is not intended for the PSTN.

To understand how a computer can be used for FAX it is worth looking at the operation of a normal, non-computer based machine. Normal Fax machines are small stand-alone units less than the size of a typical PC system unit (about the same as an Amstrad system unit). It is made up of three essential parts and shown diagrammatically in Figure 12.7. A document is inserted into the scanner and it is scanned in very thin lines. Every so often a sample is taken of the reflected light and the electronics decides on whether black or white and a digital code produced which is passed to the high speed modem. This translates it into an analogue signal and the data is sent. The process continues until the document scan is finished - length being determined by absence of document. The resolution is approximately 200 dots per inch horizontally and vertically about either 100 or 200 dots per inch. At 200 dpi (dots per inch) in both directions an 8 inch by 10 inch document requires 200x8x200x10 or 3.2 Mbits which is equivalent to 400 kbytes. By using a special algorithm to reduce the amount of data that has to be transmitted, this is reduced by a factor of ten and so requires only 40 kBytes.

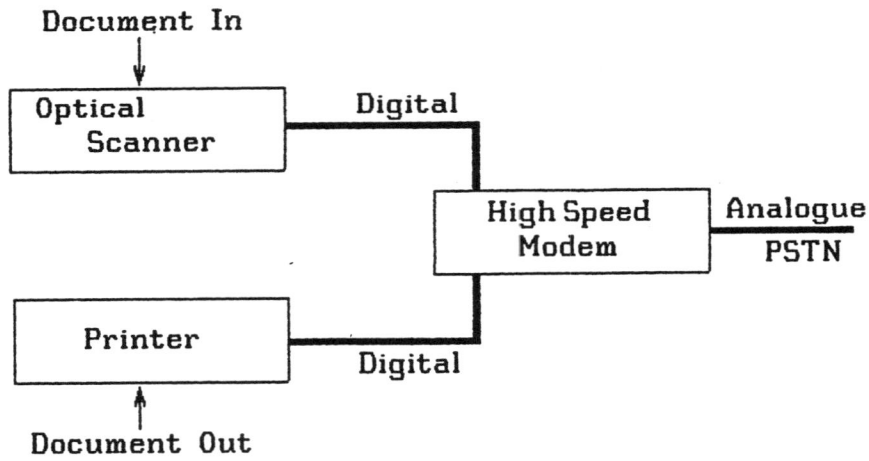

Figure 12.7 Typical Stand-alone FAX Machine

A PC contains much of the hardware required for facsimile providing the original document/image can be input to the computer. The only item that is missing is the high speed modem. A document can be created on the computer by using a wordprocessor or similar, images can be created by graphics packages and it is also possible to use image scanners as discussed previously in Chapter 8.

It should be mentioned that the cost of the FAX cards is about the same as a stand-alone unit which incorporates a scanner.

Transmission Standards

In order to transmit documents speedily the data rate used is high. However, some telephone lines are poor and noisy and in these cases a slower data rate is more desirable. The standards in use, and in the order in which they should be used are:-

V29 .. 9600 bps with fall back to 7200 and 4800 bps
V27 ter .. 4800 bps with fall back to 2400 bps
V21 .. 300 bps using channel 2 if all else fails.

These must all use a half-duplex transmission method to keep within the voice channel bandwidth; further information on these standards is given in Table 12.1.

The units must all be able to communicate with CCITT Group 3 machines otherwise you may as well send pictures to yourself!

Adding the FAX Expansion Card

There appears to be only two BABT approved FAX cards on the market, these being supplied by Dowty and Communicate and their various distributors. They are both of USA origin. There are other cards such as EZ-FAX from Veren, SmartFax from Beyond words, PC-Fax from Softech and IO-01B card from D-RAM Electronics using Group 3 but there was no indication in advertisements that these have BABT approval. This may of course be obtained during the life of this book.

They all appear to be full size expansion cards and can be fitted into any expansion slot where there is room, the width being one unit wide. There are several DIP switches on the boards and these determine the I/O address and IRQ level. The Dowty board (for example) has the following selections:-

I/O address .. 150H
250H
350H

IRQ level .. 3,4,5 or 7

Connection to the telephone line is via a standard BT 600 series plug and socket.

Facilities Offered

These are very much dependent on the software supplied with the FAX card. A typical arrangement with the telephone line, optical scanners and conventional FAX machines is shown in Figure 12.8.

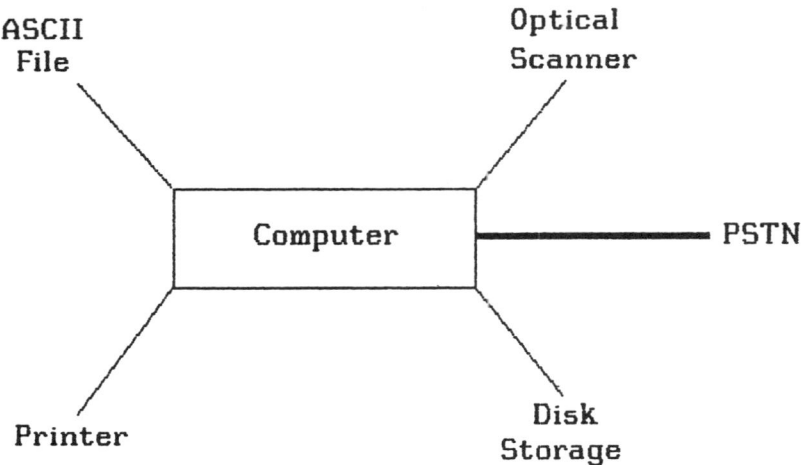

Figure 12.8 Typical Arrangement for PC Based FAX

The units all appear able to accept various types of document for transmission. They contain conversion routines to convert ASCII and graphic files from various sources to a standard FAX format and allow re-conversion at the receiving end so that they can be directly included into other software packages. The FAX images can be received whilst the computer is carrying out other functions (background mode), stored to disk if required, or output to various forms of printer, from Lasers to dot-matrix types. The final quality must change, of course.

The dialling can be pulse or tone (DTMF) and re-try on engaged tones can be automatic. It is also possible to store most frequently used FAX numbers and for the same document to be sent to multiple addresses. As can be seen the variations are vast and it is best to get more details from the firms involved. At the moment the units are not cheap but hopefully the price will fall with time and as demand increases.

Telephone Traffic Management

There is one item produced by a firm called Callbox that can act as a complete telephone line management system. It should function on any call made on a telephone line (not Telex lines) and is approved for use on BT lines. It has a very long list of facilities, only some of which are mentioned here. The firm also produces a video presentation tape giving more details.

The product consists of a half-card that fits inside the PC, an external speaker so that the progress of calls can be monitored, and software. Figure 12.9 shows how the units connect to the PC, telephone line and telephone/modem. When installed, the computer sees this as an 8 bit port at I/O address 208H (the games port).

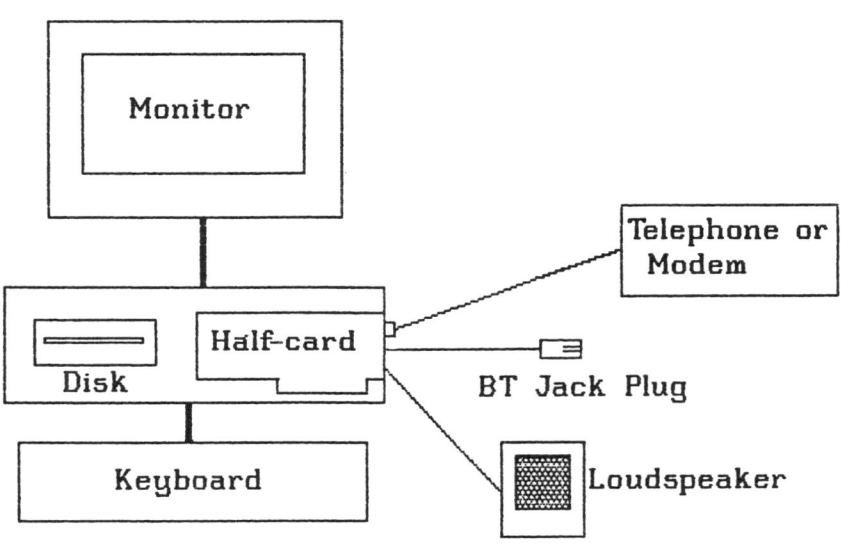

Figure 12.9 Telephone Management System

Software is provided that runs in the background and can be automatically loaded via the AUTOEXEC.BAT file - it requires 64 kBytes. Whilst this is sitting in the background other tasks can be performed and also the facility called by SHIFT-ALT (but this can be changed). The software is key driven.

As already mentioned this product has many facilities and a few are:-

auto-dialling from screen selection
tone or pulse dialling
call queuing
call made at specified time
phonebook of up to 1000 numbers
pad for note taking (with time and date stamp)
redialling
cost of call displayed
call costed to job numbers
telephone expenditure by week, month, quarter, etc.
optional logging of all calls.

A utility program is provided that allows standard maintenance on stored telephone book, notes, logs and charge rates.

Modem Manufacturers

This list gives a representative sample of modems by manufacturer, there is also some badge-engineering. Most of the following are distributed by suppliers, a list of whom follows this chapter. The modems below are all believed to be BABT approved.

MANUFACTURER	MODEL	STANDARDS	COMMENTS
Amstrad	MC2400PC	V21,V22,V22bis,V23	I
Case	410/21	V21	E
	410/22	V22	E
	410/23	V23	E
	410/213	V21,V23	E
	400/22	V22	E
	400/22B	V22,V22bis	E
	400/24+	V21,V22,V22bis,V23	E
Communicate	C-fax	FAX Group 3	I
Dacom	Unity Gold	V21,V22,V23	I
	2424MNP	V22,V22bis	E
	Quad	V21,V22,V22bis,V23	I
Dataflex	Stradcom	V21,V22	I
	Biscom	V21,V22,V22bis	I
Dataphone	Demon II	V21,V23	E
	Designer	V21,V23	E
Dowty	SB321	V21	E,M
	SB1223	V23	E,M
	SB1275/7512	V23	E,M
	SB2123	V21,V23	E,M
	SB1212	V22	E,M
	SB2426	V26,V26bis	E,M
	SB4827	V27	E,M
	SB9629	V29	E,M
	Minimo 300	V21	E,M
	Minimo 3/12	V21,V23	E,M
	Minimo Plus1	V21,V23	E,M
	Minimo Plus2	V21,V23	E
	Minimo Plus3	V21,V22,V23	E
	Duo	V21,V23	E
	Trio	V21,V22,V23	E
	Trio Card	V21,V22,V223	I
	Quattro	V21,V22,V22bis,V23	E
	Quattro Card	V21,V22,V22bis,V23	I
	Trailblazer	V21,V22,V22bis,V23,	E,F
	Microtelex	Telex	E
	Microfax	FAX Group 3	I
Epson	CX-21	V21	A,E,M
Hayes	2400	V22,V22bis	E

	1200	V21,V22,V23	E
	1200B	V21,V22,V23	I
K & N	KN300	V21	A,E,M
Mayze	48PC	V27ter	I
	24	V26	E
Miracle	WS2000	V21,V23	E
	WS3000	V2123 V21,V23	E
	WS3000	V22 V21,V22,V23	E
	WS3000	V22b V21,V22,V2bis,V23	E
	WS4000	As WS3000 models	I
	Keycard 3000	As WS3000 models	I
Pace	Linnet Card	V21,V23	I
	Linnet	V21,V23	E
	Linnet 1200	V21,V22,V23	E
	Nightingale	V21,V23	E,M
	S4,2123S	V21,V23	E
	S4,1200S	V21,V22,V23	E
	S4,2400S	V21,V22,V22bis,V23	E
PC Communications	2123	V21,V23	E
	2123X	V21,V23	I
	1200	V21,V22,V23	E
	1200X	V21,V22,V23	I
	2400	V21,V22,V22bis,V23	E
	2400X	V21,V22,V22bis,V23	I
Racal Milgo	VI1222	V21,V22	E
	VI2422	V21,V22,V22bis	E
	MPS24	V26bis	E
	VI9600VP	9600bps	E
Tandata	TM512	V21,V23	E
	PC Card 512	V21,V23	I
	TM602	V21,V22,V23	E
	TM722	V22,V22bis	E
Thorn-EMI	VX543	V21,V23	E
	VX524	V22bis	E

A - acoustic   E - external   I - internal   M - manual   F - fast adaptive

Suppliers

APL Data Communications - modems, fax, telex , software
Beyond Words - fax
Black Box - modems
Callbox - telephone traffic management
Comcat - modems
Dynatech - modems
Datalines - modems
D-RAM Electronics - fax
Libtech Ltd - fax,
Microcomms - modems
Softech - fax
Veren - fax, fax-lan

13

DATA ACQUISITION AND INDUSTRIAL CONTROL

Introduction

It is very hard to split up these two areas as many applications rely on similar techniques and processing of the incoming data. Also, with a data acquisition system the host computer may have to react on a value of the data input and then the dividing line between acquisition and control becomes very grey.

In the past much data logging and control has been done with unlinked control units and sensors. With the increasing size and complexity of industrial plant there has been more need for overall central control in various processes as well as the very important task of safety. In the larger industries this has been accomplished with the equivalent of the minicomputer but with the advent of the cheap PC and its processing power, the microprocessor can handle many of the applications and because of the low cost they can be used as dedicated units for many applications. The PC may also be used as a hub for control in one area of an industrial plant, some of the data being processed there and passing on only relevant data to another computer having overall control. Figure 13.1 gives various possible control/data collecting arrangements.

Many of the parameters to be controlled and monitored are not in a form readily input to or output from a computer. For example many measurements may be with analogue voltages and some may be in a digital form but not directly suitable for input to the computer. On the output side both analogue and digital signals may be necessary but of vastly increased power and voltage levels. The computer must also in some instances be protected from dangerous voltage levels which would "kill" an integrated circuit before one can even blink. The sensors and units to be controlled are sometimes fairly close to the computer but can also be at some distance and hence some form of communication link may have to be used which may be RS232 serial (or derivative), parallel centronics or IEEE488 - all of which have previously been discussed.

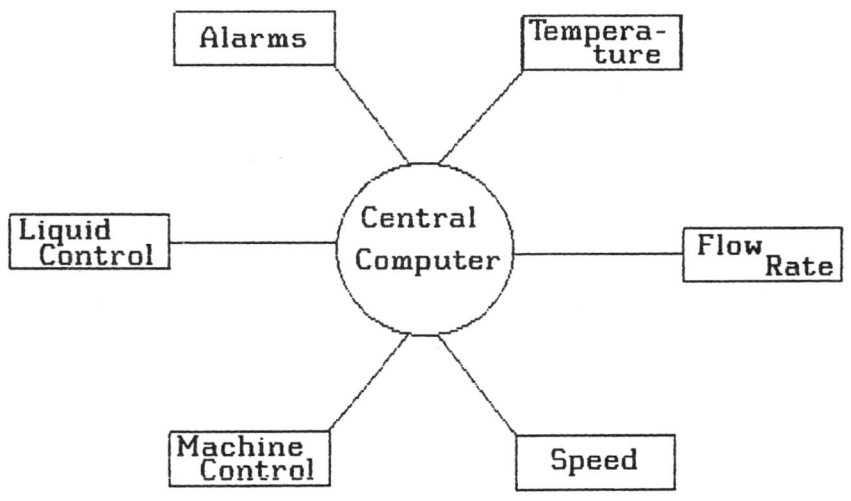

(a) Central Control

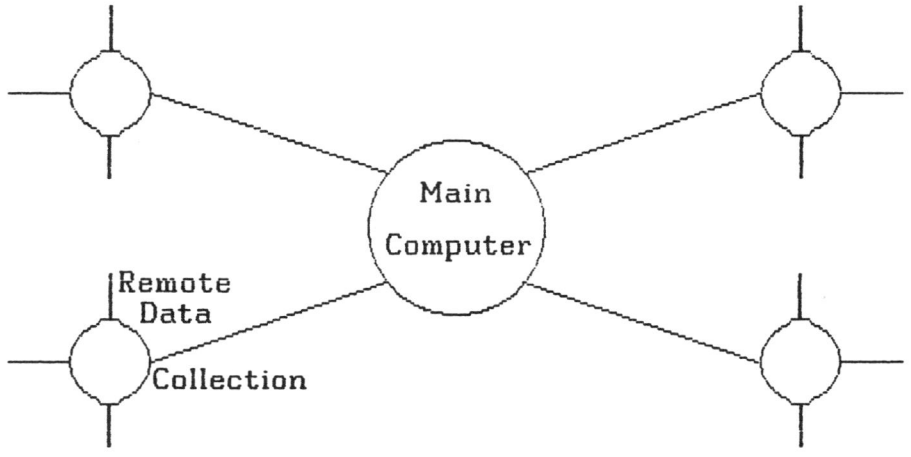

(b) De-centralised Control

Figure 13.1 Industrial Control/Data Acquisition

Signal Conditioning

This section is purely concerned with the concepts behind getting a signal into the correct form for input or output to a computer. It is also included to help the reader comprehend the facilities offered on many of the I/O boards for this type of application, and why. Further detailed work is really in the sphere of electronic engineering.

Analogue Signals

As already appreciated the computer will only cope with digital signals but many devices produce analogue signals and these must then be converted to a digital form. This is accomplished by a device called an analogue to digital converter (ADC), the converse being a digital to analogue converter (DAC). An ADC is often preceded by a sample and hold circuit which in effect takes a "snap-shot" of the input analogue voltage so that the ADC is performing on a constant input in the time it takes to carry out its conversion. Figure 13.2 gives a typical block diagram of an ADC arrangement, the input voltage assumed to be the maximum it can cope with (e.g. typically 0 - 2 volts). It should be noted that this ADC is an eight bit data device and hence has 255 different levels. This means that 00H is 0 volts and FFH 2 volts, giving a quantisation level of 2/255 = 7.84 mV.

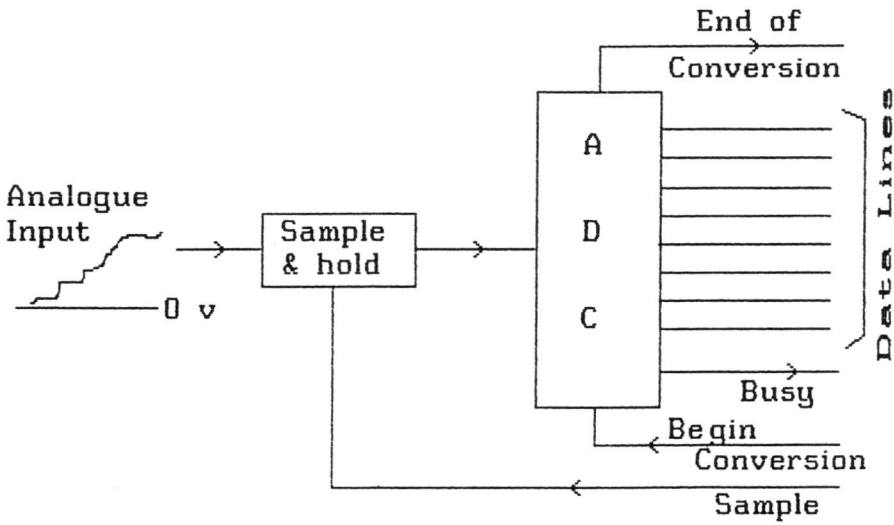

Figure 13.2 Typical Arrangement for A to D Converter

There are also various control signals, these tell the sample and hold (S/H) circuit when to take its sample, when the ADC is to begin its conversion and end of conversion to indicate when the data on the eight output lines is valid. There are ADCs with varying numbers of data lines, speeds at which they can sample, and maximum input voltages. The requirement is that the output digital signals switch between 0 and 5 volts and the input analogue voltage is within a suitable range for the ADC. There are also circuits as depicted in Figure 13.3 that will accept a number of different inputs but only one output to the sample and hold and ADC. The input is selected by a select or address signal and this type of device is referred to as a multiplexer. The address signals can be generated by the computer in any sequence.

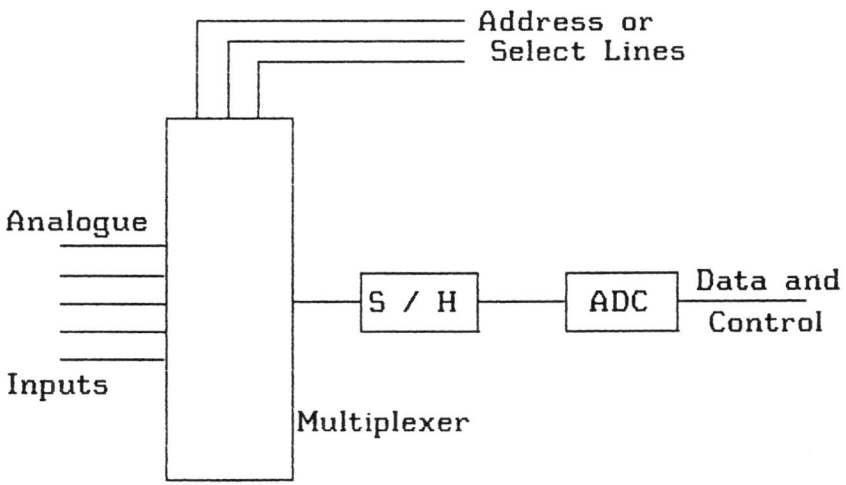

Figure 13.3 Arrangement for ADC with Multiplexer

As mentioned above, the converse is the digital to analogue converter (DAC). This accepts typical digital signals generated from the computer and re-constitutes an analogue waveform. However, because of the quantisation involved the output waveform is composed of a small number of steps and this process is shown in Figure 13.4. The small steps do not normally cause any concern and may well be smoothed out in the following amplifying process to get the analogue signal to the correct power level.

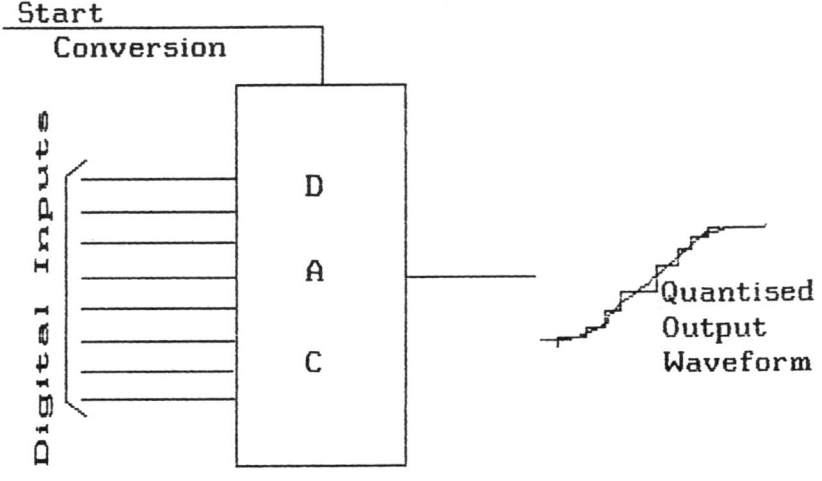

Figure 13.4 Typical DAC Conversion Process

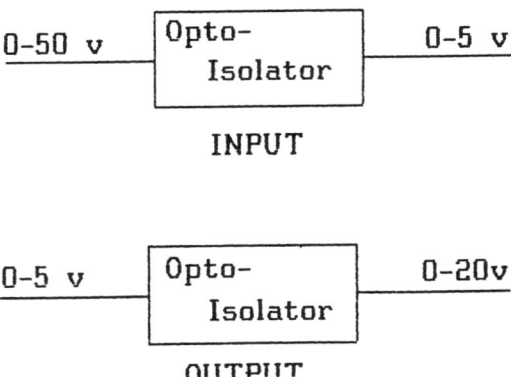

Figure 13.5 Use of Opto-isolators

Digital Signals

With digital I/O it is normally a matter of getting the signal into a suitable voltage range. For input this must be between 0 and 5 volts and at output the computer only gives this range at low current level; either way round suitable interfacing may be required. With input it may be a matter of using a few resistors or possibly the use of an opto-isolator. Opto-isolators are devices which can have an isolation between input and output of up to 4000 volts and so are also very useful for protecting the computer. Figure 13.5 gives two examples of input and output. The common relay may also be used for this application and again provides protection for the computer. In a typical application the output digital signal may still need to be converted to suitable power levels and typical of this is an arrangement using two transistors known as a darlington pair or driver (it is also possible to use these with analogue signals).

Digital & Analogue I/O

Having scanned the literature and looked at many of the products it is impossible to describe each type of expansion facility as they all appear to have different combinations of analogue and digital channels. Whilst many units are expansion cards that fit internally some are external units that interface to the PC via an RS232, parallel or IEEE488 link.

Because of all these combinations it was decided to describe briefly a fictitious internal board that contains a few of the facilities and leave it to the reader to make the decision on the type and number of channels required. The expansion boards are either full length or half length and any of the suppliers quoted below will be willing to provide assistance. The boards from Blue Chip are manufactured and designed in the UK.

In choosing a board the user should make a decision on some of the following:-

> number of analogue input channels
> number of analogue output channels
> number of digital input channels
> number of digital output channels
> input voltage range
> output voltage range
> sampling rate of above input channels.

The last item is very important for analogue inputs and it is a general rule that as the frequency of sampling increases so does the price !

A Fictitious Board

Figure 13.6 shows the block diagram of a fictitious data acquisition and control board. On some boards DMA is used and if so then a spare allocation must be found (if possible). Another possibility is the use of interrupts, especially those designated IRQx, and again it may be hard to get a spare allocation here.

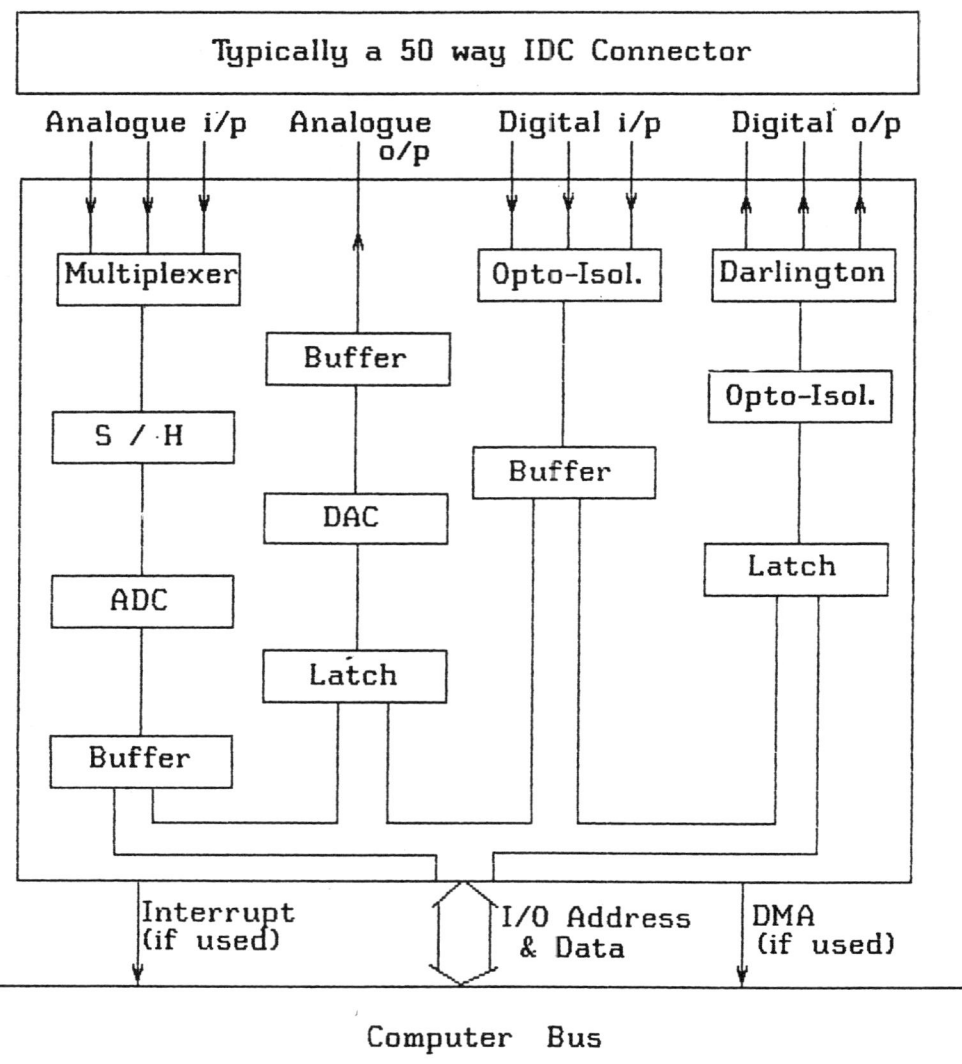

Figure 13.6 Fictitious Data Acquisition/Control Board

The boards are all accessed by using spare I/O addresses and contain jumpers/switches on the boards to determine the I/O address space and they usually require a contiguous block of I/O addresses. See Chapter 2 for nominal maps for DMA, IRQ and I/O addresses. Below is a typical list of boards seen advertised, some applications being discussed below:-

24 channel opto-isolated digital input card

24 channel opto-isolated digital ouput with darlington drivers

48 channel programmable I/O card

24 channel, 12 bit analogue input card

8 channel, 12 bit analogue output card

multi-channel digital and analogue I/O card

relay I/O board (external models also)

DMA data acquisition and control

mulitple RS232 and derivatives (see Chapter 10)

stepper motor control.

Some of the above cards may also contain a microprocessor so that this will control the data transfer to the host computer. The on-board microprocessor may also carry out some of the signal conditioning and channel selection, thus cutting down the time required by the host computer's processor in servicing input and outputs.

Some Specific Applications

This section gives a brief insight into some of the applications from specialised boards. The full range of applications is vast and possibly only limited by the imagination. Brief information is given as there are variations on the cards from the different suppliers. The data sheets on the cards provide a good introduction.

Thermocouple Boards

Thermocouples are analogue devices and because their output is in the millivolt region it requires amplification before it can be sampled and converted to a digital signal. In addition a thermocouple requires cold junction compensation (normally equivalent to 0^0C) and this can be accomplished using a sensor mounted on the conversion board or an offset voltage. It would appear for the boards available that even a multiple input board can only linearise and compensate for one type of thermocouple.

Apart from the compensation and amplification, the way in which a signal is handled is as for the analogue case described above.

Timer and Pulse Generator Boards

These are basically digital I/O cards but with a specific purpose. They are software controlled and on input allow pulse counting, stop watch timing and similar functions. On output they will also provide timing information but can also produce complex digital waveforms. These cards can all be controlled via software and the board is accessed and controlled by jumper selectable addresses and interrupts.

Waveform Capture

There are some high speed waveform digitizers (e.g. STR825 from Speedtronics) that allow the "capture" of a waveform for subsequent analysis. This might be useful in applications such as non-destructive testing, where the return waveform contains information, or in spectrum analysis. The accompanying software can perform various functions such as Fourier analysis and includes the production of displays such as an oscilloscope and spectrum analyser.

IEEE488 Cards

This standard has already been mentioned in Chapter 9 when introducing communication links. The devices in an IEEE488 system are split into three types and referred to as Control, Talker and Listener. The Control is, obviously from its name, the controller and only one can exist. The Listener is a device that takes information from the controlling device only, and the Talker will only give information to the controlling device. A device can be at least two of these units and a typical arrangement is shown in Figure 13.7.

The IEEE488 expansion card therefore has to be driven by software and the drivers are again normally provided in a mix of languages. The card will use direct memory address (normally DMA channel 1 - but hardware selectable) if at all possible plus a user settable interrupt line (IRQ). It is also possible to have a selectable base address.

Motion Control

Another application is the control of motors and at least two firms provide internal expansion cards for this purpose. The cards appear to control either a single stepper motor or up to three stepper motors, i.e. three axes in such applications as robotics.

The cards are all programmed from software and give control over such parameters as:-

      - direction   - pulse length and speed
      - acceleration   - open or closed loop control

In addition the cards have some separate digital I/O which can be used for functions such as limit control and external alarms.

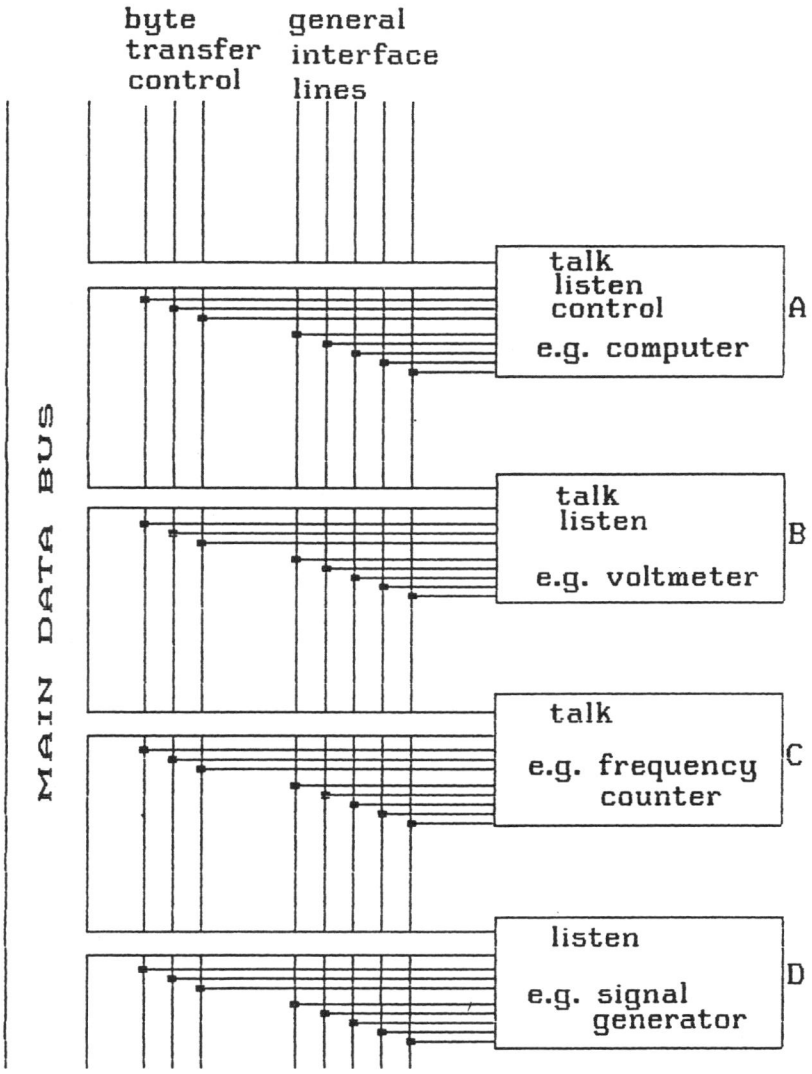

Figure 13.7 Typical IEEE488 Arrangement

Connections to the Real World

This is usually one of the biggest problems as every manufacturer of peripheral units seems to have their own idea of connectors. The IEEE488 board has a standard connector for that type of interface as it is specified in the standard, this is also true for an RS232 ouput. The other expansion boards have no standard but typical is the 50 way IDC connector. This is standard with many pieces of equipment and some suppliers also have extra boards that attach to the 50 way connector that allow options such as screw connections to be used for external devices, larger relays and so forth. These extra boards are located external to the PC and some boards may allow the inclusion of a few extra components such as resistors.

The fitting for these boards is standard as for expansion cards and as people with this type of card are likely to be from an engineering background no problems should occur. However, do not forget the DMA, IRQ and address base settings.

Software

Software may be provided without additional cost, check with the supplier concerned. The software falls into two distinct groups:-

- software for the data acquisition and control (I/O)
- software for the analysis of data collected.

How much software is required depends on the end user and the level of expertise already existing. The suppliers will no doubt provide what software that is required, but the typical approach is to offer the driving software for the expansion board in a few popular languages such as BASIC, FORTRAN, PASCAL, C and assembler. This may well be included in the cost of the board itself.

In addition, software is available for the analysis of the data acquired and the production of screen images that would be akin to equipment that has been replaced by this acquisition system. It may also allow settings to be made to initiate such functions as alarms and printer output. Several packages are available but some are also only tailored to a particular manufacturer/supplier as they also contain driver routines - consult your supplier.

Typical software packages are :-

ASYST - scientific software package. It comes in four modules which can be bought separately. These allow IEEE488 control, data analysis, statistical functions, graphics, array manipulation, control of RS232 ports and support for various data acquisition boards.

DT/NOTEBOOK - electronic laboratory netebook software. Menu driven software that gives real time data acquisition, process control, data analysis, real time graphic display, curve fitting, fast fourier transforms and interfaces with Lotus 1-2-3 and Symphony.

LOTUS MEASURE - allows access into Lotus 1-2-3 environment. Data can be collected from IEEE488 instruments, analysed, displayed and sent to the 1-2-3 environment. Allows data collection from RS2323 devices and data acquisition boards.

Suppliers

Aditi Electronics - digital and analogue I/O, IEEE488
Amplicon Liveline - digital and analogue I/O, IEEE488, software
Atomstyle Ltd - IEEE488
Biodata Ltd - IEEE488
Blue Chip Technology - digital and analogue I/O, IEEE488
CIL Group - digital and analogue I/O, IEEE488, waveform analysis
Citadel Products - digital and analogue I/O cards
Data Translation - digital and analogue I/O, software, IEEE488
Deltest - digital and analogue I/O, IEEE488
Integrated Measurement Systems - digital and analogue I/O,IEEE488
Keithley Instruments - digital and analogue I/O,IEEE488, software
Parker Digiplan - motion control
Speedtronics - highspeed ADC or waveform digitizer
U-Microcomputers - digital I/O card, external ADC and DAC

14

SMALL LOCAL AREA NETWORKS (LANS)

Introduction

Local Area Networks seem to be advertised everywhere these days and it is must be very bewildering to the reader. Everyone wants to sell you their product yet in the advertisements there sometimes appears to be very little technical information. It almost appears that advertisers want you to jump and buy their product and afterwards it is a case of lump it or buy another product if the first does not come up to expectations. The moral is tread carefully and have a good idea what the LAN is to achieve before spending the money.

This chapter looks at the concepts of small LANs, what can be achieved with them and gives a precis of some products that are on the market (this is NOT a comprehensive list). It should also give the reader some information that enables one to understand what the dealer is trying to sell. For a fuller description, the reader is advised to seek further information either from books (see the references) or a supplier who has the time to understand your problem and does not just want a hard sell.

Some LANs have been produced to attach only to their own brand of computer, and these are not considered general enough for this chapter. The systems examined are those that appear relatively easy for an end user to set up themselves with the cabling, expansion boards (if needed) and necessary software. Also only low- cost variants are examined as these will be more acceptable economically to a small business.

In looking at the merits of a LAN system one should always, as with all other applications, consider the future and how a system might expand. In this one must ponder over:-

> The number of stations that could exist
> How many peripheral devices will there be?
> Can it be integrated into a wider network?
> How easy is it to use?
> How secure is it?
> What advice and service can be expected from the supplier?
> Will multi-user software run on it?
> Physical connection problems.

What is a LAN?

A local area network is a method whereby a collection of computers and peripheral devices can be interconnected so that information can be exchanged between them and possibly also allow sharing of expensive devices. It encompasses several PCs communicating with each other as well as one PC being used by several keyboards or inputs. LOCAL also defines that the area is limited geographically (e.g. a small suite of offices or a compact factory) as opposed to the WANs (wide area networks) that are available which will cover large sites as well as site to site communications. Figures 14.1 to 14.3 show in simplified form the various ways in which devices can be interconnected.

In many instances distributed computing power may rival the central mini-computer with its multiple terminals. The LAN certainly has the advantage that if one unit fails it can be disconnected and the remaining part of the network can carry on; with a central mini-computer everything will fail if it does. As already mentioned, devices can exchange information and share other units. Typical of these units are:-

other computers	printers
plotters	hard disks
tape storage	keyboards/terminals
FAX equipment	modems
machine tools	data acquisition
point of sale terminals	

A local area network can also be a "gateway" into a much larger network which could be site-wide, country-wide or world-wide. In a small area it may provide efficient electronic mail around a building as well as remote collection of data into a central point.

LANs can be divided into various groupings by considering different parameters such as:-

topology
interconnection medium
type of signalling
access methods

These can all impose various characteristics on a network, but at first they are considered separately. Further discussion will then examine some of the accumulative characteristics.

Topology

The methods of interconnection such as Figures 14.1 to 14.3 show cover the majority of area networks (there being some variations on a theme). Common to all forms of communication system with more than two devices on a common link there must be methods of addressing who the information is for and this can be in the "packet" of information that is sent, or in some form of electrical/electronic switching.

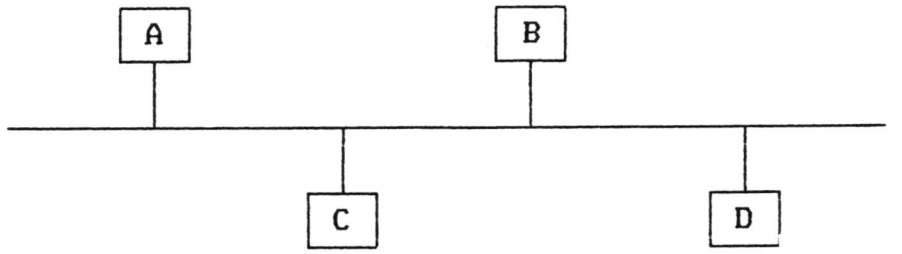

Figure 14.1 Typical Bus Type Network

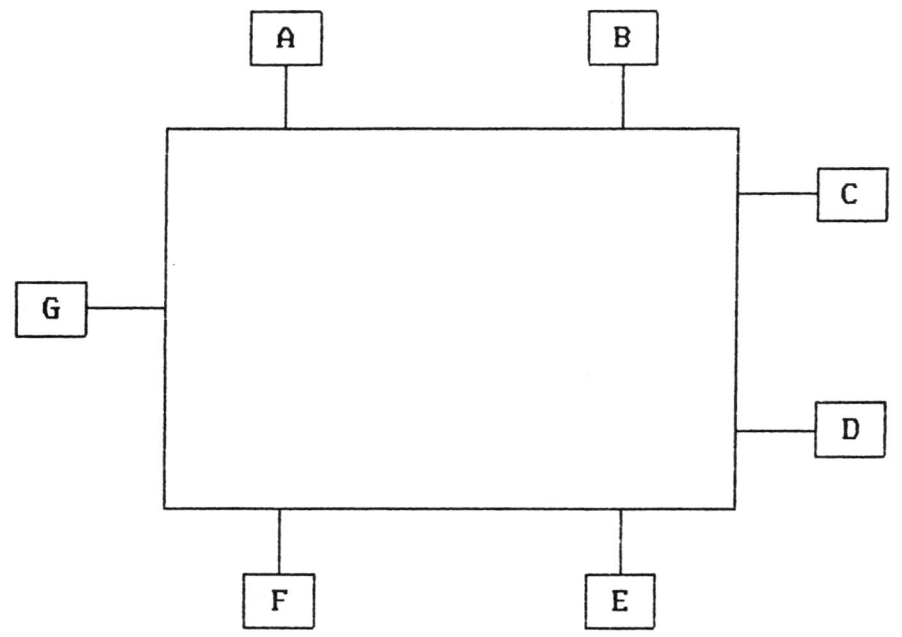

Figure 14.2 Typical Structure for Ring Type Network

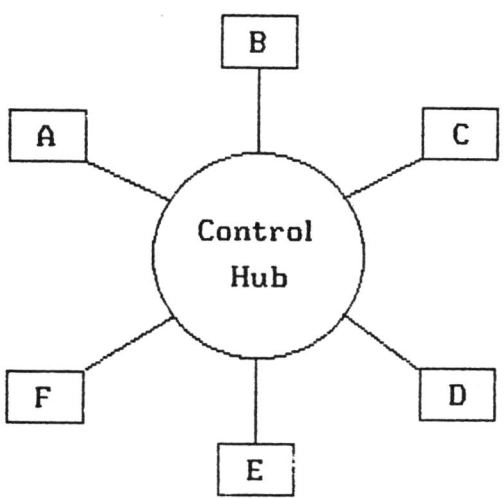

Figure 14.3 Typical Star Interconnection

Bus System

The bus system (Figure 14.1) is very similar to the mains power supply one has at home, office and factory. The nodes are just connected in parallel and more can be added as necessary wherever one is on the line. Here the analogy ends as the connection joining the nodes is not powered. Any signals sent to the line are powered from the node sending the information and so the connection can be termed "passive". Because nodes can be added up to the number that can be addressed by the controlling software, it is a good choice where the final number of nodes to be accommodated is indeterminate.

Nodes can be added anywhere along the line, not just at the ends. However, the length and type of the inter-connecting medium will limit how far the network can stretch and how fast the data can be sent. The bus network can have additional parallel branches and it may appear like Figure 14.4 and is then referred to as a tree network.

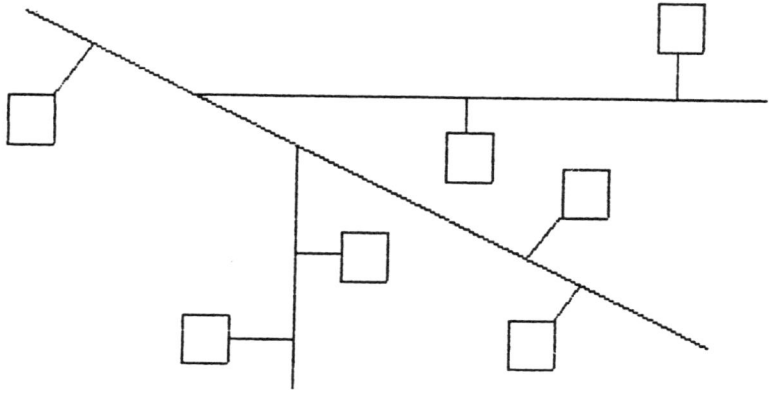

Figure 14.4 Extension of Bus into a Tree Network

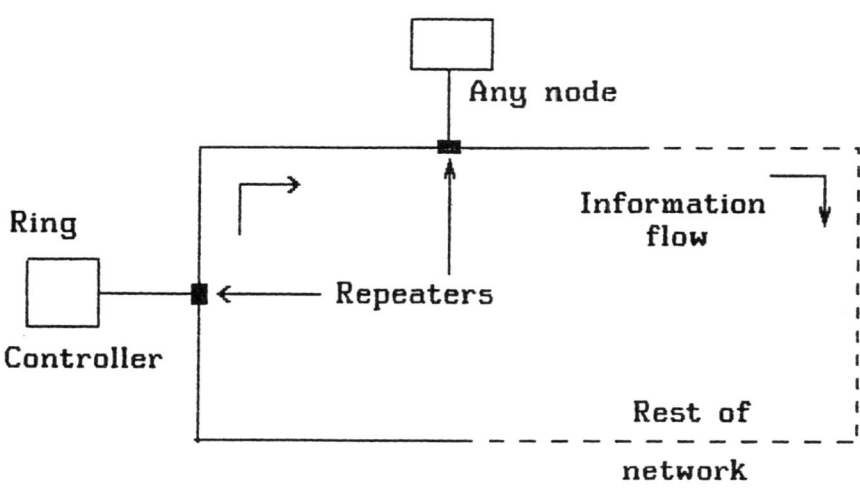

Figure 14.5 More Detail of Ring Type Network

Ring Systems

The ring network is shown diagrammatically in Figure 14.2 and in more detail in Figure 14.5. The ring has a controlling computer which merely acts in a housekeeping role. It will configure the ring correctly when switched on, remove packets of data which continuously circulate due to an error in the addressing, or the receiving node being unable to accept it. The information is encoded with the address by the transmitting node and sent sequentially from one device to the next until the correct receiving node is reached.

At each node there is a repeater which receives the circulating packet of information and re-transmits it unless it is the receiving address. The repeater will also give its attached device access to the ring, if required. If a repeater fails then the ring itself is likely to be broken and can be considered a shortcoming of this form of interconnection. However, methods have been used to overcome this drawback. Another problem is that the ring MUST be broken in order to add another node and so this has to be accomplished during quiet, maintenance or shut-down periods.

Star Sytems

The final method to be included here is the star connection as shown in Figure 14.3 where all the nodes radiate outwards from a hub like spokes on a wheel. In one sense this is not a true LAN as the central switching unit determines where the packet of data is routed and not the node itself, but the node must provide an address when it wishes to access another device. Stars can be expanded so that one node becomes the hub of another star as shown in Figure 14.6.

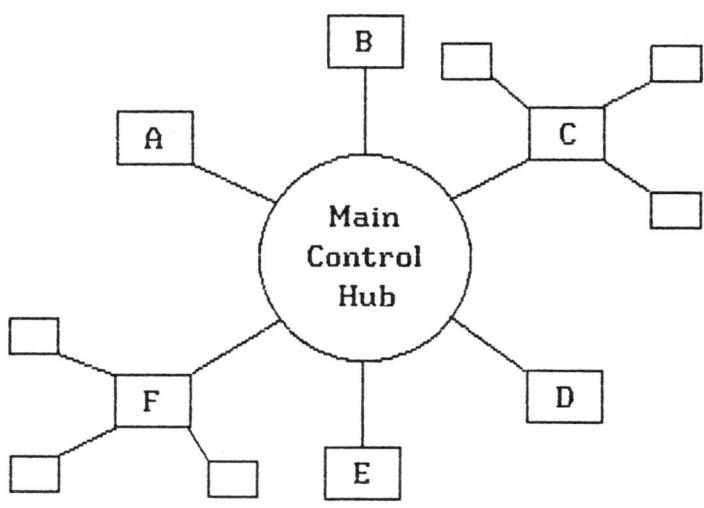

Figure 14.6 Typical Star upon Star Arrangement

Interconnecting Media

This section discusses the actual physical connection between the nodes. This is either made up from copper wire in various forms or in more sophisticated and expensive units from fibre optics.

In the majority of networks examined by a small business the copper wire will be in most and this can come in various forms such as:-

> coaxial cable
> twisted pairs (with and without shield)
> multi-core cable with screen
> ribbon cable.

Coaxial Cable

The coaxial cable is synonymous for many people as being the cable connecting the TV antenna to the TV set. It is constructed from a central core surrounded by a dielectric which is then sheathed in a copper braid followed by a protective PVC outer. The ratio of the diameter of sheath to core diameter plus the electrical parameters of the dielectric determines the characteristic impedance of this cable. Common types specified are, with their various nearest equivalents given in Table 14.1

US	UK	Belden	Alpha	UL	Other	Impedance
RG58	UR43	8262	9158	.	.	50 ohm
RG59	UR70	8263	9059B	.	.	75 ohm
RG62	.	9269	9062A	1478	.	93 ohm
"ethernet"		9880	.	.	BICC8112	50 ohm
"twin-ax"		9272	9815	2092	.	78 ohm
"twin-ax"		9207	9817 or 9818	2498	IBM7362211	100 ohm

Table 14.1 Common Coaxial Cables

Coaxial cable is often used for radio transmission type work and so can be expected to have good high frequency characteristics and so data rates on this type of cable are moderately high. The screening gives some immunity from outside interference and minimises unwanted radiation from data signals on the cables.

Twisted Pairs

A twisted pair is simply two insulated cables twisted along themselves longitudinally. There may be more than a single pair of twisted cables and these may or may not be surrounded by a screen. In any case they are encased in a PVC or similar sheath. The act of twisting the cables does help to reduce the risk of picking up unwanted signals and is further improved by an earthed screen. This also assists in reducing unwanted radiation from the cable which could interfere with sensitive electronic equipment in the proximity.

Twisted pairs have been commonly used on telephone lines for voice communications for many years and the cable available stems from this source. This means that they will not have a good high frequency response and this limits the data rate. Drivers and receivers in integrated circuit form are well established for this type of transmission medium. If multiple pairs are used in parallel for data, control and synchronisation then the data rate can be improved considerably.

Multi-core Cable

Of similar construction to the twisted pairs (but no twist in the cable) is the multi-cored screened cable. This has similar characteristics to the twisted pair and is used in similar circumstances.

Ribbon Cable

All of the above, especially if they have an outer screen, are fairly robust cables and will stand a certain amount of abuse. The other cable mentioned above is flat ribbon cable. Whilst being admirable for crimp connections to multi-way plugs and sockets it lies flat like a ribbon and is very much more susceptible to physical damage. Also, as it has no screen, it becomes susceptible to unwanted "pick-up" and radiates unwanted signals readily.

The systems with coaxial cable and twisted pair/multi-core cable should be favoured.

Fibre Optic Transmission

This was briefly mentioned in Chapter 10 and it is forming a growing method of interconnection. The electrical energy is converted to light energy and then sent on a medium that allows light transfer. As the energy is now in light form it is not susceptible to electrical interference and so may be useful where LAN connections must pass through areas where there is large electrical machinery or sources of radiating/inductive energy.

The add-on cards for this type of network must contain the appropriate electrical to optical drivers and receivers and will thus increase the cost of the network. However, it is as easy to install fibre optics as any other cable. The data rate on this type of system can be very high. As an alternative to internal fibre optic drivers it is possible to have external units which couple to the computer using a COM port.

Types of Signalling

This consists of two types, where the digital signals are either sent as they are, i.e. a voltage or a current pulse, or they are frequency encoded in a modem (see Chapter 9 for further discussion). In the first instance they are referred to as baseband and in the second broadband.

Baseband

In this case, as mentioned, the digital signals are either a current or voltage level. A positive value determines one of the binary states and a negative value the other. Typical of this transmission is using the RS232 standard which has already been explained in Chapter 10. Line drivers and receivers are readily available. The cabling here can be fairly cheap but this will limit the distance that can be covered and the data rate.

Broadband

With the broadband type, a modem is required at either end of the link for the frequency encoding and decoding. For this reason broadband systems tend to be more expensive than their baseband counterparts. To offset against this is the ease with which the information can be sent over much longer distances. If the information is by cable and the data rate high then the use of high quality cabling is essential, e.g. coaxial cable.

Access Methods

This section deals with the problem "when does a node know when to transmit a signal onto the network". This is an area that can get quite complex in structure and so only simple brief outlines are given here that are common for the low cost LAN networks considered earlier (see bibliography for more reading). Basically one gets what one pays for.

CSMA/CD/CA

The majority of low cost systems use baseband transmission and the problem is that all nodes could try and transmit at one time probably resulting in no connections being made. Many of the systems use Carrier Sense Multiple Access (CSMA) with possible enhancements. In the basic system all nodes listen constantly to the bus and if there appears to be no traffic (carrier sense) they will then try and transmit (multiple access). The problem here is that two nodes (as they are all independent) may try to transmit within a very short time of each other and so will not have "heard" each other. This of course leads to a "collision" on the bus and the data is probably corrupted.

Two variants on this theme exist and are labelled CSMA/CD and CSMA/CA. In the first case the transmitting nodes all listen briefly to the bus during their transmissions to see if anything else is happening. If there is another transmission also going on Collision Detection will cause the transmitting nodes to cease operation and all other nodes will ignore the data sent. Each transmitting node then waits a random time interval and tries to transmit again. Because of the random time interval the data should get through although other nodes may try and transmit as well.

In the second case the CA stands for Collision Avoidance. Here each node is allocated a "time slot" after cessation of any transmission when it can transmit. If it does not transmit then the time slot remains unused. If no transmissions occur during the time interval that all nodes can transmit then the network reverts to CSMA/CD. Although this probably gives better utilisation of the bus it does require the nodes to be "intelligent" as far as recognising their own "time slot". Because of the random time delay before transmitting, some devices may have to wait an unacceptable time before they can transmit and may pose problems in real time applications. CSMA/CD is most satisfactory in operations where nodes have intermittent transmission requirements.

Token Passing

Another method termed token passing is where a packet known as a "token" is passed along a bus from one node to another. When a node has possession of this token it gives permission to transmit (much the same as a token on a single track railway line is permission for the train to proceed). This removes the possibility of data clashes and when a node has finished the token is released and passed on.

The way in which the token is passed on is determined by the devices in the network, so that nodes that require to transmit most frequently can have the token passed more often to them. Although the nodes can be on a linear bus the token passing appears more like a ring as it passes between the nodes addressed. Considering Figure 14.1, if A was very important then the sequence might go: A-B-A-C-A-D-A, i.e. looking almost like a ring.

Buffer/Register Insertion

A fairly common access method for ring type networks is that of buffer or register insertion. In this scheme a repeater at a node accepts a packet of data and passes it on if it is not addressed to it. Then, if the node has something to transmit this new packet is "inserted" immediately after the previous packet and sent on its way. The repeater then accepts the next packet on the bus and passes it on.

NET/BIOS

Occasionally one may see reference to NET/BIOS or compatible with NET/BIOS. NET/BIOS derives from IBM and is a standard interface method for communicating between networks. Whilst a local area network can run its own protocols, if it wants to pass information/data to another, possibly dissimilar, network via a gateway then the NET/BIOS is one standard that could be considered. NET/BIOS can therefore be considered as a "bridge".

The Connection to the Node

This section has a brief look at how the cabling couples to the node (e.g. PC and/or peripheral device) and what this implies.

In the low cost small local area network market there appear two common methods of connecting to the PC and its bus/ring. These are :-

    use an existing COM port or
    use an interface card specifically for the LAN.

In the star network only a single cable goes from the hub to a specific node - either coaxial or otherwise. Whichever interconnection method is used the associated software must be able to select the port at the hub so that the correct device is accessed.

In the bus or ring connection the cabling must enter the node as well as leaving it. This is depicted diagrammatically in Figure 14.7. In Figure 14.7(a) the connection medium actually enters the expansion card on one socket and leaves on another. In Figure 14. 7(b) the coaxial cable is "T'ed" off just behind the computer and there is only one connection cable to the expansion card. These arrangements may also be relevant for star systems when one hub is connected to another.

In many of the LAN systems the expansion cards are identical and it does not matter which computer has which card, but in systems where there is a "master or manager" PC then this must have a specific card inserted, all the other outlying PCs then having identical cards.

Access to Attached Devices

With straightforward RS232 links in a star system there is no reason why a serial peripheral device cannot be attached and it can be accessed by the intelligent hub. In other systems items such as printers, storage devices and communication links must be

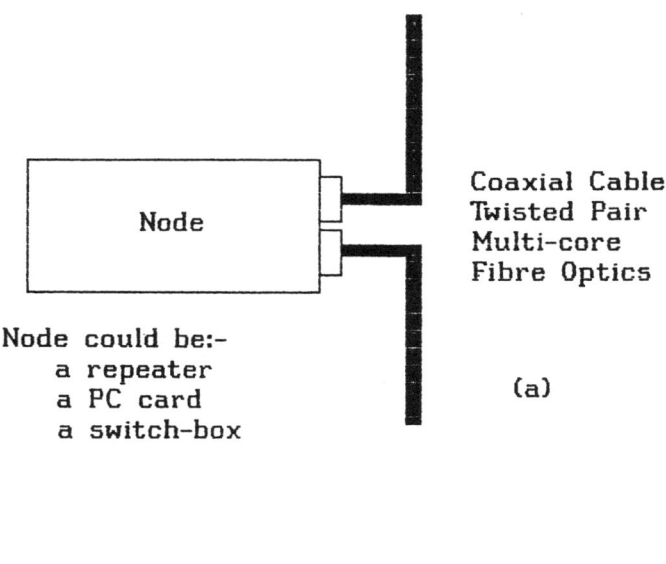

Node

Node could be:-
   a repeater
   a PC card
   a switch-box

Coaxial Cable
Twisted Pair
Multi-core
Fibre Optics

(a)

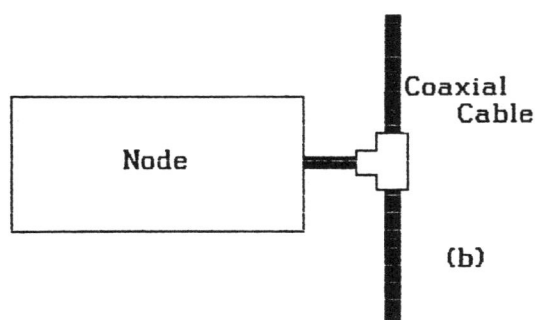

Node

Coaxial
Cable

(b)

Figure 14.7 Typical Interconnection of Nodes

associated with a computer and this PC then becomes known as a file server. The PC must be accessed so that the peripheral device can be used and this may then tie a PC up for just serving the network with its peripheral attachment. It is much more economic in a very small system for all PCs to be used for normal work and then only used as file servers when required. Therefore, care should be taken when choosing a LAN to ensure whether or not a dedicated file server is required.

Some LANs require a PC to be a "manager" for the network and this may well take note of the equipment available that can be shared on the link, to which PC it is attached and who is "logged-on". Again, for the small user this PC should also be able to act as conventional workstation.

In whichever form the network appears, there must be software for controlling the network as well as the add-on expansion cards that form the link with each of the stations. This software is usually accessed via some arrangement of soft-keys and then menu driven. Some of the aspects worth considering in the software are:-

Is it easy to use?
Is there private file storage for individual use?
Is there password selection for individuals?
Is there password selection for various groups?
Does it provide electronic mail for the site?
Does it provide gateway facilities to the outside world?
Are there in-built HELP facilities?
How easy is it to re-configure the system?

Small LAN Summary

Table 14.2 is a summary of some of the small LANs available on the market. It is meant to give the reader an insight into the variations available but is by no means a comprehensive list. The contents probably represent some of the types more often seen advertised.

Suppliers

AST (Europe) Ltd - AST networks
Citadel Products - CP-Net
Equinet Computers Ltd - DNA and Quicklink networks
Go-Mark Ltd - TOPS network
Infa Communications - RS232 based network
JVF Communications - RS232 based network
Nectar Electronics - Powerlan
Newbridge - Main Street Data Controller
.Nine Tiles - Multilink network
Persona plc - G-net products
Sagesoft plc - SageNet network
Tech-Nel - PowerNet
Technomatic Ltd - Trans-Net network
Torus Systems Ltd - Torus NetWare 86, Torus Icon and Tapestry

Parameter Type	Topo-logy	Cable Type	Length m	RAM Req'd	Data Rate	Trans-mission	Nodes	Proto-col	Comment
SAGENET	Bus	Dual Twisted pair	200	125 kByte	1 Mb/s	Broad band	2-63	CSMA	Interface Card DMA & IRQ I/O Address
MULTILINK	Ring	Twisted Pair	1000		250 kB/s	Base band	125		
POWERLAN	Bus and tree	Uses Mains Wiring		30 kbyte	110 to 56kB	Broad band	2-32	Half Dup. CSMA if req'd	RS232 + external modem
G/Net	Bus	Coaxial	1200	64 kByte	1.43 Mb/s	Base band	2-255	CSMA /CD or /CA	Interface card I/O Address selectable
Infa-plug	Ring	RS232 Twisted pair Coaxial Fibre	800		up to 115 kByte	depends on mode	up to 100	Packet Insertion	RS232 from PC. Connection to net depends on options
MAIN STREET 1008	Star	Multi-Core			50-19.2 kBd	Base band	8		RS232
TRANSNET	Bus	Twisted Pair	1200		1 Mbps	Base band	255		Interface card I/O Address IRQ, both selectable
DNA	Bus	Dual Twisted pair	1640	32 kB Mast. 6 kB Work.	2.5 Mbps	Base band	64	CSMA /CA	Interface card I/O Address IRQ, both selectable
TOPS	Bus	Twisted Pair	1200	60 to 240 kB	0.8 Mbps	Base band	100	CSMA /CA	Interface card I/O Address IRQ, both selectable
AST-RSN	Bus	Coaxial	500		5 Mbps	Base band	100	CSMA /CD	Interface card IRQ selectable

Table 14.2 Summary of Some LANs

15

SPECIALIST COMMUNICATIONS

Introduction

There has been quite a strong emphasis in this book on the theme of communications and some items have been omitted or only briefly mentioned because they lead on to more complex areas such as packet communications. This chapter looks briefly at the Integrated Services Digital Network concept and then at an interesting aspect in amateur radio.

Integrated Services Digital Network (ISDN)

This was briefly mentioned in Chapter 12 and is expanded upon in this chapter. It is essentially telephone communications but is as yet in its infancy which is why it was put into this chapter. The ISDN is now becoming a reality and the backbone of the system was due to be implemented during 1988 as the number of local digital exchanges increased.

The system will allow customers using either switched (dial up) or leased lines to access the network. A single pair of wires will give a customer two independent digital paths - one for speech or data and the other for data only and there are facilities for private branch exchanges that give up to 30 channels. The service will provide additional facilities such as access (or gateways) to other established network services such as telephony on the PSTN, data on KiloStream and Packet Switch Stream. The data rate will be up to 64 kbps and allow facilities such as fast facsimile transmission (an A4 sheet of text in about six seconds) or even slow scan television which is adequate for many surveillance and security applications.

The access to the trunk ISDN system is via local digital exchanges that implement IDA (Integrated Digital Access). The information is sent in a packet format using the

International CCITT X25 standard and is very similar in construction to that in amateur packet radio shown in Figure 15.2. The result is thus an error-corrected communication link.

There is an expansion card for the PC which provides all of the digital processing for this service and the one seen by the author was produced by British Telecom. It is a full length card that plugs into a standard expansion slot and contains its own processor and has on-board software. It allows connection of a special telephone handset for use with this service.

Amateur Radio

It must be stated that this section is not aimed at the business market, rather it is specifically for radio amateurs or "hams" as the world is wont to call them. It is therefore aimed at a hobby market, although a somewhat technical one. It shows what is possible with communications although many of the other chapters are also relevant for the hobby market also. Readers may well find an interest in this chapter but it must be stressed that a licence is required for transmitting on the airwaves.

Amateur radio has its roots way back in the mists of the ether (i.e. early days of wireless) and it still exists as a means of self-training in radio communications both technically and in operating practices. Unlike Citizens Band (CB) radio, an examination must be passed (which is set by the City and Guilds of London Institute on behalf of the DTI) to show that one is proficient in the theory and use of radio equipment as well as the prevailing licence conditions. The licence permits transmissions using:-

amplitude modulation	single sideband
frequency modulation	teleprinter
facsimile	slow scan TV
fast scan TV	data transmission
morse code (or CW)	satellite communications

Various small segments of the radio spectrum are designated for amateur radio use from 1.8 MHz way up into the microwave bands. The use and designation of the bands is mainly at international level with local variations as the national authorities permit. Further information is available from any local amateur or club as well as the national society based near London (Radio Society of Great Britain, Lambda House, Cranborne Rd, POTTERS BAR, Herts EN6 3JE). The use of amateur radio is restricted and **excludes** its use for business, advertising, religion and politics. However, it is not restricted to national boundaries.

Data Transmission

One aspect of the hobby here comes under the heading data transmission and concerns the use by radio amateurs of a form of commercial Packet Transmission (X25) modified for amateur radio use and designated AX25. Its roots stem from experimental transmissions in Canada and the USA.

At a home location a station will consist of a computer plus a control unit plus a modem together with the necessary transmitting and receiving apparatus. The data is sent over the airwaves by converting the digital data to tone frequencies just as for the application over telephone lines and therefore requires the use of modems. A typical channel should be about as wide as a normal voice channel. The computer does not necessarily have to be a PC or compatible but with the decrease in price of these units they are becoming a very attractive proposition, especially if it has to be justified to the spouse!

The unit involved with the decoding and encoding of the digital data and the modem comes in two basic forms - an external unit plus RS232 link (suitable for any computer/terminal with an RS232 port) and the internal board designed specifically for the IBM PC and compatibles.

Amateur Packet Radio

Amateur packet radio can become a very complex subject and, in the brief space in this book, it is only possible to cover certain aspects. It is best to start with the simplest arrangement where two stations wish to communicate directly with each other using packet radio - shown on Figure 15.1.

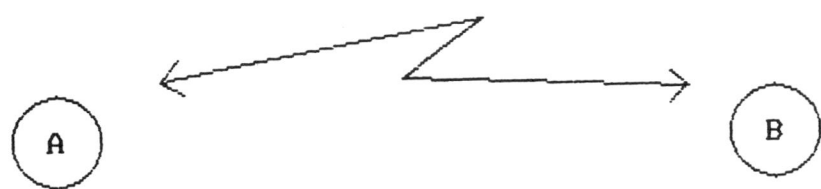

Figure 15.1 Simple Direct Communication

Using voice one merely picks up the microphone and calls the other station using the callsigns allocated by the national authority and these callsigns are recognised aurally. With packet communications these callsigns are embedded into the digital data and a simple format is shown in Figure 15.2. The inclusion of source and destination callsigns is necessary so that receiving equipment can recognise that a message is being sent to it over the airwaves - unlike a telephone line where the sender and receiver are purely connected by a single dedicated communication channel.

Flag	Destination	'Source	Information	FCS	Flag

Figure 15.2 Simple Packet or Frame of Data

The purpose of the FLAGS is to signify beginning and end of the packet, whilst the frame check sequence (FCS) performs error checking. On recognition of a valid incoming packet, communication can then take place between the end users. Because the signal is "addressed" it is possible for more than one communication link to co-exist on the same channel although "clashes" of packets of data can corrupt the packets.

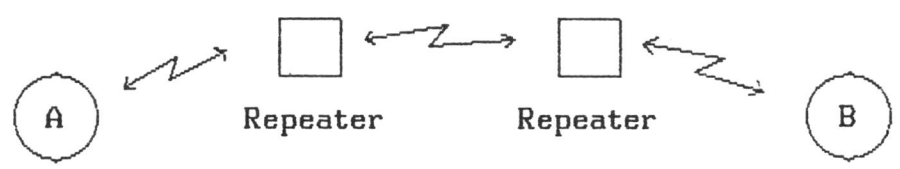

Figure 15.3 Communications via a Repeater

An extension to the above simple arrangement is the possibility of other stations being able to relay a message en-route - see Figure 15.3. To be able to do this the originator of the packet will know which stations can be used and this information can then be included into the packet format (in fact up to 8 repeating stations can be used). The format of the packet then becomes as shown in Figure 15.4.

Packet transmission is possible on both the high frequency bands (HF or 2-30 MHz) and higher bands such as VHF, UHF and microwaves. On the HF bands audio frequency shift keying is used (AFSK) and in most other instances frequency modulation is used. The audio tones derived from the modem are fed in via the microphone socket to the transmitter and on receive the audio is normally tapped off from the loudspeaker output. This arrangement saves internal modification of the receive/transmit (transceiver) equipment. It is shown diagrammatically in Figure 15.5. Transmit control of the push to talk (PTT) is also via the microphone socket.

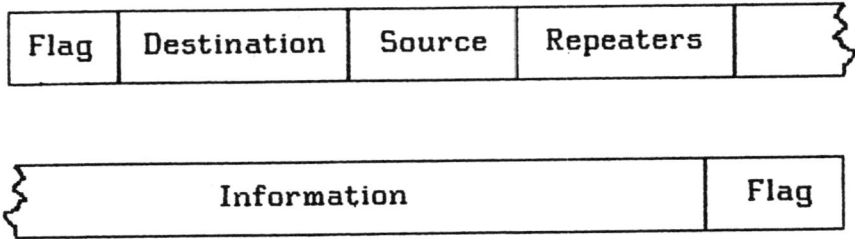

Flag	Destination	Source	Repeaters	{

{	Information	Flag

Figure 15.4 Data Packet or Frame to Include Repeaters

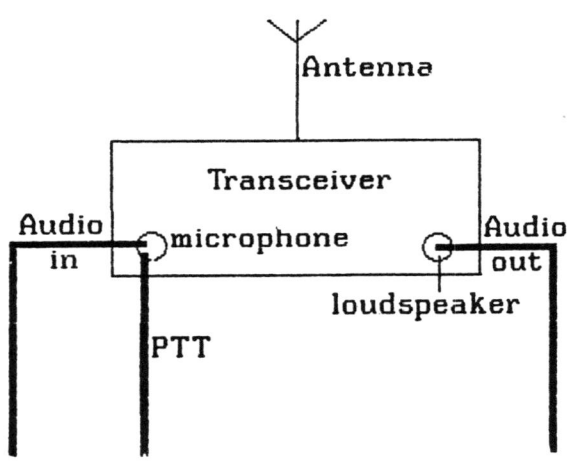

Figure 15.5 Connection of Audio and Transmit Controls

The equipment into which the transceiver is connected is referred to as the Terminal Node Controller (TNC) - a station being referred to as a node as in the case of Local Area Networks. The TNC has several functions, these being:-

a modem
baseband digital encoding
baseband digital decoding
error checking (Rx)
error code production (Tx)
frame assembling
frame disassembling
communication to computer/terminal
communication from computer/terminal
data rate generator to Tx/Rx

This unit is shown in block diagram form in Figure 15.6.

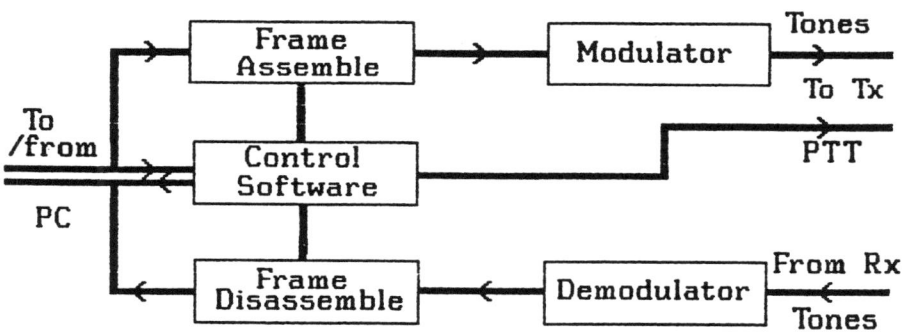

Figure 15.6 Block Diagram of Terminal Controller

	HF	VHF/UHF
Logic 1	1600 Hz	1200 Hz
Logic 0	1800 Hz	2200 Hz
Data Rate	300 Baud	1200 Baud
Shift	200 Hz	1000 Hz

Figure 15.7 Data Standards used at Present

The data rates and tone frequencies used on the HF and VHF bands are shown in Figure 15.7. There is pressure under some circumstances for higher data rates, but these are very much in an experimental stage at present.

Gateways

The concept of gateways is similar to that for the LAN, that is, one node will allow access to other facilities. The gateway for amateur packet radio is the transition from local packet networks to networks which may cover a single county, country, continent or the world. Different frequency allocations provide different transmission characteristics and distances covered.

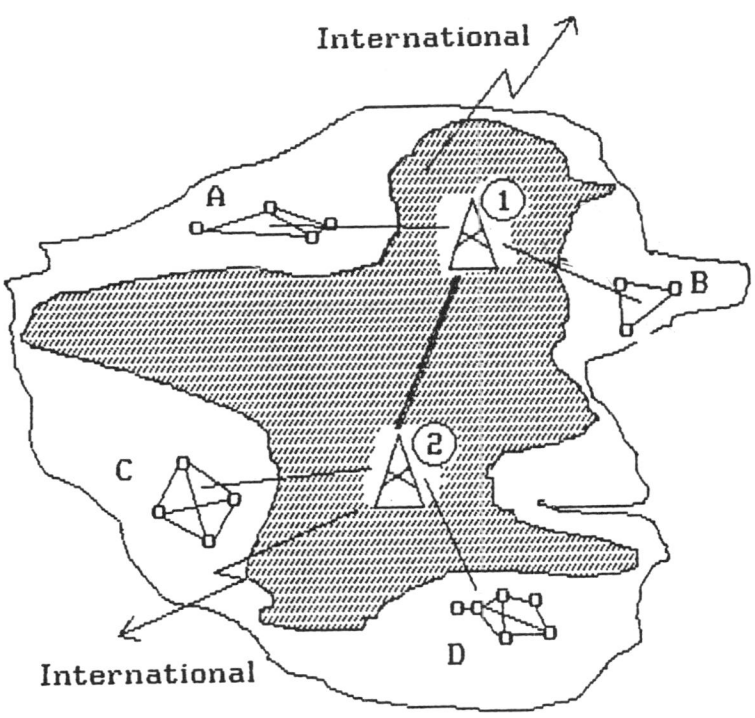

Figure 15.8 Typical Arrangement of Stations on Packet Radio

Consider a fictitious island, as shown in Figure 15.8 where there are several pockets of amateurs, normally associated with urban areas. These all have good local communications but not group to group. The terrain is such that groups A and B can get access to each other via repeater 1 whilst groups C and D can use repeater 2. A network could be arranged so that repeater 1 could communicate with repeater 2, thus giving all stations in the groups A,B,C and D the ability to inter-communicate. Thus repeater 1 would act as a gateway to repeater 2 and groups C and D and similar for repeater 2. In addition to this it is possible that each repeater could act as a gateway to long distance communication to other places in the world.

Mailboxes

The above concepts explain how a packet system could function, the only element missing is that of mailboxes. This is a means whereby messages can be sent and held for a period of time whilst awaiting collection by the recipient. It is not always possible to be in a position to receive information from another station or it may be desirable to pass out a general message for many stations and so messages can be left at a mailbox. These mailboxes are also a gateway to a mailbox network whereby messages can be left in remote mailboxes, not necessarily in the same country.

To be able to perform this function mailboxes must be able provide some of the following:-

be a node in a packet network
be a gateway into a mailbox network
store information
delete information
add routeing information.

To perform these functions mailboxes are normally based on the ubiquitous and relatively cheap PC with a hard disk and the appropriate software and hardware with the ability to interface into transmitting/receiving equipment. Therefore, in setting up a mailbox much of the information already covered in this book is highly relevant.

The Terminal Node Controller

This is the heart of a packet station and the two possible options are shown in Figure 15.9.

In the first instance a communications package is all that is necessary for controlling the RS232 link to the TNC. The TNC is intelligent in that it will accept commands to set up the protocols, data rates, tone frequencies, destination and source callsigns, repeater stations and many other functions. The data rate on the RS232 to TNC link need not match that of the actual transmission data rate. (This is very similar to the concept of intelligent modems in Chapter 12.) There is, however, at least one software package in the public domain that is specific for packet radio and known as YAPP. This is of American origin and allows screen scrolling, storage to disk, transmission from disk, input direct to printer, direct transmission from keyboard and other useful utilities.

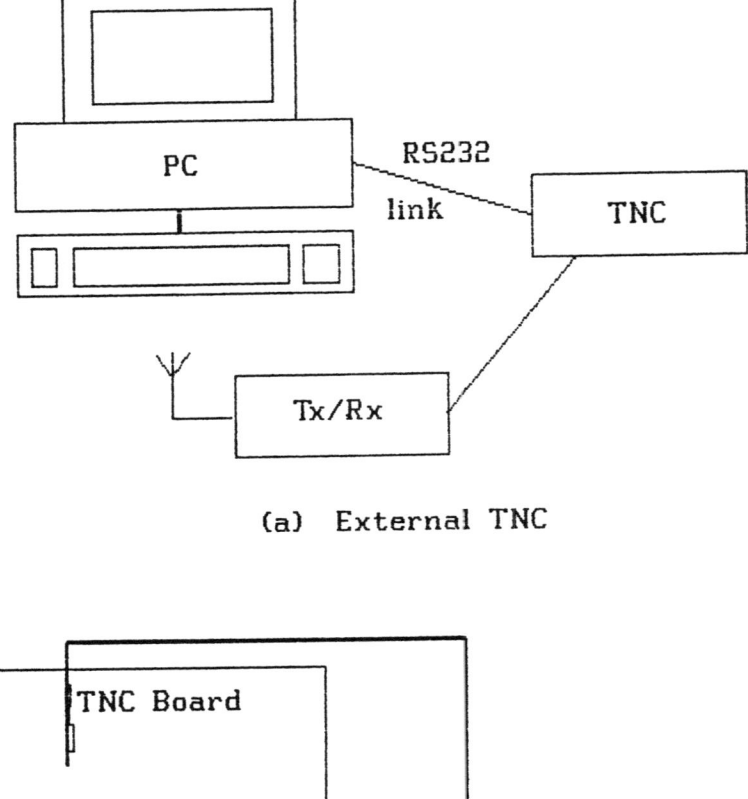

(a) External TNC

(b) Internal

Figure 15.9 The Arrangements for a TNC

The internal type of TNC is very much the same as any other expansion card and can be fitted to any expansion socket in the way described for other cards. It is also similar in many ways to the internal modem card. The board can usually be configured as a COM port, in which case it can be accessed by any communications package. Alternatively, to avoid conflicts with other equipment, it can be addressed as an I/O port which is jumper or switch selectable on the expansion board. In the latter case the driving software must be capable of variable I/O port selection and addressing.

Operating

This is normally covered well in the accompanying manual with a TNC. It will take some time to get used to as will the quirks of some units on the market. It is not feasible to go through the options here but a list of possibilities is:-

    set data rates
    set tones
    set destination callsign
    make sure one's own callsign is present
    set up repeating route
    prepare any long messages
    and connect

The world literally is the limit!

Suppliers

AMDAT - amateur packet radio equipment
BT - ISDN expansion boards
ICS Electronics - amateur packet radio equipment
Siskin Electronics - amateur packet radio equipment

Appendix1

ASCII REFERENCE CHART

ASCII	Decimal	Hex	Binary	Control Code	ASCII	Decimal	Hex	Binary
					.	046	2E	00101110
NUL	000	00	00000000	<CTRL> @	/	047	2F	00101111
SOH	001	01	00000001	<CTRL> A	0	048	30	00110000
STX	002	02	00000010	<CTRL> B	1	049	31	00110001
ETX	003	03	00000011	<CTRL> C	2	050	32	00110010
EOT	004	04	00000100	<CTRL> D	3	051	33	00110011
ENQ	005	05	00000101	<CTRL> E	4	052	34	00110100
ACK	006	06	00000110	<CTRL> F	5	053	35	00110101
BEL	007	07	00000111	<CTRL> G	6	054	36	00110110
BS	008	08	00001000	<CTRL> H	7	055	37	00110111
HT	009	09	00001001	<CTRL> I	8	056	38	00111000
LF	010	0A	00001010	<CTRL> J	9	057	39	00111001
VT	011	0B	00001011	<CTRL> K	:	058	3A	00111010
FF	012	0C	00001100	<CTRL> L	;	059	3B	00111011
CR	013	0D	00001101	<CTRL> M	<	060	3C	00111100
SO	014	0E	00001110	<CTRL> N	=	061	3D	00111101
SI	015	0F	00001111	<CTRL> O	>	062	3E	00111110
DLE	016	10	00010000	<CTRL> P	?	063	3F	00111111
DC1	017	11	00010001	<CTRL> Q	@	064	40	01000000
DC2	018	12	00010010	<CTRL> R	A	065	41	01000001
DC3	019	13	00010011	<CTRL> S	B	066	42	01000010
DC4	020	14	00010100	<CTRL> T	C	067	43	01000011
NA	021	15	00010101	<CTRL> U	D	068	44	01000100
SYN	022	16	00010110	<CTRL> V	E	069	45	01000101
ETB	023	17	00010111	<CTRL> W	F	070	46	01000110
CAN	024	18	00011000	<CTRL> X	G	071	47	01000111
EM	025	19	00011001	<CTRL> Y	H	072	48	01001000
SUB	026	1A	00011010	<CTRL> Z	I	073	49	01001001
ESC	027	1B	00011011		J	074	4A	01001010
FS	028	1C	00011100		K	075	4B	01001011
GS	029	1D	00011101		L	076	4C	01001100
RS	030	1E	00011110		M	077	4D	01001101
US	031	1F	00011111		N	078	4E	01001110
SP	032	20	00100000		O	079	4F	01001111
!	033	21	00100001		P	080	50	01010000
"	034	22	00100010		Q	081	51	01010001
#	035	23	00100011		R	082	52	01010010

Char	Dec	Hex	Binary
$	036	24	00100100
%	037	25	00100101
&	038	26	00100110
'	039	27	00100111
(	040	28	00101000
)	041	29	00101001
*	042	2A	00101010
+	043	2B	00101011
,	044	2C	00101100
-	045	2D	00101101
]	093	5D	01011101
	094	5E	01011110
_	095	5F	01011111
	096	60	01100000
a	097	61	01100001
b	098	62	01100010
c	099	63	01100011
d	100	64	01100100
e	101	65	01100101
f	102	66	01100110
g	103	67	01100111
h	104	68	01101000
i	105	69	01101001
j	106	6A	01101010
k	107	6B	01101011
l	108	6C	01101100
m	109	6D	01101101
n	110	6E	01101110
o	111	6F	01101111
p	112	70	01110000
q	113	71	01110001
r	114	72	01110010
s	115	73	01110011
t	116	74	01110100
u	117	75	01110101
v	118	76	01110110
w	119	77	01110111
x	120	78	01111000
y	121	79	01111001
z	122	7A	01111010
{	123	7B	01111011
:	124	7C	01111100
}	125	7D	01111101
~	126	7E	01111110
DEL	127	7F	01111111
S	083	53	01010011
T	084	54	01010100
U	085	55	01010101
V	086	56	01010110
W	087	57	01010111
X	088	58	01011000
Y	089	59	01011001
Z	090	5A	01011010
[	091	5B	01011011
\	092	5C	01011100

Definitions

NUL	null
SOH	start of heading
STX	start of text
ETX	end of text
EOT	end of transmission
ENQ	enquiry
ACK	acknowledge
BEL	sound bell/buzzer
BS	backspace
HT	horizontal tab
LF	line feed
VT	vertical tab
FF	form feed
CR	carriage return
SO	shift out
SI	shift in
DLE	data link escape
DC1	device control 1
DC2	device control 2
DC3	device control 3
DC4	device control 4
NAK	negative acknowledge
SYN	synchronous idle
ETB	end of block
CAN	cancel
EM	end of medium
SUB	substitute
ESC	escape
FS	file separator
GS	group separator
RS	record separator
US	unit separator
SP	space
DEL	delete

Appendix 2

LIST OF CCITT RECOMMENDATIONS

The following definitions are included for the sake of completeness and reference.

V series recommendations, covering data transmission over telephone circuits.

V.1   Equivalence between binary notation symbols and the significant conditions of a two conditioned code.

V.2   Power levels for data transmission over telephone lines.

V.3   International Alphabet No.5.

V.4   General structure of signals of International Alphabet No.5 code for data transmission over public telephone networks.

V.5   Standardisation of modulation rates and data signalling rates for synchronous data transmission in general switched networks. V.6 As for V5 except for leased telephone type circuits.

V.10   Electrical characteristics for unbalanced double-current interchange circuits for general use with integrated circuit equipment in the field of data communications.

V.11   Ditto but for balanced double-current interchange circuits.

V.13   Answerback unit simulator.

V.15   Use of acoustic coupling for data transmission.

V.16   Recommendation for modems for transmission of medical analogue data.

V.19   Modems for parallel data transmission using telephone signalling frequencies.

V.20   Parallel data transmission modems standardised for universal use in the general switched network.

V.21   300 bps modem standardised for use in the switched telephone network.

V.22   1200 bps full duplex 2-wire modem standardised for use in the general switched telephone network.

V.22bis   2400 bps full duplex 2-wire modem standardised for use in the general switched telephone network.

V.23   600/1200 bps modem standardised for use in the general switched telephone network.

V.24	List of definitions for interchange circuits between data terminal equipment and data circuit terminating equipment i.e. modem.
V.25	Automatic calling and/or answering equipment on the general switched telephone network including disabling or echo suppressors on manually established calls.
V.25bis	Bit synchronous auto-dialling protocol for use over PSTN.
V.26	2400 bps modem for use on 4-wire leased point to point circuits.
V.26bis	2400/1200 bps modem standardised for use in the general switched telephone network.
V.26ter	2400 bps dial or 2-wire leased line modem.
V.27	4800 bps modem standardised for use on leased circuits.
V.27bis	4800/2400 bps modem with automatic adaptive equaliser standardised for use on leased circuits.
V.27ter	4800/2400 bps modem standardised for use in the general switched telephone network.
V.28	Electrical characteristics for unbalanced double-current interchange circuits.
V.29	9600 bps modem for use on leased circuits.
V.31	Electrical characteristics for single-current interchange circuits controlled by contact closure.
V.32	9600 bps full duplex 2-wire modem standardised for use in the general switched telephone network with 4800 bps fallback speed.
V.33	14.4 kbps full duplex 4-wire modem for use over leased lines using Trellis encoded modulation.
V.35	Data transmission at 48 kbps using 60-108 kHz group band circuits.
V.36	Modems for synchronous data transmission using 60-108 kHz group band circuits.
V.40	Error indication with electromechanical equipment.
V.41	Code independent error control system.
V.42	Error control using LAP-M as primary and MNP as secondary method.
V.50	Standard limits for transmission quality of data transmission.
V.51	Organisation of the maintenance of international telephone type circuits used for data transmission.
V.52	Characteristics of distortion and error rate measuring apparatus for data transmission.
V.53	Limits for the maintenance of telephone type circuits used for data transmission.
V.54	Loop test devices for modems.
V.55	Specification for an impulsive noise measuring instrument for telephone type circuits.
V.56	Comparative tests for modems for use over telephone type circuits.
V.57	Comprehensive data test set for high data signalling rates.

X series recommendations covers data networks

X.1	International user classes of service in public data networks.
X.2	International user facilities in public data networks.

X.3	Packet assembly/disassembly facility (PAD) in a public data network.
X.4	General structure of signals of International Alphabet No.5 code for data transmission over public data networks.
X.20	Interface between data terminal equipment and data circuit terminating equipment for start-stop transmission services on public data networks.
X.20bis	V21 compatible interface between data terminal equipment and data circuit terminating equipment for start-stop transmission services on public data networks.
X.21	General purpose interface between data terminal equipment and data circuit terminating equipment for synchronous operation on public data networks.
X.21bis	Use on public data networks of data terminal equipment which is designed for interfacing to synchronous V-series modems.
X.24	List of definitions of interchange circuits between data terminal equipment and data circuit terminating equipment on public data networks.
X.25	Interface between data terminal equipment and data circuit terminating equipment for terminals operating in the packet mode on public data networks.
X.26	Electrical characteristics for unbalanced double current interchange circuits for general use with integrated circuit equipment in the field of data communications (identical to V10).
X.27	Electrical characteristics for balanced double current interchange circuits for general use with integrated circuit equipment in the field of data communications (identical to V11).
X.28	DTE/DCE interface for a start-stop mode data terminal equipment accessing the packet assembly/disassembly (PAD) on a public data network situated in the same country.
X.29	Procedures for exchange of control information and user data between a packet mode DTE and a packet assembly/disassembly facility (PAD).
X.92	Hypothetical reference connections for public synchronous data networks.
X.95	Network parameters in public data networks.
X.96	Call progress signals in public data networks.
X.121	Defines the International packet-switched networks numbering scheme.

Appendix 3

SUMMARY OF BELL STANDARDS

This listing gives a summary of the Bell standards as commonly used in modems in the USA and shows their compatibility with the CCITT V.XX standards.

Bell Code	Speed bps Forward	Reverse	Modulation	Frequency Hz	Compatibility
103/113	0-300		Async	Originate	No
			FSK	1070 (0)	
				1270 (1)	
				Answer	
				2025 (0)	
				2225 (1)	
202	1200		Async	Forward	V23
			FSK	1200 (1)	sometimes
			HDX	2200 (0)	
		5*	OOK	Reverse*	
				387	
212A	1200		Sync	Originate	V22
			4DPSK	1200	at 1200 bps
				Answer	
				2400	
	300(F)		FSK	As Bell 103	
201CR	4800		Sync	Carrier	V26(bis)
			4DPSK	1800	at 2400bps
208BR	4800		Sync	Carrier	No
			8DPSK	1800	

230

203	3600	Sync	No
	4800		
	5400		
	6400		
	7200		
	9600		
	10800		
209A	9600	Sync	No
		QAM	

QAM = quadrature amplitude modulation   DPSK = differential FSK
FSK = frequency shift keying   F = fallback speed

* only used for error and control codes if fitted

Appendix 4

HAYES COMMAND SUMMARY

The following is a brief list of the Hayes command summary which is almost a *de facto* standard now for intelligent modems. It is included to give the reader an insight into the range of commands available. The ATtention code AT precedes all command lines, e.g. ATD. The line is finished by a <RETURN> except for A/. **PLEASE NOTE** not all items are implemented by the various modems and this list is not exhaustive.

Commands

A		answer call immediately
A/		repeat last command
Cn	n=0 or 1	Carrier control
		0=off 1=on
Dan	a=T,P,R	used if needed. T=tone dialling, P=pulse dialling R=reverse dial (calls an originate only modem)
	n=0 to 9	represents telephone number to be dialled, can be interspersed with , (pause 1 second) or ; (return to command state after dialling)
En	n=0 or 1	local echo command: 0=no echo, 1=echo
Fn	n=0 or 1	format command: 0=half duplex, 1=full duplex
Hn	n=0 or 1	hook mode: 0=hang up, 1=seize line
In	n=0,1,2	identify: 0=request product code, 1=request check sum, 2=RAM check: other options may exist
K		clock timer: modem responds with call duration
Ln	n=1,2,3	loudspeaker volume: 1 is low, 3 is high
Mn	n=1,2,3	mute control: 1=always, 2=when on-line,3=never
Nn		used to dial telephone number from store n
Nn?		displays telephone number from store n
On	n=0,1,2	on-line state: 0=go on-line, 1=remote digital loop off:2=remote digital loop on
Qn	n=0 or 1	quiet mode: 0=result codes sent, 1=codes not sent
Sr=n		set register r to value n: n=0..255,

Sr?	read register r
U	dial until answer: repetitively re-dial number according to parameters in an S register
Vn n=0 or 1	verbose mode: 0=response in code, 1= in text
Xn n=0 to 6	extended mode: 0=basic set, 1= extended set, 2=detect dial tone. 3=detect busy tone, 4=detect dial and busy tone, 5= as 3 plus ARQ, 6=as 4 plus ARQ
Yn n=0 or 1	long space disconnect: 0=disabled, 1=enabled
Z	reset modem to initial factory parameters
&An n=0 or 1	automatic rate detection: 0=line speed less than or equal to interface speed: 1=automatic detection
&Bn n=0,1,2	delayed make busy: 0=make busy cleared, 1=make busy no loopback, 2=make busy with loopback
&Cn n=0 or 1	data carrier detect options: 0=signals DCD and DSR maintained ON: 1=operate as V24
&Dn n=0 to 3	data terminal ready options: 0=DTR ignored, 1=if DTR drops whilst on-line modem reverts to command mode, 2=DTR function as normal, if it drops while on-line call disconnected, 3=transition high to low same as powering modem off then on
&En n=0 to 3	error correction: 0=disabled, 1=enabled in transparent mode as slave, 2=enabled in transparent mode as master, 3=enabled in non-transparent mode
&F	default configuration
&Gn n=0,1,2	select guard tone: 0=no guard tone, 1=550 Hz guard tone, 2=1800 Hz guard tone
&In n=0,1,2	constant speed interface: 0=disabled, 1=enabled, CONNECT message shows line speed, 2=as 1 but interface speed shown
&Jn	telephone jack selection
&Kn n=0 to 3	flow control method: 0=no flow control, 1=Xon/Xoff ennabled, 2=CTS control enabled, 3=both 2 & 3
&Ln n=0 or 1	select line type: 0=PSTN use, 1=private circuit
&Mn n=0 to 3	async/sync operation: 0=async, 1=sync but call initiated using async, 2=sync stored number dial, 3=sync, manual dial DTR control
&N	directory display (&N99 clears directory)
&On n=0 or 1	register output format:0=decimal, 1=hexadecimal
&Rn n=0 or 1	RTS options: 0=CTS follows state of RTS, 1=RTS ignored
&Sn n=0 or 1	front panel switch control: 0=disabled, 1=enabled
&Tn n=0 to 8	various tests performed - see user manual
&Vn n=0,1,2	command mode control: 0=normal command mode, 1= escape sequence disabled, 2=modem in dumb mode
&W	store active configuration
&Xn n=0,1,2	transmit clock timing source: 0=internal, 1=external, 2=slave receive timing
&Yn n=0 or 1	command port control: 0=disabled, 1=enabled
&Z	stores a number entered with N command

Response Codes

Basic

Code	Verbose
0	OK
1	CONNECT (300)
2	RING
3	NO CARRIER
4	ERROR

Extended set (may vary according to modem and manufacturer)

5	CONNECT 1200
6	NO DIAL TONE
7	BUSY
8	NO ANSWER
9	CONNECT 600
10	CONNECT 2400
11	CONNECT 75
12	RDL GRANTED Test mode only
13	RDL DENIED Test mode only
14	Trying to Connect:
15	(Aborted!)
16	(Timeout)
20	ARQ ON
21	NO ARQ

S Registers

These registers determine configuration settings, some of which can be altered. They normally contain a default or factory set ting. They are held in non-volatile RAM.

S0	controls number of rings before answering
S1	records number of incoming rings
S2	ASCII value of escape code sequence
S3	ASCII value of CR or end-of-line character
S4	ASCII value of line-feed character
S5	ASCII value of backspace character
S6	wait time for dial tone
S7	wait time for data carrier
S8	pause time for comma in dial command
S9	carrier detect response time
S10	time for loss of carrier to hang up
S11	duration and spacing of DTMF tones
S12	escape code guard time
S13	for internal use
S14	holds status settings of various command registers
S15	for internal use
S16	for internal use

From this point on there appears to be no standard use of the S registers by different manufacturers.

ABBREVIATIONS USED

ACK acknowledgement
ANSI American National Standards Institute
ARQ automatic request for retransmission
ASCII American Standard Code for Information Interchange
BIOS basic input output system
CCITT Comite Consultatif Internationale de Telegraphique et Telephonique
CD carrier detect
CGA colour graphics adapter
CPU central processor unit
CR carraiage return
CRC cyclic redundancy check: error detection scheme
CSMA carrier sense multiple access: acces in LANs
CSMA/CA as CSMA with collision avoidance
CSMA/CD as CSMA with collision detection
CTS clear to send
DCD data carrier detect
DCE data communications equipment or data circuit terminating equipment; typically modem or similar
DIL dual in line
DPSK differential phase shift keying: a form of modulation that helps conserve bandwidth, also 2DPSK, 4DPSK and 8DPSK
DSR data set ready
DTE data terminal equipment: typically equipment controlling a link, e.g. computer
DTMF dual tone multiple frequency: frequency pairs used for telephone dialling instead of pulses
DTP desk top publishing
DTR data terminal ready
EGA enhanced graphics adapter
EIA Electronics Industries Association (American organisation)
EPROM electronically programmable read only memory
FD full duplex
FDC floppy disk controller
FDD floppy disk drive
FM frequency modulation
FSK frequency shift keying

HDC hard disk controller
HDD hard disk drive
HDX half duplex
IC integrated circuit
IDA integrated digital access: access method by subscriber for ISDN
IEEE Institute of Electrical and Electronic Engineers (USA)
IEEE488 bus organisation for instrumentation adopted by IEEE
ISDN integrated services digital network: CCITT standard under development for future digital data communications
LAN local area network
LAP line access procedure superseded by LAP-B (also LAP-D and LAP-M)
LF line feed
MDA monochrome display adapter
MFM modified frequency modulation
MNP Microcomms Networking Protocol
PAD packet assembler/disassembler
PDN public data network
PM phase modulation: form of modulation
PSK phase shift keying; form of modulation
PSTN public switched telephone network
QAM quadrature modulation: a combination of AM and PM to con serve bandwidth
RAM random access memory
RxD received data
RI ring indicator
RLL run length limited
ROM read only memory
RS232,RS422,RS423,RS449 serial transmission standards
RTC real time clock
RTS request to send
TTL transistor-transistor logic
V.xx transmission recommendations from CCITT - see Appendix 2
VGA video graphics array
WAN wide area network
X.xx transmission recommendations from CCITT - see Appendix 2
Xon/Xoff protocol for flow control of information

Appendix 6

BIBLIOGRAPHY

The following is a list of books that may provide additional reading or be useful for reference. In addition to this, much information can be gleaned from the manuals for specific products.

Amstrad Personnal Computer PC1640, Technical Reference Manual,
        Amstrad Part No. 50016

Communications with Microcomputers, Cullimore,I (Sigma Press)
        ISBN 1-85058-055-3

IBM PC & PC XT User's Reference Manual, Held G (Pitman)
        ISBN 0-81046427

Low Cost Local Area Networks Bridges, S P M (Sigma Press)
        ISBN 0-905104-86-2

Microprocessor Interfacing Techniques Zaks, R, Lesea A (Sybex)
        ISBN 0-89588-029-6

OPUS PCII User's Guide

Supercharging Your PC Perdue (McGraw Hill
        ISBN 0-0788100000

The ARRL Handbook for the Radio Amateur (ARRL, 1986)
        ISBN 0-87259-063-1

8088 Personal Computer Introductory Guide

8088/8086 Assembly Language Programming, Yeung B C (John Wiley)
        ISBN 0-471-90463-5

1987 Applications Handbook (Image Processing & Data Acquisition)
        (Data Translation Ltd)

Appendix 7

ADDRESSES OF SUPPLIERS

Aditi Electronics, 46B High St, HURSTPIERPOINT, W.Sussex BN6 9TT

Altek Instruments Ltd, 44-46 Terrace Rd, WALTON-ON-THAMES, Surrey KT12 2SD

Amdat, Crofters, Harry Stoke Rd, Stoke Gifford, BRISTOL BS12 6QH

Amplicon, Centenary Ind Est, Hollingdean Rd, BRIGHTON BN2 4AW

Amstrad plc,Brentwood Hse,169 Kings Rd, BRENTWOOD, Essex CM14 4EF

APL Data Communications, Unit 8, Fleetway North Business Park, 715b N Circular Rd, LONDON NW2 7AT

AST Europe Ltd, AST House, 2 Goat Wharf, BRENTFORD, Middx TW8 0BA

Atomstyle Ltd, Millmead Bus. Centre, Millmead Rd, LONDON N17 9QU

Audiocard, STC Mercator, S. Denes, Gt Yarmouth, Norfolk NR30 3PX

Ayden Controls, 64 Wilbury Way, HITCHIN, Herts SG4 0TP

Bentley Computers, PO Box 368, FLINT, Clwyd CH6 5XQ

Beyond Words Ltd, Wessex Hse, St Leonards Rd, BOURNEMOUTH BH8 8QS

Biodata, 10 Stocks St, MANCHESTER, M8 8QG

Black Box, 15 Cradock Rd, READING, Berks RG2 0JT

Blue Chip Technology, Main Ave, Hawarden Ind Park, DEESIDE, Clwyd CH5 3PP

Brigden Technology, Unit 24,Erith Business Centre, Erith High St, Erith, Kent DA8 1QY

BT, Anzani Hse, Trinity Ave, FELIXSTOWE, Suffolk IP11 8XB

Callbox Ltd, 18 Agincourt Sq, MONMOUTH, Gwent NP5 3DY

Case Comm. Ltd, PO Box 254, Watford Bus. Park, WATFORD WD1 8XH

CIL, 4 Wayside, Commercial Way, LANCING, W.Sussex BN15 8TA

Cipher, Cipher Hse, Ashville Way, WOKINGHAM, Berks RG11 2PL

Citadel Products Ltd, 50 High St, EDGWARE, Middx HA8 7EP

Comcat, as Trend Datalink

Computers by Post, 14 Emmabrook Ct,Sea Rd, RUSTINGTON BN16 2NG

Computer Marketing, CMA Hse, Lansbury Est, Lower Guildford Rd, KNAPHILL, Surrey GU21 2EW

Connexions plc, Unit 3, Huggins La, WELHAM GREEN, Herts AL9 7LE

Continental Ltd,4 Royal Cres, CHELTENHAM GL50 3DA

Control & Display Technology Ltd, Brookside, S.Kilvington, THIRSK, N.Yorks YO7 2NL

Core Int'l, Kingswick Hse, SUNNINGHILL, Berks SL5 7BH
CPU Peripherals, Cpsoe Rd, St John's, WOKING, Surrey GU21 1SX
Cristie Electronics Ltd, Bonds Mill, STONEHOUSE, Glos GL10 3RG
CRT Displays, 16 Kelvinhaugh St, GLASGOW G3 8NU
Data Design Techniques, Unit 16B, Severn Br Ind Est, PORTSKEWETT,
Gwent NP6 4YU
Dataflex Design, Merton Pk Hse, 2 Jubilee Way, LONDON SW19 3XD
Datalines, 27 Heathfield, Stacey Bushes, MILTON KEYNES MK112 6HR
Dataphone Ltd, 22 Alfric Sq, Woodston, PETERBOROUGH PE2 0JP
Datastripe, 461 London Rd, CAMBERLEY, Surrey GU15 3JA
Data Translation, The Mulberry Business Pk, WOKINGHAM, Berks RG11 2QJ
Deltest, PO Box 24, Pottery Rd, POOLE, Dorset BH14 8RQ
Digithurst, 7 Church Lane, ROYSTON, Herts SG8 9LG
Digitask, Unit 2,Gatwick Metro Centre,Balcombe Rd, HORLEY RH6 9GA
Digivision, Parker Dr, LEICESTER LE4 0JP
Dowty Inform. Systems Ltd, London Rd, NEWBURY, Berks RG13 2PZ
DRAM Electronics, Unit 12, Kingston Mill, Chestergate, STOCKPORT SK3 0AL
Dynatech Comms Ltd,Britannica Hse, High St, WALTHAM CROSS EN8 7DR
First Software, Wade Rd, BASINGSTOKE, Hants RG24 0NE
Electro+Graphic Products, 37 Darton Rd, Cawthorne, BARNSLEY,S.Yorks S75 4HU
Electronic Studio Products, Unit 8, The Cam Centre, Wilbury Way HITCHIN
SG4 0TW
Eltime Vision Systems, 10/14 Hall Rd, Heybridge, MALDON CM9 7LA
Equinet, 114/116 Curtain Rd, LONDON EC2A 3AH
Europa Ltd, Mill Works, Mill Cr, TONBRIDGE, Kent TN9 1PE
Formscan Ltd, Apex Hse, West End, FROME, Somerset BA11 3AS
Golden Gate, Winchester Hse, Gardener Rd, MAIDENHEAD, Berks SL6 7RL
Go-Mark, 29 Harper Rd, LONDON SE1 6AW
GP Industrial Electronics, Unit E, Huxley Close, Newnham Ind Est, PLYMOUTH
PL7 4JN
Headway Comp. Products, Headway Hse,Christy Est, Ivy Rd, ALDERSHOT
GU12 4TX
Hitachi, Station Rd, HAYES, Middx UB3 4DR
HK Systems Ltd, 6 Sunbeam Rd, LONDON NW10 6JL
ICS Electronics, PO Box 2, ARUNDEL, W.Sussex BN18 0NX
Ideal Hardware, Ltd, 3rd Flr, Low Rise, Tolworth Twr, SURBITON, Surrey KT6 7EL
Infa Communications,Copas Hse,8 Adam Ct, HENLEY-ON-THAMES RG9 2BJ
Integrated Measurement Systems, Unit 3-06, Solent Business Centre
Millbrook Rd West, SOUTHAMPTON SO1 0HW
Intel Corporation (UK) Ltd, Pipers Way, SWINDON, Wilts SN3 1RJ
JVF Communications,4 Loughborough Rd, MOUNTSORREL, Leics LE12 7AT
Keithley Instruments, 1 Boulton Rd, READING, Berks RG2 0HN
Kudos Systems Ltd, Capitol Way, Edgware Rd, LONDON NW9 0ED
Libtech Ltd, Heatherbrow, Holyport Rd, MAIDENHEAD, Berks SL6 2EY
Link Intnl Products Ltd, Prince of Orange Lane, LONDON SE10 8JQ
Lloyd Research, 28 Warsash Rd, Warsash, SOUTHAMPTON SO3 6HX

Logic 2000, Beaver Hse, Victoria Rd, SWINDON, Wilts SN1 3BU

Logitech UK, Linford Forum, Rockingham Dr, MILTON KEYNES MK14 6LY

Loughborough Sound Images, The Technology Centre, Epinal Way, LOUGHBOROUGH LE11 0QE

Manitron Displays, Sandy La, Moston Rd, SANDBACH, Ches. CW11 9HT

Maplin Electronics,PO Box 3, RAYLEIGH, Essex SS6 8LR

Mayze Systems Ltd, Delta 900, Grt Western,Way, SWINDON SN5 7XQ

Mektronic, Linden Hse, 116 Rectory Lane, Prestwich, MANCHESTER M25 5DB

Memorex, 120 Buckingham Ave, SLOUGH, Berks SL1 4PF

Memory Corporation, Logsys Hse, Ashville Way, WOKINGHAM, Berks RG11 2PL

Microcomms, The Old Mill, Chapel Hill, Ponsanooth, TRURO TR3 7ES

Micro Macro Distrbtrs, Martela House, Rooksley, MILTON KEYNES MK13 8PD

Microprocessor Eng. Ltd,133 Hill Lane,Shirley,SOUTHAMPTON SO1 5AF

Microvitec, Futures Way, Bolling Rd, BRADFORD BD4 7TU

Miracle Technology (UK) Ltd, 10-12 St Peters St, IPSWICH IP1 1XB

Mitsubishi, Travellers Lane, HATFIELD, Herts AL10 8XB

MQP Electronics,Unit 2,Park Rd Centre,MALMESBURY, Wilts SN16 0BX

Mutek Ltd,Farleigh Hse,Frome Rd,BRADFORD-ON-AVON, Wilts BA15 1LE

NEC (UK) Ltd, PO Box 594, LONDON N14 6QQ

Nectar Electronics, Dyson Hse, Hetton Lyons Est, HOUGHTON LE SPRING, Tyne and Wear DH5 0BT

Newbridge Networks, 22 Welsh St, CHEPSTOW, Gwent NP6 5LL

Nighthawk Electronics, PO Box 44, SAFFRON WALDEN, Essex CB11 3ND

Nine Tiles,Beach Hse, 25 Greenside, Waterbeach, CAMBRIDGE CB5 9HW

N.L.Ford & Associates,21 South St, SHERBORNE, Dorset DT9 3NA

NTS, 16 Dock St, Sandport Est, EDINBURGH EH6 6EY

Numonics,The Creative Workshop,Lovel Rd,WINKFIELD, Berks SL4 2ES

Orchid (Europe) Ltd,Unit 2,Intec 2,Wade Rd, BASINGSTOKE RG24 0NE

Oxford Hard Disks, Kings Copse Park, GARSINGTON, Oxford OX9 9BU

P & P Micro, Todd Hall Rd, Carrs Ind Est, Haslingden, ROSSENDALE Lancs BB4 5BR

Pace Micro Technology, Allerton Rd, BRADFORD, W Yorks BD15 7AG

Parker Digiplan, 21 Balena Close, Creekmoor, POOLE BH17 7DX

Persona, Unit 1, Silverglade Business Pk, Leatherhead Rd, CHESSINGTON, Surrey KT9 2NQ

PC Communications Ltd, Elmsdale Hse, 31 The Green, WEST DRAYTON Middx UB7 7PN

PC Relative - PO Box 4, POYNTON, Cheshire SK12 1NY

Peripherals Connections Ltd, 3 The Mall, LONDON W5 2PJ

Philips Electronics (Monitors), PO Box 298, CROYDON CR9 3QR

Pinna Electronics, 522 APL Centre, Stevenston Ind Est, STEVENSTON Ayrshire KA20 3LR

Plus 5 Engineering Ltd, Crowborough Hill, Crowborough, TN6 2EG

Racal Milgo, Landata Hse, Station Rd, HOOK, Hants RG27 9PE
Rapid Systems, Denmark St, HIGH WYCOMBE, Bucks HP11 2ER
Ringdale Peripherals, 11 Decoy Rd, WORTHING, Sussex BN14 8ND
Rodime Ltd, Nasmyth Rd, Southfield Ind Est, GLENROTHES, Fife KY6 2SD
RS Components Ltd,PO Box 99, Weldon, CORBY, Northants NN17 9RS
Sagesoft, NEI Hse, Regent Centre, Gosfirth, NEWCASTLE UPON TYNE,
NE3 3DS
Samuelson Communications Ltd,120 Cricklewood Lane, LONDON NW2 2DD
Savtec, 11A Wrecclesham Hill, FARNHAM, Surrey GU10 4JP
Seagate, use CPU Peripherals
Semaphore Systems Ltd, 7 Moreland Ct, Finchley Rd, LONDON NW2 2PJ
Sharp Systems, PO Box 8, MANCHESTER M10 9BB
Siskin Electronics, PO Box 32, Hythe, SPOUTHAMPTON SO4 6WQ
Specialix Systems Ltd, Rosenheath Hse, Giggs Hill Rd,
THAMES DITTON KT7 0TR
Speedtronics, PO Box 52, Somersham, HUNTINGDON, Cambs PE17 3JH
Softech,9 Tonbridge Chambers, Pembury Rd, TONBRIDGE, Kent TN9 2HZ
Sony (UK) Ltd, Sony Hse, South St, STAINES TW18 4PF
Stag Electronic Designs, Stag House, Tewin Ct, WELWYN GARDEN CITY
Herts AL7 1AU
STC Electronic Services, Edinburgh Way, HARLOW, Essex CM20 2DF
Stem Computing, 3 Blackness Ave, DUNDEE DD2 1ER
Tandata Hldgs plc, Albert Rd North, MALVERN, Worcs WR14 2TL
Tandon Computer (UK) Ltd, Hunt End, REDDITCH, Worcs B97 5XP
Taxan (UK), Taxan Hse, Cotsham Rd, BRACKNELL, Berks RG12 1RB
Tech-nel, 8 Haslemere Way, BANBURY, Oxon OX16 8TY
Technomatic Ltd, 17 Burnley Rd, LONDON NW10 1ED
Thame Systems, Thame Park Rd, THAME, Oxon OX9 3XD
Thorn EMI Datatech Ltd, Spur Rd, FELTHAM, Middx TW14 0TD
Torus Systems, Science Pk, Milton Rd, CAMBRIDGE CB4 4GZ
Trend Datalink Ltd, Knaves Beech Estate, Loudwater, HIGH WYCOMBE
Bucks HP10 9QX
U-microcomputers, 12 Chetham Ct, Calver Rd, Winwick Quay,
WARRINGTON WA2 8RF
Vanilla Computer Co Ltd, 112-116 New Oxford St, LONDON WC1A 1HJ
Veren Computer Systems, 520 Reading Rd, WINNERSH, Berks RG11 5EX
Verspeed, Boyatt Wood, EASTLEIGH, Hants S05 4ZY
Visualex Ltd, 18 Reading Rd,HENLEY-ON-THAMES, Oxon RG9 1AG
West Coast Ltd, 20 Boulton Rd, READING, Berks RG2 0PH
Western Digital Corp,B & W Hse,55 East St,EPSOM, Surrey KT17 1BP
Zenith, Cranfield Rd, Wavendon, MILTON KEYNES, MK17 8AT

BEST SELLERS AND NEW TITLES FROM SIGMA PRESS

Mastering Your Hard Disk *Alan Balfe*

This is for everybody with a hard disk (or hard card) who needs to organise their work efficiently and to maximise the benefits of a hard disk. It provides a basic introduction to how hard disks work and how to get a hard disk system set up and running. For users of floppy-based machines, it even tells how to install your own hard card or hard disk. A unique feature is its extensive description of hard disk utility programs - including secure back ups, system testing and user friendly commands (PC BOSS, NORTON utilities, Power Menu and PC TOOLS are included).

Spring 1989　　　*ISBN: 1-85058-146-0*　　　*250 pages £11.95*

The PCW Project Book *Alan Foster and Gabriel Jacobs*

This is a compilation of approximately 30 hardware and software projects for both beginners and the more experienced. Each project has been thoroughly tested and the components can be obtained easily - no hard-to-find parts and no special knowledge of electronics required. The projects include: Memory upgrades; test equipment; input interface for joysticks etc; output port for motors, relays and so on; analogue-to-digital and digital-to-analogue converters (e.g. for temperature or motor control); I/O interfaces at a fraction of the commercial prices; speech synthesiser; building a modem; bio-feedback unit; adding extra disk drives; non-volatile RAM.

Winter 1988　　　*ISBN: 1-85058-113-4*　　　*250 pages £11.95*

Personal Computing with the Sinclair PC200 *Patrick Hall*

First in the field with a book on the Sinclair PC200, Patrick, Hall's new book is also an excellent beginner's guide to MS-DOS, including version 3.2. The contents include: Sinclair PC-200 hardware and software; operating systems, GEM; GEM applications; MS-DOS basics; MS-DOS for advanced users; the Sinclair 'Organiser' package - word processing spreadsheets, database. Additional software packages for the PC-200.

Spring 1989　　　*ISBN: 1-85058-150-9*　　　*250 pages £11.95*

Manage Your Business - Computerise your Accounts *Malcolm Briggs*

After word processing, most PC users need an accounting package. Although this book uses the Mini Office Accounts package as an illustration, the principles are sufficiently general for any other package to be used. It explains the principles of small business accountancy and how to transfer smoothly from a manual system. Contents include: simple accounting;setting up a computerised system; nominal ledger; sales (or debtors) ledger; stock control and order processing; benefits of integration.

Spring 1989　　　*ISBN: 1-85058-147-9*　　　*250 pages £12.95*

Inside dBASE IV *Mike Lewis*

One of the first books on dBase IV - the long-awaited successor to dBase III from Ashton-Tate. It is comprehensive whilst being more readable than the official manual. The contents include: designing the database; using the Control Centre; creating a working application; using the application generator; enhancing the application - indexing, sorting, multiple databases, views, query by example; programming with dBase IV; macros; programming the user interface; building large applications; advanced features - networks, SQL, links, tools.

Spring 1989　　　*ISBN: 1-85058-133-9*　　　*280 pages £12.95*

Packet Switched Networks: Theory and Practice *Richard Barnett and Sally Maynard-Smith;*

This highly praised book has two main aims. The first is to provide the basic theory of packet switched networks and their protocols. The second is to provide sufficient information to allow the reader to implement a packet switched network in a real situation. Contents: Packet switched network basics and components; Network Protocols; International standards; Open Systems Interconnection (OSI); Security; Private Networks; Equipment for packet switched networks; Network management; Future Developments.

Summer 1988　　　*ISBN: 1-85058-095-2*　　　*274 pages £19.95*

Timeworks Desktop Companion *Ray Morrissey*

This is a 'hands on' approach to using the popular, low- cost Timeworks package. The package has been widely acclaimed as having many features only found on Ventura, Pagemaker and other high-cost packages. With Timeworks and a low-cost PC, you really can get started in desk-top publishing. Contents: Word Processing and DTP; Introduction to typography; Installing Timeworks; Designing the layout - using the 'toolbox'; Text and graphics manipulation; Preparing single page and multi-page documents; Choosing printers; Advanced applications.

Summer l989   *ISBN: 1-85058-149-5*   *250 pages £12.95*

Pathways to Concurrent DOS *Richard Trebilcock*

This is a comprehensive guide to the operation of Digital Research's Concurrent DOS, and also a handbook for improving the effectiveness of the user's system. Concurrent DOS enables users to add extra terminals at low cost and also exploit its multi-tasking abilities. Contents include: installation; C-DOS commands shared with MS-DOS plus extended and unique commands; utilities; printer management; menus, window management, batch files: advanced concepts - multitasking, multi-user; networking.

Winter 1988   *ISBN: 1-85058-132-0*   *280 pages £12.95*

All-in-One Business Computer: Amstrad PCW and Mini - Office Professional *John M. Hughes*

Our best seller for 1988! This will open your eyes to the business potential of your Amstrad PCW 8256 or 9512. A clear and invaluable guide to using Mini Office Professional's powerful modules, including the word processor, and how to include the results from the spreadsheet module in your word-processed letters. Create your own graphics wisee how you can turn your spreadsheets into attention-grabbing charts.Use the Database option to store stacks of information and revolutionise your stock control. And the Communications module enables you to connect to on-line services including Prestel, Telecom Gold, Microlink and bulletin boards.

July 1988   *ISBN: 1-85058-124-X*   *232 pages £11.95*

Ventura Adventure - moving up to Version 2.0! *Philip Crookes*

This explains what the manual never told you - and it also shows the differences between version 1.1, 1.2 and the new, greatly enhanced version 2.0. See how to deal with the ordinary and extraordinary problems of desktop publishing, and how you can use Xerox's Ventura Publisher packages even on such a low-cost machine as the Amstrad PC1512. After an introduction to DTP and Ventura, you'll see how to: read in text from word processors spreadsheets, and databases; how to edit and typeset on the screen; exploiting the full character set; creating graphic not just from Ventura, but also from GEM, from spreadsheets and from CAD programs; placing pictures in the text letting the computer do the work of indexing, preparing contents pages, building tables

Winter 1988   *ISBN: 1-85058-123-1*   *240 pages £12.95*

Communications and Networks - a handbook for the first time user *Philip Croucher*

Phil Croucher explains how to transfer files from other computers, or to network hardware so that expensive resources such as laser printers are shared between computers. The first part covers computer communications and includes: Principles; Protocols; Communication packages (including Kermit); Hardware (modems, fax cards, telex cards) ; Troubleshooting. The second part describes networking: Advantages; Networking versus multi-user Hardware and software; Packet switched systems; Security.

Spring 1989   *ISBN: 1-85058-136-3*   *200 pages £11.95*

Inside Lotus/Release 3 - developing applications *Howard James*

This is a book for the spreadsheet 'Power User' and for all those who need to develop spreadsheets beyond the basics. It emphasises the use of Lotus 1-2-3 and includes features of the latest version - Release 3. Contents include Effective memory usage; Data processing in a spreadsheet; Interactive spreadsheets - why macros are needed Assembling macros; Macro examples; Deeper than macros - add-ins and add-ons; The Developer's Tool Kit; Linking Lotus into networks; Exporting and importing data; 3D spreadsheets; Spreadsheets as data receivers and processor.

Spring/Summer l989 *ISBN: 1-85058-138-X*   *280 pages £12.95*